CONTENTS

Chapter 1

"IT'S GOING TO CHANGE YOUR LIFE"

Chapter 2

NURSERY NECESSITIES: CRIBS, DRESSERS & MORE

Chapter 3

Baby Bedding & Decor

Chapter 4

The Reality Layette: Little Clothes for Little Prices

OVER 1 MILLION COPIES SOLD!

BABY
Bargains

Secrets to saving
20% to 50%
on baby cribs,
car seats, strollers,
high chairs,
and much,
much more!

Money-Back
Guarantee

Denise & Alan Fields
Authors of the best-seller, Bridal Bargains

Copyright Page and Free Range Production Credits

The reviews in this book are made from scratch
The ink used to print this book contains no GMO's
The paper used in this book is locally sourced and gluten-free
The cover/interior design by Epicenter Creative is hormone-free
The index in this book was wild caught and contains no preservatives
The back cover photograph by Moses Street utilizes all-natural light
Computers used to produce this book were powered by fair trade electrons

To order this book, go to BabyBargains.com or call 1-800-888-0385. Baby Bargains is published by Windsor Peak Press, 436 Pine Street, Boulder, CO 80302. Questions or comments? E-mail the authors at authors@babybargains.com. Call us at (303) 442-8792.

Learn more about this book online at
BabyBargains.com

Distributed to the book trade by Ingram
Publisher Services, 866-400-5351.

Library Cataloging in Publication Data

Fields, Denise
Fields, Alan
   Baby Bargains: Secrets to saving 20% to 50% on baby cribs, car seats, strollers, high chairs and much, much more/ Denise & Alan Fields
   288 pages.
   Includes index.
   ISBN 978-1-889392-57-8
   1. Child Care—Handbooks, manuals, etc. 2. Infants' supplies—Purchasing—United States, Canada, Directories. 3. Children's paraphernalia—Purchasing—Handbooks, manuals. 4. Product Safety—Handbooks, manuals. 5. Consumer education.
   649'.122'0296—dc20. 2017.

Version 12.0

Chapter 5

FEEDING BABY: BREASTFEEDING, BOTTLES, HIGH CHAIRS

Chapter 6

Around the House: Monitors, Diaper Pails, Safety & More

Chapter 7

CAR SEATS

Chapter 8

STROLLERS, DIAPER BAGS AND OTHER TO GO GEAR

Chapter 9

CARRIERS

Chapter 10

CONCLUSION: WHAT DOES IT ALL MEAN?

CHAPTER 1

"It's Going to Change Your Life!"

Inside this chapter

That had to be the silliest comment we heard while we were pregnant with our first baby. Believe it or not, we even heard this refrain more often than "Are you having a boy or a girl?" and "I'm sorry. Your insurance doesn't cover that." For the friends and relatives of first-time parents out there, we'd like to point out that this is a pretty silly thing to say. Of course, we knew that a baby was going to change our lives. What we didn't realize was how much a baby was going to change our pocketbook.

Oh sure, we knew that we'd have to buy triple our weight in diapers. What we didn't expect was the endless pitches for cribs, gear, toys, clothing and other items parents are required to purchase by FEDERAL BABY LAW.

We quickly learned that having a baby is like popping on the Juvenile Amusement Park Ride from Consumer Hell. Once that egg is fertilized, you're whisked off to the Pirates of the Crib ride. Then it's on to marvel at the little elves in StrollerLand, imploring you to buy brands with names you can't pronounce. Finally, you take a trip to Magic Car Seat Mountain, where the confusion is so real, it's scary.

Consider us your tour guides—the Yogi Bear to your Boo Boo Bear, the Fred to your Ethel, the . . . well, you get the idea. Before we enter BabyLand, let's take a look at the Four Truths That No One Tells You About Buying Stuff For Baby.

The Four Truths That No One Tells You About Buying Stuff for Baby

1 BABIES DON'T CARE IF THEY'RE WEARING DESIGNER CLOTHES. Babies just want to be comfortable. They can't even distinguish between the liberals and conservatives on "Meet the Press," so how would they ever be able to tell the difference between Baby Gucci crib bedding and another less famous brand that's just as comfortable, but 70% less expensive? Our focus is on making your baby happy—at a price that won't break the bank.

2 MOST BABY GEAR ISN'T TESTED FOR SAFETY. One of the biggest myths about baby gear is that every product you see on the shelf at a baby superstore is safety tested before it hits the market. Sadly, that isn't true.

Here are the scary facts: 65,800 children under age five were injured (requiring emergency room visits) by nursery products in 2015 (the latest year figures are available). During a recent three-year period, those same baby products caused 100 deaths per year. (Source: 2016 Consumer Product Safety Commission report based on 2015 data).

Yes, there are safety regulations for a couple of baby gear categories (cribs and car seats). But most other categories only have *voluntary* safety rules and standards. You read that right—anyone can sell a baby gizmo that doesn't meet safety guidelines. (Maybe federal regulators will catch it before it injures children—or maybe not).

So it is up to you as a parent to understand the basic safety guidelines for baby gear. Each chapter of this book will go over safety basics to arm you with in-depth advice on keeping your baby out of trouble. We'll tell you which products we think are dangerous and how to safely use other potentially hazardous products.

3 MURPHY'S LAW OF BABY TOYS SAYS YOUR BABY'S HAPPINESS WITH A TOY IS INVERSELY RELATED TO THE TOY'S PRICE. Buy a $200 shiny new wagon with anti-lock brakes, and odds are baby just wants to play with the box it came in. As we survey baby gear, we will point out the wastes of money (spoiler alert: smart baby monitors—not worth your money).

4 IT'S GOING TO COST MORE THAN YOU THINK. Whatever amount of money you budget for your baby, get ready to spend more. Here's a breakdown of the average costs of bringing a baby into the world today:

The Average Cost of Having a Baby

(based on industry estimates for a child from birth to age one)

Crib, mattress, dresser, rocker	$1570
Bedding / Decor	$350
Baby Clothes	$615
Disposable Diapers	$865
Maternity / Nursing Clothes	$1300
Nursery items, high chair, toys	$515
Baby Food / Formula	$1015
Stroller, Car Seats, Carrier	$730
Miscellaneous	$490
TOTAL	**$7,450**

The above figures are based on a survey of 1000 readers, buying name brand products at regular retail prices.

Bedding/Decor includes not only bedding items but also lamps, wallpaper, and so on for your baby's nursery. Baby Food/Formula assumes mom breastfeeds for the first six months and then feeds baby jarred baby food ($385) and formula ($630) until age one. If you plan to bottle-feed instead of breastfeed, add another $630 on to that figure. (Of course, the goal is to breast-feed your baby as long as possible—one year is a good target.)

Sure, you do get a tax credit for that bundle of joy, but that only amounts to about $1000 this year (if you are in the 25% tax bracket). Plus, there is a child care tax credit for up to $3000 depending on your income. But those tax goodies won't nearly offset the actual cost of raising a child. And as you probably realize, our cost chart is missing some expensive "extras" . . . like medical bills, childcare, saving for college, etc. Here's an overview of those extras.

Scary Number: The Cost of Raising Baby to 18

$233,610. That's what the federal government says it costs to raise a child born in 2017 to age 18. Those costs include food, transportation, housing, clothes and child care.

But let's talk about child care. Critics say the federal government grossly underestimates this cost (the feds say parents spend $2,200 to $5,500 on child care each year for the first two years).

So what does child care really cost? According to the National Association of Child Care Resource and Referral

Agencies, the average annual bill for center care for an infant ranges from $5754 (Louisiana) to $17,082 in Massachusetts.

College is another expense the government leaves out of their figures. The College Board estimates that four years at a public college averages $80,360 (tuition, fees, room and board). At a private college, that same figure is $181,480. Given current rates of return, you have to put away $465 per month every year for 18 years to afford that public school.

The take-home message: raising a baby ain't cheap. It's important to start saving your pennies now, so you can start saving for those important items (college, etc.) down the road.

Reality Check: Does it Really Cost That Much to Have a Baby?

Now that we've thoroughly scared you enough to inquire whether the stork accepts returns, we should point out that children do NOT have to cost that much. Even if we focus just on the first year, you don't have to spend $7450 on baby gear. And that's what this book is all about: how to save money and still buy the best. Follow all the tips in this book, and we estimate the first year will cost you $4323. Yes, that's a savings of over $3100!

Now, at this point, you might be saying "That's impossible! I suppose you'll recommend shopping garage sales and dollar stores." On the contrary, we'll show you how to get *quality* name brands and safe products at discount prices. Most importantly, you will learn how not to WASTE your money on dubious gear. And much more. Yes, we've got the maximum number of bargains allowed by federal law.

A word on bargain shopping: when interviewing hundreds of parents for this book, we realized bargain seekers fall into two frugal camps. There's the "do-it-yourself" crowd and the "quality at a discount" group. As the name implies, "do-it-yourselfers" are resourceful folks who like to take second-hand products and refurbish them. Others use creative tricks to make homemade versions of baby care items like baby wipes and diaper rash cream.

While that's all well and good, we fall more into the second camp of bargain hunters, the "quality at a discount" group. We love discovering a name brand stroller for 75% off on Craigslist. Or the discount version of an expensive designer furniture brand, sold at a 20% discount. We also realize savvy parents save money by not *wasting* it on inferior goods or useless items.

While we hope that *Baby Bargains* pleases both groups of

bargain hunters, the main focus of this book is not on do-it-your-self projects (exception: IKEA furniture assembly). Our emphasis is on identifying best buys for the dollar and not wasting your money, as well as on the best discount online sources.

What? No One Paid You to Recommend Their Product?

Yes, it's true. We don't get paid by the brands we review.

We also do not accept samples or other freebies from companies we review—if we are doing a first-hand inspection of a product, we purchase it on our own at regular retail prices. When we visit factories or other company facilities, we pay for our all our travel expenses. We don't accept gifts from companies we review.

Why? We believe that when you take a freebie, there is an obvious quid pro quo—a baby gear company isn't going to give you a $500 stroller and not expect anything less than a nice review in return. To remain objective, you can't accept free samples, gift baskets, etc.

Here's how we make a living: we sell the book you are reading. We also have affiliate links on our free web site (BabyBargains.com). When you read our review of a car seat and you click through on a link to purchase it, we may make a small commission from the site selling the product. If you hate the car seat and return it, we don't make any commission. FYI: Affiliate links do not affect the price you pay.

We also use software to affiliate links posted by users of our message boards, which are free. There are ads on our message boards (visible only to unregistered users) and other parts of our web site. These revenue sources are used to pay for bandwidth and server maintenance.

Of course, given the sheer volume of baby stuff, there's no way we can personally test everything. To solve that dilemma, we rely on reader feedback to help us figure out which are the best products to recommend. We receive over 200 emails a day from parents; this helps us spot overall trends on which brands/products parents love. And which ones they want to destroy with a rocket launcher.

Of course, one bad review from one parent doesn't mean we won't recommend a product—we combine multiple review sources to come up with an overall picture as to which brands are best.

The prices you see in our book were accurate as of press time. We aim to print actual selling prices (versus suggested retail prices) in our book—we do this by surveying stores and web sites. While the publisher makes every effort to ensure their accuracy, errors and omissions may exist. That's why we update this book with every new printing—make sure you are using the most recent version (go to BabyBargains.com and click on Book and then Which Version?).

Our door is always open—we want to hear your opinions. Email us at authors@BabyBargains.com or call us at (303) 442-8792 to ask a question, report a mistake, or just give us your thoughts.

So, Who Are You Guys Anyway?

Why do a book on saving money on baby products? Don't new parents throw caution to the wind when buying for their baby, spending whatever it takes to ensure their baby's safety and comfort?

Ha! When our first child was born, we quickly realized how darn expensive this guy was. Sure, as a new parent, you know

The 7 Commandments of Baby Bargains

Yes, we've come down from the mountain to share with you our SEVEN commandments of *Baby Bargains*—the keys to saving every parent should know. Let's review:

1 SAFETY IS JOB ONE. As a parent, your baby's safety is paramount. We never compromise safety for a bargain—that's why we don't recommend hand-me-down cribs or used car seats, no matter how cheap they are. Good news: you can subscribe to our free blog to get an email or text message when a baby product is recalled. Go to BabyBargains.com/blog and enter your email address in the box at the right.

2 FOCUS ON THE BASICS. Big box baby stores are so overwhelming, with a blizzard of baby products. Key on the basics: setting up a safe place for baby to sleep (the nursery) and safe transport (car seats). Many items like high chairs, toys, and so on are not needed immediately.

3 WEED OUT THE FLUFF. Our advice: take an experienced mom with you when you register. A mom with one or two kids can help you separate out needed items from the rest.

you've got to buy a car seat, crib, clothes and diapers . . . but have you walked into one of those baby "superstores" lately? It's a blizzard of baby stuff piled to the ceiling, with a bewildering array of "must have" gear, gadgets and gizmos, all claiming to be the best thing for parents since sliced bread.

Becoming a parent in this day and age is both a blessing and curse. The good news: parents today have many more choices for baby products than past generations. The *bad* news: parents today have many more choices for baby products than past generations.

Our mission: make sense of this stuff, with an eye on cutting costs. As consumer advocates, we've been down this road before. We researched bargains and uncovered scams in the wedding business when we wrote *Bridal Bargains*. Then we penned an exposé on new homebuilders in *Your New House*.

Yet, we found the baby business to be perplexing in different ways—instead of outright fraud or scams, we've instead discovered some highly questionable products that don't live up to

4 TWO WORDS: FREE MONEY. As a parent, you NEVER pass up free money! From tax deductions to tax credits, being a parent means freebies. And don't overlook your employer: take advantage of benefits like dependent care accounts—using PRE-TAX dollars to pay for child care will save you HUNDREDS if not THOUSANDS of dollars.

5 MORE FREEBIES. Many companies throw swag at new parents, hoping they will become future customers. We keep an updated freebie list on our web site—get free diapers, bottles, and more. Go to BabyBargains.com/freebies for the latest update!

6 SHOP AT STORES THAT DO NOT HAVE "BABY" IN THEIR NAME. Costco for diapers? Pet web sites for safety gates? IKEA for high chairs? Yes! Yes! Yes! You can save 30% or more by not buying items at baby stores.

7 ONLINE SHOPPING SAVVY. Let's face it: as a new mom and dad, you probably won't have much time to hit the mall. The web is a savior—but how do you master the deals? One smart tip: ALWAYS use coupon codes for discounts or FREE shipping. Our readers post codes/sales daily to the Bargain Alert Forum on our free message boards (BabyBargains.com).

What you need, when

Yes, buying for baby can seem overwhelming, but there is a silver lining: you don't need ALL this stuff immediately when baby is born. Let's look at what items you need quickly and what you can wait on. This chart indicates usage of certain items for the first 12 months of baby's life:

Item	Months of Use				
	Birth	3	6	9	12+
Nursery Necessities					
Cradle/bassinet	███				
Crib/Mattress	██████████████████				
Dresser	██████████████████				
Glider Rocker	███████████████				
Bedding: Cradle	███				
Bedding: Crib	██████████████████				
Clothing					
Caps/Hats	█████████				
Blanket Sleepers	██████████████████				
Layette Gowns	███				
Booties	████				
All other layette	██████████████████				
Around the House					
Baby Monitor	██████████████████				
Baby Food (solid)			████████████		
High Chairs				██████	
Places to Go					
Infant Car Seat	█████████				
Convertible Car Seat*				██████	
Full-size Stroller/Stroller Frame	██████████████████				
Umbrella Stroller				██████	
Front Carrier	█████████				
Backpack Carrier				██████	
Safety items			████████████		

You can use a convertible car seat from birth (instead of an infant car seat) if you prefer.

their hype—and others that are outright dangerous. We learned that most juvenile items face little (or no) government scrutiny when it comes to safety, leaving parents to sort out true useful-ness and safety from sales hype.

So, we've gone on a quest to find the best baby products, at prices that won't send you to the poor house. Sure, we've sam-pled many of these items first hand. But this book is much more than our experiences—we interviewed over 17,000 new parents to learn their experiences with products. Our message boards have over 48,000 members, buzzing with all sorts of product feedback and advice. We also attend juvenile product trade shows to visit with manufacturers and retailers to discover what's new. The insights from retailers are especially helpful, since these folks are on the front lines, seeing which items unhappy parents return.

Our focus is on safety and durability: which items stand up to real world conditions and which don't. Interestingly, we found many products for baby are sold strictly on price . . . and sometimes a great "bargain" broke, fell apart or shrunk after a few uses. Hence, you'll note some of our top recommendations aren't always the lowest in price. To be sensitive to those on really tight budgets, we also identify "budget-friendly" picks in our recommendations.

We get questions: Top 6 Questions & Answers

From the home office here in Boulder, CO, here are the top six questions we get asked here at *Baby Bargains*:

1 How do I know if I have the current edition? We strive to keep *Baby Bargains* as up-to-date as possible. As such, we update it periodically with new editions. But if you just bor-rowed this book from a friend, how do you know how old it is? First, look at the copyright page. There at the bottom you will see a version number (such as 12.0). The first number (the 12 in this case) means you have the 12th edition. The second num-ber indicates the printing—every time we reprint the book, we make minor corrections, additions and changes. Version 12.0 is the initial printing of the 12th edition, version 12.1 is the first reprint of the 12th edition and so on.

So, how can you tell if your book is current or woefully out-of-date? Go to our web page at BabyBargains.com and click on Book and then "Which version?"—this shows the most cur-rent version. (One clue: look at the book's cover. We note the edition number on each cover. And we change the color of the cover with each edition.) We update this book every two years (roughly). About 30% to 40% of the content will change with each edition. Bottom line: if you pick up a copy of this book that is one or two editions old, you will notice a significant number of changes.

2 **I AM LOOKING FOR A SPECIFIC PRODUCT BUT I DON'T KNOW WHERE TO START! HELP!** Let's say you are in a store and are wondering which infant car seat to purchase. Flip to our car seats chapter and you'll discover our recommendations, from best infant car seat (overall) to best budget-friendly pick, best pick for urban parents and so on.

What if the car seat you are looking at isn't in our car seat chapter? Then odds are, we've reviewed it on our web site— we've got 30+ infant car seats reviewed there. Go to BabyBargains.com and type the car seat name in the search box (from your phone, click on the three lines you see at the upper right. This opens the search box).

3 **WHAT IS ONLINE THAT ISN'T IN THIS BOOK?** In addition to individual product reviews, we also have our famous baby gear checklist—everything you need to be ready for baby.

We also have a section on car seat adapters, with links as to what adapters work with which strollers. Check out our popular message board where you can discuss gear, parenting and more with other parents to be.

Looking for breaking news items about safety recalls and other baby gear news? Check our social media: Facebook (facebook. com/babybargains) or Twitter feed (@babybargain-book).

4 **CAN I ASK A QUESTION?** Sure, our door is always open— email us at authors@babybargains.com. We value your feedback, so feel free to tell us how to make our book or web site better.

5 **WHY DO YOU SOMETIMES RECOMMEND A MORE EXPENSIVE PRODUCT THAN A CHEAPER OPTION?** Yes, this is a book about bargains, but sometimes we will pick a slightly more expensive item in a category if we believe it is superior in quality or safety. In some cases, it makes sense to invest in better-quality products that will last through more than one child. And don't forget about the hassle of replacing a cheap product that breaks in six months.

To be sure, however, we recognize that many folks are on tight budgets. To help, we offer budget-friendly recommendations as well.

Another note: remember that our brand reviews online cover many options in a category, not just the cheapest. Don't be dismayed if we give an expensive brand an "A" rating—our ratings are based on quality, construction, innovation and more. Yes, we will try to identify the best values in a category as well.

6 **WHAT OTHER PARENTING BOOKS DO YOU PUBLISH?** We have three other best-selling books: Expecting 411, *Baby 411* and *Toddler 411*. Co-authored by an award-winning pediatrician, these books answer your questions about pregnancy, your baby's sleep, nutrition and more. See the back of this book for details.

What's New in This Edition?

Welcome to the 12th edition—this year marks our 24th year of covering the baby biz. Yes, we started writing this book way back in 1993. Before Amazon shipped its very first book. Before Google. When dinosaurs roamed the Earth.

We've streamlined Baby Bargains in this new edition, focusing more on specific recommendations for different parenting lifestyles (strollers for runners, car seats for those who don't own a car and rely on Uber, etc). And let's not forget our grandparent readers—we've got specific ideas for you on cribs, high chairs and more.

We've expanded our eco-friendly recommendations this year, calling out specific ideas for furniture, diapers, organic baby food and more.

By moving our specific product/brand reviews online, we've freed up space to include recommendations for products such as baby food processors and related gear.

Of course, we've kept the features you love about *Baby Bargains*, such as our ever-popular baby registry at-a-glance

(Appendix B).

Don't forget to check out our other extensive online offerings—click on the Bargain forum on our message boards (shortcut: BabyBargains.com/coupons) to get news on the latest discount codes and more. Our "Bargain Alert" message board has dozens of posts by readers each day, sharing deals, steals and more.

Ebooks

Prefer to read this book as an ebook? We've got you covered with ebook versions of this book available for your Kindle, iPad/iPhone, Android device and other e-readers.

Let's Go Shopping!

Now that all the formal introductions are done, let's move on to the good stuff. As your tour guides to BabyLand, we'd like to remind you of one key rule: the Baby Biz is just that—business.

The juvenile products and baby care (food, diapers) industry is a $23 BILLION DOLLAR business in the US. Yes, stores and brands are out there to "help" you care for your baby—but their job is also to *sell* baby gear.

But that's not *our* job! We want to help you prepare for baby and her safe without breaking the bank. So let's get going . . .

CHAPTER 2

Nursery Necessities: Cribs, Dressers & More

Inside this chapter

What's the best crib on the market today? For space-challenged parents? For design enthusiasts? This chapter covers cribs, crib mattresses, dressers, rocker gliders, bassinets and more.

We've got a bit of ground to cover in outfitting your nursery— so let's begin at the beginning: your baby's crib.

The Best Baby Crib

Yes, job #1 for any new parent is to set up a safe sleep space for your new baby. And buying a crib should be straight forward, right?

Yet step into a baby megastore and you'll quickly note they have 20+ different nursery "vignettes"—cleverly put-together looks that match a crib, dresser and a zillion accessories.

Ditto for typing "crib" into Amazon's search box—out pops 69 *pages* of results. That's when you feel your head start to spin . . . and now you've got crib overload.

Deep breath! Let's cut through the clutter and go over some basics.

7 Things No One Tells You About Buying A Crib!

1 **WHETHER THEY COST $70 OR $700, ALL CRIBS SOLD IN THE U.S. AND CANADA MEET MANDATORY SAFETY RULES.** Yes, you read that right— that crib at IKEA for under $100 is just as safe as the European designer model from a fancy boutique that runs $2000.

Do cheap cribs have dangerous designs? No. Long gone are the days when you had to measure slats to make sure they were the correct distance. If a crib is sold in a major store or reputable online site, you can rest assured it meets current safety standards. Unlike other baby gear, safety standards for cribs are *mandatory* in the US and Canada.

That said, we would suggest buying from an *established* brand name (in addition to the top picks in this chapter, we review top brands BabyBargains.com). Yes, some web sites sell cribs from obscure brands with little or no history in the U.S. The concern here is whether you'd be able to contact them to buy replacement parts. Or how would they handle a safety recall?

2 ALMOST ALL CRIBS SOLD TODAY ARE IMPORTED FROM ASIA. YES, EVEN THOSE WITH ITALIAN-SOUNDING NAMES. China and Vietnam are the two biggest exporters of cribs to North America. In fact, we'd estimate that 97% of the cribs sold in the U.S. are imported from Asia. The rest are imported from Eastern Europe (Latvia, Romania) with a smattering from Italy and Canada. And yes, there is a company or two left in the U.S. that makes cribs domestically (El Greco, for example).

We realize some readers are concerned about products from China, which has been through various product safety scandals over the years. For those folks, we recommend a crib or two made in North America (later in this chapter). Fair warning: this will cost you much more than an imported crib.

3 CRIBS ARE SOLD A LA CARTE. AND REQUIRE ASSEMBLY. When you shop for cribs, you often will find pictures like this:

But when you *buy* a crib, what you get is actually this:

Yep, that is it. Crib mattress? Extra. Sheets? Extra. Fancy bedding decor? Extra. You get the picture.

Obviously, some of these items are required (mattress) and most are optional (besides sheets, just about everything else). And those extras (crib mattresses) can sometimes cost more than the crib itself. Just a heads up as you plan that nursery room budget!

4 Size matters. Not the size of the crib, but the size of your baby's bedroom. Full-size cribs are all the same size: about 29" wide and 53" long. That's the *interior* dimensions. Cribs with fancy headboards or curved sides can be several inches wider/longer.

Fitting a full-size crib into a tiny secondary bedroom (or urban condo) can sometimes be a challenge. We recommend some options for those who are space-challenged later in this chapter.

And remember that the crib is just the start of your nursery furniture saga—most nurseries also have a dresser to store clothes. And perhaps a place to sit and nurse baby. Later you might want a desk and chair. Plan out space considerations before shopping.

Where the baby's crib should go in a nursery is another factor. The safest place for a crib is away from any heat or cooling source (ducts, radiators, etc). And you'll want to keep baby's crib away from windows and window coverings/blinds (cords are a strangulation hazard). Got a baby monitor as a gift? Keep the cord at least three feet from the crib.

We should note not all cribs are your standard rectangle. There are some funky cribs out there like round cribs (see right).

But remember this equation: more funky = more money. A round crib needs a special round mattress, round bedding, and so on . . . at prices typically much more than standard size crib accessories.

5 To convert? Or not to convert? Full-size cribs today come in two basic flavors: convertible. Or not convertible.

Non-convertible cribs (we call them basic cribs) are just, well, cribs. They don't morph into other piece of furniture. As such, they are typically less expensive than convertible cribs.

As the name implies, convertible cribs . . . well, convert into several different stages as your child grows. Many "4-in-1" cribs are first cribs, then toddler beds (with a toddler rail replacing one side), "day beds" (no toddler rail) and then full-size beds. The different configurations look like this:

The four different configurations of a convertible crib: crib, toddler bed with rail, day bed (no rail for older toddlers) and then finally full-size bed.

In order to do all this presto-change, you need (wait for it) an extra "conversion kit" which includes bed rails to make a full-size bed, connecting the headboard and footboard. These kits range from $100 to $200—that's on top of the crib price. And convertible cribs are more pricey than basic cribs—convertibles *start* around $250 and can easily soar into the $500's.

You could argue that even with this extra expense, you would save money in the long run because you are not buying a separate bed when a child outgrows a crib. But basic (non-convertible) cribs start around $100 and you can buy a twin bed for as little as $139. Like this one:

Homelegance twin platform bed with headboard. $139 on Amazon.

The take home message: convertible cribs aren't really money savers, but more of a choice in aesthetics.

Confusingly, there are several variations on convertible cribs. Some manufactures say they are "convertible" when all they mean is you can take the side rail off and then have a toddler bed. Doh! That doesn't count as convertible in our book. On the other hand, some crib makers include a toddler rail for free (the rail keeps a toddler from rolling out of the crib once the side rail is removed).

There is no right or wrong answer when it comes to whether to buy a basic or convertible crib. Some considerations: if space is tight, remember that using a standard crib and then buying a twin size bed may make much more sense than a convertible that morphs into a full size bed (full size beds are 15″ wider than a twin).

Think about how the crib will look when converted. Is the headboard higher than the footboard? Some folks think that looks better than converted cribs where the headboard and footboard are similar in height, which is more common in lower price convertible cribs. Your choice, of course!

Some convertible cribs (like the affordable and popular Fisher-Price models) don't require special conversion kits or rails— you can use standard bed frames like this:

This bed frame can morph from a twin bed to full-size, queen or king. $40 on Amazon.

These rails run about $40. If you plan to have more than one child, it might make sense to buy an affordable basic crib you can re-use from child to child. Then as each one outgrows the crib, you can move then into a twin bed (headboard or footboard optional, of course).

6 IT MAY TAKE 14 WEEKS TO SPECIAL ORDER THAT FANCY CRIB. YES, WE SAID 14 WEEKS. NOT DAYS. WEEKS. There are three basic places to buy a crib: online, chain stores and specialty boutiques. Most online sites deliver in about a week.

Chain stores stock many cribs, while some styles require two to four week lead times (to ship in from a distribution center).

Specialty boutiques, however, are a mixed bag. Some do stock cribs for immediate purchase. Most, however, require you to special order. And that is where the 14 week wait can come in, which usually is an unpleasant surprise.

Most specialty stores carry upper-end crib brands that cost $500 to $2000. Some of these brands require a wait of 8-12 weeks for delivery, with a few up to 14 weeks. And sometimes deliveries can be delayed (port strike? earthquake? Chinese new year?), causing your furniture to go on back order for, say, 20 weeks. Plan accordingly!

7 SAY NO TO . . . used or hand-me-down cribs. Buy a brand-new crib to make sure it meets current standards.

Crib safety standards have changed over the years—not more than a few years ago, cribs had drop-sides that were implicated in safety issues (sides detached, resulting in injuries and in some cases, deaths). These cribs were outlawed in 2011.

We know well-meaning family members want to help by dusting off that family heirloom your grandfather used in the "old days." Or a friend has a crib in the attic from 1998 they are dying to ~~pawn off~~ graciously give you.

Here (right) is an antique iron baby crib, like many cribs lurking in relative's basements and attics. Does it meet current safety standards? That would be a big fat NO!

Remember that even a late-model crib can be dangerous if it is missing hardware or instructions. Buying new ensures your crib meets current safety standards and has all its parts and hardware.

The Best Baby Cribs

Enough with the safety advice! Let's get down to the recommendations! Here's what we are going to cover in this section:

◆ Best Crib Overall
◆ Best Budget-Friendly Crib (Convertible)
◆ Best Budget-Friendly Crib (Basic)
◆ Best Crib for City Dwellers (and those with little space)
◆ Best Eco Baby Crib
◆ Best Crib Made In the USA.
◆ Best High Style Crib
◆ Best Travel/Portable Crib
◆ Best Crib for Short Parents
◆ Best Crib For Grandma's House

The Best Baby Crib (Overall)

After researching and reviewing 87 different crib brands, we pick the **Pali Imperia crib** ($400 on Amazon) as the Best Baby Crib (Overall).

Clean, simple lines set the Pali Imperia apart from its competition. This crib converts into a full-size bed (with conversion rails, a separate purchase for $190). For folks who want a simple crib for $400 or less, it is an excellent buy.

Pali touts its eco-friendly bona fides with the Imperia, claiming that the woods used to make the crib are "sustainably harvested from trusted and reliable sources that are committed to minimizing environmental impact." Pali doesn't have any third-party certifications to verify this claim, so you have to take their word for it. The Imperia is made from rubber wood "pine solids" and birch veneer.

So why is this crib a "best pick"? Part of what you are paying for here is the Pali brand, an Italian crib brand with a long and successful track record here in North America. FYI: The Imperia crib is imported from Thailand.

Another plus for the Imperia: the large number of accessory pieces you can choose from to build a complete nursery. The Imperia matches Pali's Novara collection, which enables you to customize your baby's nursery with a double dresser, armoire, night stand, and/or bookcase hutch. Less expensive brands typically only have one or two accessory pieces.

The Best Crib: Pali Imperia
Available in both white and espresso, the Pali Imperia is an excellent crib with simple lines and quality construction. $399 on Amazon.

Also Great: DaVinci Kalani 4-in-1 Convertible

Looking for a more affordable crib that is traditionally styled? We recommend the ***DaVinci Kalani 4-in-1 Convertible Crib***. This affordable $200 crib is made by DaVinci, which is part of the Million Dollar Baby furniture company. The Kalani crib includes curved rails and is made of New Zealand pine in eight finishes.

The Kalani offers four different configurations: toddler bed, daybed and full-size bed. Included in the box is the toddler rail—which is a nice bonus, as other brands charge $20 to $80 as an accessory. (Of course, the bed rails to convert the Kalani into a full size bed are an extra $89 purchase, as is customary).

We like the little touches DaVinci has added to the Kalani—note the design detail at the feet and the eight color finishes. Most cribs in this price range have just two or three finish options.

The Kalani has a metal spring platform, which we prefer. Other $200 cribs sometimes have MDF or solid wood boards.

Nursery Design: Two Schools of Thought

There are two theories of nursery design: either a baby's room should look, well, babyish . . . or it should be more adult-looking, able to adapt as the child grows. There is no right or wrong answer. If you subscribe to the baby-theme, then go with a basic (non-convertible) crib and dresser that you will later swapped out for a twin bed and desk/hutch. If you prefer the other path, then buy a convertible crib (which converts to a full size bed) and dresser that can do double duty. Some brands have dressers that are first a changing area for diapers . . . and then convert to a computer area complete with pull out keyboard drawer.

Best Budget-Friendly Crib (Convertible)

The Fisher-Price Newbury is our pick as the best budget-friendly convertible crib. Made of New Zealand pine, the Newbury converts to a full-size headboard and is available in four colors (white and three shades of brown: praline, espresso and cherry).

The Fisher-Price Newbury is a simple crib for $150 with a "4-in-1" pitch—it coverts from crib to toddler bed, daybed and finally a headboard for a full-size bed. The toddler and daybed configuration requires the separate purchase of a toddler rail.

We should point out that even though this crib is touted as convertible, it isn't as convertible as other brands. With more expensive cribs, you get both a headboard and footboard—therefore, you only have to get conversion rails ($100-$200) to make it into a full-size bed.

For the Newbury, you get a headboard but no footboard—so you can purchase a bedframe for $40 or so on Amazon. The result is a simpler look, which we think is just fine. And remember that most convertible cribs that convert into a headboard and footboard are two to three times the price of the Newbury.

Price-wise it is probably a wash, but with other cribs you are getting both a headboard and footboard. With the Newbury, it is just the headboard.

Best Budget-Friendly Crib (Basic)

Another affordable simple crib is the **IKEA Sniglar** at $80. No, that's not a typo! A simple, modern crib for less than a $100. The crib is just a crib—it doesn't convert to a full-size bed, etc. Also: the Sniglar only has two mattress positions. Very simple, but well made.

You can have any color for the Sniglar as long as it is beech, which is similar to maple in color (that is, light brown). If you want a simple white crib, look at the **IKEA Hensvik** is $99. Like the Sniglar, the Hensvik is a basic crib without any frills.

If you are into minimalist style, either of these cribs will fit the bill. Note that even though IKEA cribs are simple, they meet all U.S. safety standards. We've recommended this brand for years and heard from many readers who were happy with this simple crib for under $100.

Who Is Jenny Lind?

You can't shop for cribs and not hear the name "Jenny Lind." Here's an important point to remember: Jenny Lind isn't a brand name; it refers to a particular *style* of crib. But how did it get this name? Jenny Lind was a popular Swedish soprano in the 19th century. During her triumphal U.S. tour, it was said that Lind slept in a "spool bed." Hence, cribs that featured turned spindles (which look like stacked spools of thread) became known as Jenny Lind cribs. All this begs the question—what if today we still named juvenile furniture after famous singers? Would we have Drake cribs and Beyonce dressers? Nah, probably not a good idea.

Best Crib For City Dwellers
(and those with little space for a nursery)

If you live in the city, space may be at a premium. We have two solutions here, although both have drawbacks.

Our best pick for cribs for city dwellers is the **Stokke Sleepi.** Norwegian juvenile gear maker Stokke pitches its oval crib as a "system" that grows with your child: the Sleepi morphs from a bassinet to a crib, then a toddler bed and finally two chairs . . . all for a mere $1000. You can buy just the crib for $799 (without the toddler bed conversion kit).

The Sleepi's oval shape and wheels makes it easier to move through narrow doors. The Sleepi is 29″ wide; standard full-size cribs are 30″ and more. That may not sound like much, but it can make the difference between fitting through a doorway—or not. Plus few cribs come with wheels these days, as the Stokke does.

Also: you can use the Sleepi in bassinet mode for up to six months. The bassinet mode takes up just 26″ in width. And the bassinet's simple style wins fans for its minimalist aesthetic.

So what's not to like about Sleepi, besides its steep price? Well, an oval crib requires a special oval crib mattress ($200); and oval crib bedding ($35 for a sheet). As you might guess, choices are limited.

We also noted that Stokke has struggled with quality control issues in recent years, as expressed by our readers as well as customer reviews posted to Amazon. As a result, we currently give them an overall grade of B-.

If the price and concerns about the Stokke Sleepi have you wishing for another alternative, consider plan B: a portable crib.

About 10% of all cribs sold in North America are portable/mini cribs, sometimes also called folding cribs.

As you can guess from the name, these cribs are narrower in

both width (25″ width versus 30″ or more for full-size cribs) and length (about 39″ vs 52″).

Our top pick for best mini crib is **Babyletto's Origami Mini Crib** ($250). This simple crib folds away when not in use and comes with wheels to move it about a small apartment or condo. (Using the wheels is optional). Overall, we found the construction quality to above average for this type of crib.

The downside to the Babyletto Origami Mini Crib? Well, it does take a while to assemble (a few users complained it was over an hour). And the crib only comes with a one-inch

pad; you should probably replace this with a mattress that snugly fits it (37 x 23.875 mattress), such as this one from Babyletto sold at Target for $99.

Here's the biggest drawback to the Origami mini crib—and it's the same drawback that affects nearly ALL mini crib: babies often outgrow them before they are old enough to go into a toddler or big kid bed.

Babyletto says the Origami crib can't be used "when a child begins to climb." Well, a typical child will hit that milestone around six to ten month when they can pull themselves up to a standing position. A mini crib has lower rails than a standard size crib—and that makes climbing out easy for infants under a year old.

Hence, mini cribs are more like bassinet replacements. Keep in mind that most babies will use a crib for two or three years (and sometimes up to age four). And a crib is the safest place for babies to sleep.

Yes, there are stories floating around out there that a small baby can make it in a mini crib to age 3, but that is the exception.

So what happens when your baby outgrows a mini crib before their first birthday? Well, then you have to move to a full-size crib. Hence, you can use a mini crib as a bridge until you have more room in your apartment or condo . . . or you find living accommodations with more space!

Bottom line: a mini crib can make do for a while, but you'll be finding yourself purchasing a full-size crib as your baby nears one year of age.

Best Eco-Friendly Baby Crib

Eco-Chic Baby Dorchester Classic Island 4-in-1 Convertible Crib is our pick for top eco-friendly crib. This $500 crib ticks all the boxes for our eco-friendly pick: GREENGUARD Gold certified and made by an established nursery furniture company with a good quality track record.

Exclusive to Babies R Us, Eco-Chic Baby is part of the Baby Appleseed family of nursery furniture brands. The company's mojo is to combine eco-friendliness and elegant design. The eco-pitch: when you buy one of their cribs, the company will plant ten trees in your baby's name, thanks to a partnership with the non-profit American Forests.

GREENGUARD Gold is an independent third-party certification that the nursery furniture item is low-emission—that is, emission of volatile compounds (VOC's) which can contribute to bad indoor air quality.

The Dorchester is made of American poplar wood, which is more durable than pine (commonly seen in sub-$300 cribs). We consider poplar wood to be sustainable—and since it is harvested in the U.S., this process must meet U.S. environmental standards.

This crib has several matching accessories, including a five drawer dresser, double dresser and armoire. Here's what the Dorchester Island crib looks like when converted:

Crib   Toddler Bed

Daybed   Full Size Bed

So what's not to like? Well, like most convertible cribs, the optional toddler rail ($100) and conversion rail kit ($200) are extra purchases. While the toddler rail (for the toddler bed mode pictured above) is optional, if you plan to convert this crib to a full-size bed, that $200 conversion rail kit makes the Dorchester a $700 total purchase.

And you can have any color you wish for this crib as long as it is "slate." Yep, at the time of this writing, that is your only option.

The Eco-Chic Dorchester Island crib is only available at Babies R Us—so there's no price shopping this to online competitors. If you don't live near a BRU or prefer to buy from Amazon, Eco-Chic's sister brand Karla DuBois has a similar style crib (the Oslo) for just $400 (right).

Yes, the Oslo crib has the same GREENGUARD Gold certification and quality as Eco-Chic Baby, but is $100 lower in price.

True Colors: Swatches and Samples

What's the difference between oak and pecan? When you order baby furniture, those terms don't refer to a species of wood, but the color of the stain. And many parents have been frustrated when their expensive nursery furniture arrives and it looks nothing like the "cherry" furniture they expected. Here's our advice: when ordering furniture, be sure to see ACTUAL wood samples stained with the hue you want. Don't rely on a web site picture or even a printed catalog. And remember that different types of wood take stain, well, differently. If you order your furniture in a pecan finish and the crib is made of beech wood while the dresser is pine, they may NOT match. That's because beech and pine would look slightly different even when stained with the exact same finish.

Ordering online makes this more of a challenge. Most sites don't offer wood samples—you have to rely on an online picture (and how that is displayed on your monitor). Bottom line: you'll have to be flexible when it comes to what the final stain looks like. But if you have your heart set on a particular hue for your nursery furniture, it might be best to order off-line . . . and see a stained wood sample first.

Best Crib Made in the USA

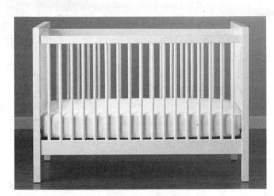

The ***El Greco Andersen crib*** ($799 at Land of Nod) is our pick for the best made-in-the-USA crib. (FYI: 97% of all cribs sold in the US are made in Asia, mostly China and Vietnam).

Based in Jamestown, New York, El Greco has been making furniture since 1975 but largely flies under the radar of the industry. Why? Because most of El Greco's cribs and dressers are sold as private label offerings by Land of Nod and Room & Board (El Greco's web site lists which cribs they make for each chain). Yes, the brand is also sold in a handful of furniture stores, but most are regular furniture stores, not baby retailers.

Quality is excellent—the Andersen crib is made of solid maple or walnut (depending on the finish), which is rare to find in nursery furniture these days. El Greco has never had a safety recall in 40+ years (!) of business and their finishes are GREENGUARD-certified. El Greco posts detailed info on their manufacturing process on the their web site (elgrecofurniture.com).

The Andersen crib comes in three finishes (maple, walnut or white).

So what are the drawbacks? Well, the Andersen is a basic crib that doesn't convert into a full-size bed like many other cribs in this price range. That makes the $799 investment here steep. But if you plan to use this crib for more than one baby, you could justify the expense.

FYI: If you like El Greco but don't like the simple style of the Andersen, the company sells a handful of other crib at Room & Board, a 16 store chain of modern furniture stores. If you don't have one of those stores nearby, you can order El Greco cribs online at Room & Board's web site.

What if you don't have that much money but still want an American-made crib? Unfortunately, there isn't much beyond El Greco.

Yes, there are a handful of modern furniture companies like DucDuc that make cribs in the US, but most of these are $1000+ and even $2000+ (see below for an expanded discussion). And we found El Greco's quality superior to these alternatives.

Not made in China

From lead paint in toys to tainted baby formula, China has had its share of, uh, quality control issues. And some of our readers have asked us, not surprisingly, how to furnish a nursery with products NOT made in China. While that sounds simple, it isn't: 97% or more of baby furniture sold in the U.S. is made in China—so avoiding Chinese-made items takes some effort.

But there is good news: there ARE a handful of companies that make their furniture somewhere other than China. And yes, there are still firms that make furniture in the U.S.: ducduc, Capretti, El Greco, and Newport Cottages. Oak Designs (oakdesigns.com) makes dressers and twin beds domestically. Lolly & Me's "Eco-Friendly" collections are made in the U.S.

Other furniture makers import goods from countries other than China: Romina makes furniture in Romania; Bratt Décor and Bivona's Dolce Babi and Tiamo have factories in Vietnam. Oeuf imports its furniture from Latvia. Natart is made in Canada and Denmark. Baby's Dream is imported from Chile.

A few caveats to this advice: first, production often shifts, so before you order, reconfirm with the manufacturer or retailer where the furniture is being made. Second, manufacturers that split production between China and other countries often don't publicize which furniture is made where. You have to ask.

Best High-Style Crib

The **Ubabub Pod** crib is a futuristic show stopper—yes, insanely expensive ($2300) but wins our pick for best high style crib with its curved wood panels and acrylic sides with funky cut-outs. The detail and craftsmanship on this crib is something to behold.

The Pod comes with a custom-fitted mattress and a conversion kit to turn into a toddler bed that looks like something out of a movie set in 2093.

Distributed in the US by the Million Dollar Baby family of nursery brands, Ubabub (pronounced "uber-bub") is actually based in Australia and sells its goods in both Oz and New Zealand. Ubabub has a good reputation for quality and a solid track record for safety.

Best Travel/Portable Baby Crib

After evaluating and testing 17 portable baby cribs, we pick the **BabyBjorn Travel Crib Light** ($200) as the best travel/portable baby crib. While not the cheapest option out there, we judged this ultra-light play yard (which folds up like an umbrella and fits in a small carry case) to be worth the investment.

Parent feedback has been universally positive. At 11 pounds, it is half the weight of a standard Graco Pack N Play.

The Travel Crib Light ($267; 13 lbs.) has breathable mesh sides with exterior metal poles and comes with an organic fitted sheet and mattress. The top edge includes a padded cover and it folds into a 19″ x 23.5″ x 5.5″ bag. You'll note that the shape is rather different from a traditional play yard and it uses poles like you'd see on a camping tent.

Overall, readers like the Travel Crib Light. Fans love the easy set up and break down, and note that the fabric is nicer than other similar travel cribs. The mattress is pretty thick for a travel crib and the light weight makes it easy to lug around.

The only complaints: short parents may have a tougher time lowering baby into the crib and the exterior poles jut out at an angle, creating a tripping hazard. Yes, it is pricey, but if you plan to travel frequently with your baby it may be worth the expense.

Also Great:
Guava Family Lotus Everywhere Travel Crib

If you are an occasional traveler, the **Lotus Everywhere Travel Crib** is a lightweight travel solution with a twist.

The Lotus has a similar design to the Bjorn Travel Crib Light, but the frame poles are thicker and one of the mesh sides has a zipper (with a locking zipper so toddlers can't escape; a toddler replies: *how much do you want to bet?*).

At 13 lbs., this is definitely a lighter option for travel than a

Pack N Play and it comes in a backpack bag for easy carrying. The Lotus is $200, similar to the Bjorn.

But what really makes the Lotus different from the Bjorn and other travel play yards are the accessories. Need a bassinet? You can purchase an Bassinet Conversion Kit ($110). FYI: Lotus sells a Bassinet Kit + Crib Bundle in one package for $300. Guava also makes three types of sheets for the travel crib, a Fun Shade for sunny days, and a mosquito net.

So what's the real difference between the Bjorn and the Lotus? The mattress in the Bjorn is thicker and the fabric is better quality, in our opinion. The footprint of the Lotus is slightly larger than the Bjorn but both have leg poles that stick out and could be a trip hazard.

Some parents complained that the Lotus' Velcro straps used to secure the mattress and sheet are difficult to thread, since you have to do it by touch. Bjorn calls out it's attachments more clearly. Finally, we wondered if the zippered side mesh was a really useful feature. We like that you could open the side and make the Lotus into a fort or hideaway for older toddlers with a blanket or even the sunshade over the top—but that's not a necessity, just a nice side benefit.

Yes, the Bjorn outpaces the Lotus on fabric quality and ease of set-up/take down, but the Lotus does have more accessories.

Best Crib for Short Parents

If you are under 5'5", you may find reaching into a standard-size stationary crib challenging. Since most cribs sit a foot or two off the floor and drop-side cribs were phased out in 2011, shorter parents may find it difficult putting baby in a standard crib when the mattress in its lowest position.

For those parents, a lower profile crib may be just the ticket. A good bet: babyletto's Modo 3-in-1 crib (pictured) is made from New Zealand pine and is relatively affordable at $279. At only 34" tall, the Modo sits low to the ground making it much easier to put baby in and out of the crib.

The Modo is available in six color combinations including two-tone options (white top with brown or grey base) that gives it a modern spin.

We like that Modo is GREENGUARD Gold certified, plus it has four mattress levels.

While Babyletto touts the Modo's "3-in-1" conversion feature, the Modo only coverts into a toddler bed (the toddler rail is included, which is a nice touch). Hence, the Modo doesn't convert into a full-size bed for older kids.

Best Crib for Grandma's House

The best crib for the grandparents must be easy to set up and take down.

We suggested one of two options here: a portable crib like the **Dream On Me 2 in 1 Portable Folding Stationary Side Crib** ($110) hits all the right notes—easy to assemble, folds away for storage and is affordable.

The biggest drawback: the Dream on Me crib is actually a mini crib that is only 38" long (versus 52" for a full-size crib). That means babies older than one year of age or larger infants may outgrow this crib before they are old enough to sleep in a toddler bed. One solution: go for one of our travel crib picks (see earlier in this section).

(FYI: Babies typically stay in a crib to age three or later. Once a child regularly climbs out of a crib, it is time for a big kid bed.)

cribs

Hence the key issue with any mini crib is safety—older babies (younger toddlers) can easily escape a mini crib. Full-size cribs? Not as much.

Therefore, our second option here is a full-size crib that is easily to assemble. Yes, such cribs do exist. Our pick for this would be the **Delta Canton** crib ($220; right)—Delta includes all the tools (basically, one allen wrench) and that makes the assembly easy-peasy, say our readers.

More crib reviews online at BabyBargains.com

On our free web site, BabyBargains.com, we include detailed reviews for 50+ crib brands. Yes, over 50! Find a brand you are looking at by doing a quick search from our home page.

Also check out our social media channels (Facebook: BabyBargains, Twitter: @BabyBargainBook) for breaking news on safety recalls and more.

On the next two pages, you'll see a chart that summarizes our current ratings for the most popular nursery furniture brands. (Ratings are accurate as of press time, but go to our web site to make sure things didn't change since then!).

Of course, in reading all this, you may ask yourself a simple question: why should I trust you? Glad you asked.

We've been rating and reviewing cribs since 1993. In addition to hands on inspections of nursery furniture, we have also visited manufacturer facilities and met with safety regulators—and when we travel, we pay our all of our own expenses.

We also gather reader reviews posted on our message boards (which have 1.1 million-plus views a month), as well as consumer reviews posted on sites like Babies R Us and Amazon.

Here's another key point: we don't take money from the brands we review. No free samples, no sponsors, no "partnerships." Baby Bargains is your independent and unbiased source for expert baby gear reviews.

Next up: let's look at the best crib mattress for that new crib.

CRIB RATINGS

Name	Rating	Cost	Where Made?
BABY APPLESEED	A	$$ TO $$$	VIETNAM
BABYS DREAM	C	$$ TO $$$	CHILE/CHINA
BABYLETTO	B+	$$ TO $$$	CHINA/TAIWAN
BASSETTBABY	B+	$$$	CHINA
BIVONA & CO	A	$ TO $$$	VIETNAM
BLOOM	B-	$$ TO $$$	CHINA
BRATT DECOR	C+	$$$	VIETNAM/CHINA
CAFEKID	B+	$$ TO $$$	THAILAND
CAPRETTI	B+	$$$	USA
CHILD CRAFT	C+	$	ASIA
CORSICAN KIDS	C+	$$$	USA
DELTA	C	$ TO $$	ASIA
DOREL	F	$ TO $$	CHINA
DREAM ON ME	B-	$	CHINA
DUCDUC	B	$$$	USA
DUTAILIER	B+	$$$	CANADA
DWELL STUDIO	B-	$$$	CANADA
EL GRECO	A-	$$$	USA
EVOLUR	B	$$ TO $$$	VIETNAM
FRANKLIN & BEN	B+	$$ TO $$$	ASIA
IKEA	A-	$	ASIA
JCPENNEY	C+	$$ TO $$$	ASIA
KIDZ DECOEUR	B	$$$	CANADA
LAND OF NOD	A	$$$	VARIES
LOLLY & ME	F	$$ TO $$$	USA/VIETNAM
MILLION $ BABY/DA VINCI	B+	$ TO $$$	ASIA
MIRA/KOLCRAFT	C	$ TO $$	VIETNAM/CHINA
MUNIRE	B	$$ TO $$$	INDONESIA
NATART	A	$$$	CANADA
NEWPORT COTTAGE	C	$$$	USA
OEUF	B+	$$$	LATVIA
PALI	A	$$ TO $$$	VIETNAM/ITALY
POTTERY BARN KIDS	C	$$ TO $$$	ASIA
RESTORATION HARDWARE	F	$$$	ASIA
ROMINA	A	$$$	ROMANIA
SIMMONS	C+	$$ TO $$$	CHINA/VIETNAM
SORELLE	C+	$ TO $$$	CHINA/VIETNAM
STOKKE/SLEEPI	B-	$$$	SLOVENIA
STORK CRAFT	C-	$ TO $$	CHINA
UNION	B	$	ASIA
WESTWOOD	A-	$$ to $$$	CHINA, VIETNAM

Key: **RATING:** Our opinion of the manufacturer's quality and value.
COST: $=under $250, $$=$250-500, $$$=over $500.
GREENGUARD: Are these cribs GREENGUARD certified?

GREENGUARD?	COMMENTS
◆	Eco-friendly, traditionally styled. Many at BuyBuyBaby.
	Still have some folding rails; long waits for backorders.
◆	Mid-century vibe, made from New Zealand pine.
	Cribs good; case pieces bad. Sold in Restoration Hardware.
	3 brands: Fisher Price, Ti Amo mid-price; Dolce Babi pricey.
	Alma mini crib good bassinet alternative for urbanites.
	Vintage looks, bright colors. Long lead times.
	Sold in Costco; includes conversion rails. Good value.
	Very pricey, made by Amish. Cribs start at $1100!
	Affordable, but freight damage issues. Skip dressers.
	Very pricey wrought-iron cribs; vintage feel.
	Entry price level, many cribs can be assembled without tools.
	Affordable, but quality issues. Soft pine wood.
	Affordable mini crib maker, also big in crib mattresses.
	Retro, modernist furniture. Expensive.
	Quality has improved; expensive, 32 finishes.
	Pricey, mid century looks. Exposed hardware disappoints.
	Excellent quality, sold at Land of Nod, Room & Board.
	Newer brand with high-end adult looks.
	Early American, distressed vintage looks.
	Do-it-yourself assembly; low prices; very simple styling.
	Sells furniture under several private label brands.
	Eco-focus. Pricey. 16 finshes.
	Stylish but pricey; good service, Made by El Greco.
	Sold in Target; eco-friendly with some items made in U.S.
	Da Vinci brand sold online; focus on traditional styling.
	Kolcraft offers better value; limited styles.
	Baby Cache is lower priced version in Babies R Us.
◆	Innovative storage; whimsical touches but very pricey.
	Two-tone, distressed finishes; quality/service inconsistent.
◆	Eco-style meets modernism; lowest price of modern group.
	Very good quality; traditional design.
	Design leader but overpriced; high shipping charges.
◆	Very pricey, complaints about customer service/returns.
◆	Pricey, but very well-made furniture. Solid wood.
	Owned by Delta; average quality, plain styling.
	Decent prices; mixed customer service reputation.
	Pricey crib "system" best for those with little space.
	Opening price point cribs sold in chains, Amazon.
	Simple crib sold on Amazon; made by Million $ Baby.
	Traditional looks; good quality. Affordable line is Imagio.

The Best Baby Crib Mattresses

Odds are, you've already bought a mattresses for yourself before and have a working knowledge of mattress lingo (box spring, memory foam). But as always, the baby version of mattresses is more a bit more complex. And confusing.

Babies need to sleep on a firm mattress for safety reasons, probably much firmer than an adult would prefer. And because diapers leak, a waterproof pad to protect that mattress may be necessary.

And what about pricey $300+ mattresses? Are they really better or healthier than a $100 basic crib mattress?

Before we get too deep in the weeds, let's start with a quick primer on buying a crib mattress.

7 Things No One Tells You About Buying A Crib Mattress!

1 **FORGET ALL THE FANCY CLAIMS: ALL YOU NEED IS A FIRM MATTRESS WITH A WATERPROOF COVER.** What's inside the mattress (foam, coil, latex, mohair, etc) is a matter of personal preference. After reviewing dozens of studies on crib mattress safety, there is no evidence that one material is healthier than another . . . despite what you might read online!

A simple crib mattress starts around $50. It should snuggly fit your crib with no gaps more than two fingers length between the mattress and the crib (see graphic at right).

And while you'd think it would be no-brainer, there are some crib mattresses sold with NON-waterproof covers, so buyer beware.

2 **THAT CRIB MATTRESS COULD COST MORE THAN YOUR CRIB.** Especially if you opt for a eco-friendly mattress or another specialty mattress. Many of these mattresses top $300 and even $400.

3 **THERE'S NO SUCH THING AS A "BREATHABLE MATTRESS."** Many parents are understandably concerned about SIDS (Sudden Infant Death Syndrome). Unfortunately, some crib mattress makers play on this fear by claiming their super-duper mattress made from special material (unicorn hair and magic fibers?) is "breathable" and a lower suffocation risk than non-unicorn mattresses. Quick fact check: that's FALSE.

These magical claims may lead some parents to think it is ok to put baby to sleep on their stomach. Please don't—the safest way for baby to sleep in a crib is on their back . . . on a firm mattress. (We have a full discussion of SIDS and how to prevent it in our other book *Baby 411*, co-authored by a pediatrician who is a spokesperson for the American Academy of Pediatrics).

4 KEY QUALITY FEATURE TO LOOK FOR: TRIPLE LAMINATED/REINFORCED VINYL COVERS. These covers are more durable and less likely to tear (when you move the mattress around to change the sheets). Lower quality mattresses just have a single or double layer of vinyl.

5 SAY NO TO THAT HAND-ME-DOWN. Your friend's cousin has a crib mattress sitting in her attic that she'd love give you. Politely refuse. Why? Bacteria and mold can grow in an old mattress, even if it has a waterproof cover—and especially if it has been stored in a dank basement or unventilated attic. Plan to have more than one kid? We also suggest a new mattress with each baby.

6 LIGHTER = BETTER. Babies do all sorts of things in cribs other than occasionally sleep. When it is time to change the sheets, you have to wrestle with that crib mattress. And here, lighter mattresses (usually foam) are much easier to handle than heavier options (most likely coil mattresses). Another option: go for quick change sheets that don't require you to wrestle with the mattress.

The added weight of coil mattresses doesn't add any benefits for baby or parent, so our rule stands: lighter = better.

7 CONVENTIONAL CRIB MATTRESSES ARE NOT DANGEROUS. Many expensive, eco-friendly crib mattresses are marketed with dark hints that conventional crib mattresses (made of foam or coils) are somehow dangerous. The online world is full of such claims:

> "Common materials in crib, bassinet, cradle and porta-crib mattresses may be harmful and even potentially life threatening to your baby. The majority of mattress manufacturers use toxic, unsafe materials." —web site of an expensive eco-baby crib mattress.

So let's state it for the record: there is NO scientific evidence that sleeping on a conventional crib mattresses is harmful to your baby. Zip. Zero.

What about mattress materials giving off chemical odors? Yes, crib mattresses are made of chemicals and some do off-gas when first removed from packaging. We do recognize concerns about bad indoor air quality, especially with newly built homes that are tightly sealed. If this fits your situation, look for crib mattresses that are GREENGUARD certified—this is an independent third-party test standard for mattresses that are low in VOC's

8 tips to lower the risk of SIDS

Sudden Infant Death Syndrome (SIDS) is the sudden death of an infant under one of year of age due to unexplained causes. Sadly, SIDS is still the number one killer of infants under age one—over 2000 babies die each year.

So, what causes SIDS? Scientists don't know, despite studying the problem for two decades. We do know that SIDS is a threat during the first year of life, with a peak occurrence between one and six months. SIDS also affects more boys than girls; and the SIDS rate in African American babies is twice that of Caucasians. Despite the mystery surrounding SIDS, researchers have discovered several factors that dramatically lower the risk of SIDS. Here is what you can do:

Put your baby to sleep on her back. Infants should be placed on their back (not side or tummy) each time they go to sleep. Since the campaign to get parents to put baby to sleep on their backs began in 1992, the SIDS rate has fallen by 50%. That's the good news. The bad news: while parents are heeding this message, other care givers (that is, grandma or day care centers) are less vigilant. Be sure to tell all your baby's caregivers that baby is to sleep on his back, never his tummy.

Encourage tummy time. When awake, baby should spend some time on their tummy. This helps prevent flat heads caused by lying on their backs (positional plagiocephaly). Vary your child's head position while sleeping (such as, turning his head to the right during one nap and then the left during the next nap). Minimize time spent in car seats (unless baby is in a car, of course!), swings, bouncer seats or carriers—any place baby is kept in a semi-upright position. A good goal: no more than an hour or two a day. To learn more about plagiocephaly, go online to plagiocephaly.org.

Forget gadgets. Special mattresses, sleep positioners, breathing monitors—none have been able to reduce the risk of SIDS, says the American Academy of Pediatrics. Just put baby to sleep on her back.

Use a pacifier. Consider giving baby a pacifier, which has been shown in studies to reduce the rate of SIDS. Why? Scientists don't know exactly, but some speculate pacifiers help keep the airway open.

(volatile organic compounds).

Since babies sleep 12+ hours a day on their crib mattress, we can understand the concern that baby has a safe sleep space. But crib mattress marketers that play on these fears to sell $400 eco options often peddle junk science—these folks claim "polyurethane foam" and "waterproof covers made of polyvinyl chloride or PVC" are dangerous, cause cancer, etc.

crib mattress

Okay, we should acknowledge that pacifiers are controversial—key concerns include breastfeeding interference, tooth development and ear infections. But if you introduce the pacifier after breast-feeding is well-established (around one month), there are few problems. Stop using the pacifier after one year (when the SIDS risk declines) to prevent any dental problems. While pacifiers do increase the risk of ear infections, ear infections are rare in babies when the risk of SIDS is highest (under six months old). Bottom line: Use pacifiers at the time of sleep starting at one month of life for breastfed babies. If the pacifier falls out once the baby is asleep, don't re-insert it. Stop using pacifiers once the risk of SIDS is over (about a year of life).

Don't smoke or overheat the baby's room. Smoking during pregnancy or after the baby is born has been shown to increase the risk of SIDS. Keep baby's room at a comfortable temperature, but don't overheat (do not exceed 70 degrees in the winter; 78 in the summer). Use a wearable blanket or swaddle baby with a blanket.

Bed sharing: bad. Room sharing: good. Why does bed sharing increase the risk of SIDS? Scientists say the risk of suffocation in adult linens (pillows, etc) or entrapment between bed frame and mattress, or by family members is a major contributor to SIDS. That said, *room sharing* (having baby in the same room as the parents, either in a bassinet or crib) is shown to reduce the rate of SIDS. Again, researchers don't know exactly why, but it's possible parents are more attuned to their baby's breathing when baby is nearby.

No soft bedding. Baby's crib or bassinet should have a firm mattress and no soft bedding (quilts, pillows, stuffed animals, bumpers, etc). We will discuss soft bedding more in depth in the next chapter. Also: consider using a swaddling blanket, footed sleeper or SleepSack instead of a blanket. More on these items in Chapter 3.

Make sure all other caregivers follow these instructions. Again, you might be vigilant about back-sleeping . . . but if another caregiver doesn't follow the rules, your baby could be at risk. Make sure your day care provider, grandma or other caregiver is on board.

Most of these conspiracy theories trace their origins to a widely discredited SIDS prevention campaign by a late New Zealand forensic scientist we'll call Dr. S. He claimed toxic gases from waterproof (PVC) covers and other chemicals in mattresses caused SIDS. If you wrapped a crib mattress in a special plastic wrap, SIDS could be eliminated, Dr. S. claimed. Several companies sprung up to sell such wraps online.

(Dr. S, who died in 2014, was apparently a controversial character in New Zealand. At one point, after analyzing blood alcohol tests, he said alcohol was not at fault in auto accidents. Instead, Dr. S. blamed rugby and "aggressive" males).

The UK investigated the "toxic gas hypothesis" in the 1990's (Limerick Report, 1998).

After an exhaustive investigation of the toxic gas hypothesis lasting three and a half years, methodically examining every aspect of the claim both by reviewing existing research, as well as by commissioning new research, the Limerick Report concluded that there is no evidence to support the claim that fire retardants in crib mattresses cause SIDS.

But that hasn't stopped the fever swamps of the internet fron keeping this false theory alive. Dozens of crib mattress web sites still quote this discredited theory, peddling all sorts of "non-toxic" crib mattresses.

Professor Barry Taylor, of the pediatrics department at Otago University, said SIDS researchers did not wish to comment on Dr S's passing in 2014, but they viewed his legacy with regret, noting the large amounts of time and money that were spent investigating his theories.

The take-home message: conventional crib mattresses are safe.

The Best Baby Crib Mattresses

We break down our picks for mattresses into these categories:

◆ Best Crib Mattress (Overall)
◆ Best Budget-Friendly Crib Mattress
◆ Best Eco Crib Mattress
◆ Best Travel/Portable Crib Mattress
◆ Best Waterproof Pad
◆ Best Changing Table Pad

FYI: If you'd like to dive deeper, we have 15 detailed reviews of top crib mattress brands on our web site, BabyBargains.com.

The Best Baby Crib Mattress (Overall)

After comparing 15 different crib mattress brands, we pick the **Naturepedic No Compromise Organic Cotton Classic Crib Mattress crib** ($259 on Amazon) as the Best Baby Crib Mattress.

Yeah, it is a mouthful: Naturepedic's No Compromise Organic Cotton Classic Lightweight mattress features closed-cell air pockets made from food-grade polyethylene. As a result, this mattress is half the weight of a traditional coil mattress. It runs $259; a dual-firmness model is $289. If you prefer a coil mattress, Naturepedic makes a version of this mattress with coils, dubbed the Organic Cotton Classic 150 coil mattress. It runs $299.

In a nutshell, Naturepedic balances the best of both worlds: organic cotton filling, a firm foam or coil innerspring AND a waterproof cover. All of Naturepedic's mattresses contain no PVC's, polyurethane foam or chemical fire retardants.

Reader feedback on this mattress and Naturepedic as a brand has been quite positive. Quality is very good and all Naturepedic's mattresses are GREENGUARD certified to be low emission. We also liked the company's detailed web site, with extensive FAQ's, articles and a blog about shopping for a natural mattress.

The Best Baby Crib Mattress: Naturepedic No Compromise Organic Cotton Classic Crib Mattress incorporates all the features we're looking for in a crib mattress: light weight, no chemical fire retardants, waterproof cover, organic fabrics. $259 on Amazon.

Also Great: Moonlight Slumber Little Dreamer Dual Firmness All Foam Crib Mattress

Moonlight Slumber's Little Dreamer foam crib mattress ($196) features welded seams and a PVC-free, "hospital grade" vinyl cover. Bonus: it has two firmness zones (firm for baby, more comfy for toddler). Below is a graphic that explains the different layers in the mattress.

The mattress comes with square corners for a tight fit, an internal fire barrier (no toxic chemicals) and medical-grade foam partially made form soybeans (making it just 7 to 10 lbs.).

The Little Dreamer is easy to clean and made in the US. The company also touts its mattresses as hypoallergenic. Priced under $200, we thought this one was a good buy as competitors are creeping closer to $300.

Got an unusual size crib? Moonlight Slumber offers custom sizes of their mattresses. That's unusual as most makers sell one standard size.

Overall reader reviews of Moonlight Slumber are quite positive. Parents note that the mattress doesn't sag even after months and years of use.

crib mattress

Best Budget-Friendly Crib Mattress

Yes, you can buy a safe foam mattress for as little as $52. The **Safety 1st Heavenly Dreams White Crib Mattress** is our top pick for budget-friendly crib mattress.

Sure, it is no frills—a basic foam mattress with a single-layer vinyl layer cover that is easy to clean. Quality is good, but the single-layer vinyl cover will probably only last for one kid. No fancy eco materials or seamless edges, but an excellent deal is the budget is tight.

The **Sealy Soybean Foam-Core crib mattress** ($122) is a great runner up to the Safety 1st mattress. It is GREENGUARD certified to be low emission and, yes, the foam is partially made from soybeans. At just 8.3 pounds, this lightweight but firm mattress makes changing sheets easy. At $122, you can get the eco-friendly features without shelling out over $300.

Best Eco-Friendly Crib Mattress

Lullaby Earth's Healthy Support crib mattress is made of polyethylene foam (a non-toxic, food-grade foam that requires no fire retardant chemicals) and weighs just 7 lbs. (Most other foam mattresses on the market are made of polyurethane). It features seamless edges and GREENGUARD-certification. Price: $170. A 2-Stage version of this crib mattress is $200. The Healthy Support is an excellent, lightweight option at an affordable price.

Also Great: Naturalmat Coco Mat

UK-based Naturalmat offers three organic mattresses made of coir (the husk of a coconut), latex or mohair. Our favorite is **Naturalmat Coco Mat crib mattress.** The filling is made from coconut husk wrapped in organic lamb's wool and then an organic cotton cover. Yes, it's an expensive option ($350 on Magic Beans), but checks all the boxes for both an eco-friendly and sustainable crib mattress.

While the Coco Mat generally gets good reviews, it does have a significant disadvantage over other mattresses: there is no waterproof cover. That means you'll have the extra expense of purchasing a mattress protector (Naturally, Naturalmat sells one from organic cotton for $40). And at $350, you're already shelling out a significant amount of cash for all this eco-good-ness. On the other hand, if you want to splurge, at least you know this is a high quality product.

Best Travel/Portable Crib Mattress

What separate mattress do we recommend for travel or portable cribs? The answer: none. It is unsafe to purchase a sep-arate mattress for portable cribs or play yards.

The Consumer Product Safety Commission says that when it comes to travel cribs or play yards, only use the mattress pad provided by the manufacturer (most, if not all, come with a mat-tress). Do not add an additional pad or mattress on top of the original mattress.

We discuss the best travel cribs earlier in this chapter.

Best Waterproof Pad

Even though most crib mattresses we recommend have waterproof covers, a crib mattress-size waterproof pad or mattress protector may be necessary if diaper leaks are a problem.

Our top pick for waterproof crib mattress pads is the **American Baby Company Waterproof Fitted Crib and Toddler Protective Pad**. ($24). The front and back of this pad have a sandwiched waterproof vinyl layer to keep the mattress dry. Readers tell us they love this pad; it washes well and the price is a bargain. (An organic version of this pad, where the outer cover is made from 100% organic cotton, runs a couple of dollars more).

Also Great: Carter's "Keep-Me-Dry" Fitted Quilted Crib Pad

Carter's Keep-Me-Dry pad is an affordable ($19) waterproof pad that features a soft, quilted polyester top and waterproof vinyl backing. We like the all-around elastic and reinforced corners. The pad is machine washable.

Best Changing Table Pad

Changing table pads help turn a dresser or any surface into a changing table. A couple of shopping tips: look for a pad with elevated sides (see photo). This will help keep your baby on the pad. A word of caution: elevated sides don't guarantee your baby won't still roll off the changing pad, so never walk away when changing your baby.

The best pick: **Simmons' Two Sided Contour Dressing Table Pad with Non-Skid Bottom** ($25, pictured). Also good: **Summer Infant's Contoured Changing Pad** ($18, pictured). Both pads are available at Amazon.com, Target, Babies R Us and Walmart. If you're looking for an organic or natural changing pad, consider **Naturepedic's Organic Cotton Contoured Changing Table Pad** ($100).

NURSERY NECESSITIES

The Best Bassinet

To encourage breast-feeding, pediatricians recommend "rooming in" with your baby for the first few weeks. That means having your baby close at hand for night-time feedings.

While baby can sleep in a full-size crib from birth, a bassinet is a handy way of bringing baby into your room until breast-feeding is established. As you'll read below, there are several different options when it comes to bassinets.

Let's go over a quick intro course to bassinets before our picks.

7 Things No One Tells You About Buying A Bassinet!

1 NO MATTER WHERE YOU PUT YOUR BABY DOWN FOR A NAP OR OVERNIGHT, FOCUS ON THE FOUR BASIC SAFETY RULES FOR SAFE SLEEP:

◆ Do not use any soft bedding in the crib/bassinet/cradle/ Moses basket.
◆ Place baby to sleep on his/her back, side or stomach.
◆ Keep the room temperature in baby's room at about 68° F.
◆ Don't overdress your baby. A light blanket sleeper is all you need.

2 MANY STROLLER MANUFACTURERS SELL BASSINETS AS ACCESSORIES. If allowed by a stroller's maker, you can use these detachable stroller bassinets as free standing bassinets in your home, not just on your stroller. You'll find manufacturers like UPPAbaby, Peg Perego , and Britax enable you to use their stroller bassinet as a stand-alone sleep space at home. Stroller bassinets typically cost around $200 to $250, about the same as a free standing bassinet but with the added feature of attaching to your stroller too.

UPPAbaby's bassinet (right) works with the Vista and the Cruz strollers and sells for $190 to $200. A stationery stand is also available for another $250.

3 CRADLES ARE ANOTHER OPTION FOR NEWBORN SLEEP. If the idea of a plastic bassinet doesn't appeal to you, consider a cradle. Unlike bassinets, cradles are typically made of wood and can be rocked. Prices range from $100 to $250 or more. If you plan on having more than one child, a cradle is a very sturdy option. You can also create a family heirloom with a cradle by passing it along to others in your family. Typically a cradle comes with a mattress pad, although replacement pads are available in a variety of sizes to fit different cradles.

This Dream on Me cradle runs about $100. As is typical of cradles, the style is rather plain. Other than a sheet for the mattress pad, no other bedding should be added.

4 **MOSES BASKETS CAN ONLY BE USED FOR A SHORT TIME.** Moses baskets are woven baskets with liners and carry handles. You can put your newborn in a Moses basket for naps, and move your baby around the house without disturbing her. Unfortunately, these baskets are useful for only a few weeks before they reach their maximum weight limit. If you get one for a gift, it might be useful, but it probably doesn't make sense to buy one on your own.

Badger Basket makes quite a few Moses baskets like this one which run around $50.

5 **PLAY YARDS NOW COME WITH BASSINET ATTACHMENTS.** If you're going to buy a play yard anyway, consider buying a version with a bassinet attachment. You can find our top picks for play yards in the "Around the House" chapter.

Graco makes a number of Pack N Play play yards with bassinet features. This version, the Graco Pack N Play Playard Bassinet with Automatic Folding Feet sells for $76.

6 **MINI CRIBS ARE YET ANOTHER OPTION FOR NEWBORN SLEEP AND CAN BE REPURPOSED AT GRANDMA'S HOUSE.** Mini cribs are sized similarly to a cradle at about 38 long by 24 wide. For comparison, a full size crib is about 52 long and 28 wide. Mini cribs have to adhere to similarly stringent safety standards as full size cribs, so they are quite safe.

The disadvantage of mini cribs? Babies often outgrow them LONG before they are old enough to go into a toddler or big kid bed—that means you'll have to then use a full-size crib.

Some mini crib manufacturers note their mini cribs can't be used "when a child begins to climb." Well, a typical child will hit that milestone around six to ten months, when they can pull themselves up to a standing position.
A mini crib has lower rails then a standard size crib—and that makes climbing out easy for infants under a year old . . . which, of course, is dangerous.

The take-home message: a mini crib does NOT replace the need for a full-size crib. A mini-crib replaces a bassinet.

Babyletto's Origami Mini Crib ($270) might be an option for moms who want their newborns to room in. But you need to take baby out of the Origami "when your child begins to climb," according to the instructions. This means you may need a full size crib by the time baby is as young as six months of age.

7 **IF YOU HAVE THE SPACE IN YOUR BEDROOM, YOU CAN JUST USE A FULL SIZE CRIB FROM BIRTH.** That's right. After all our prattling on above, you really don't have to purchase a bassinet, cradle, mini crib or Moses basket. A full size crib will do the trick . . . and save you some money!

But . . . what if you don't have room for a full-size crib in your bedroom? And you want your baby to room in to make sure breastfeeding is established during those first weeks? That's where the bassinet comes in!

The Best Bassinets

We've divided our bassinet picks into two categories:

◆ Best Bassinet (Overall)
◆ Best Travel Bassinet

The Best Bassinet (Overall)

bassinet

After researching bassinets for the last 20 plus years, we pick The **HALO Bassinest** as the best bassinet for parents of newborns. This bassinet achieves two goals: allowing rooming in for newborns (to help with breastfeeding) while providing a safe sleep space separate from a parent's bed.

The HALO Bassinest has side walls that compress down for quick access to the baby; it also sits on a base that allows you to rotate or swivel it 360 degrees. The Bassinest includes a waterproof mattress pad and sheet; extra sheets are $15.

The Bassinest comes in four versions: a basic model for $220 (called the Essentia), a deluxe version for $250 (Premiere), the Luxe for $280 and the Luxe Plus for $300 .

For the more expensive versions, HALO adds vibration, sounds and lullabies, nightlight and additional storage. While those frills are nice, we recommend going with the basic model—it's all most parents need. Vibration and lullabies aren't necessary for a newborn.

The Best Bassinet:
HALO Bassinest Swivel Sleeper Bassinet (Essentia)

We pick the HALO Bassinest as one of the safest options for newborns up to five months of age. With a swivel basket and adjustable base, the Bassinest pulls up to your bed for convenient feeding in the night. While the Bassinest is available in four different iterations, we recommend the basic Essentia version for $200 .

Best Travel Bassinet

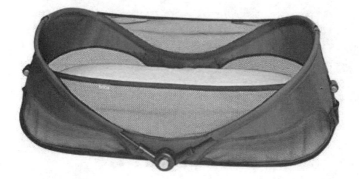

Got a road trip ahead? Here's a solution for hotel rooms. The **BRICA Fold N' Go** travel bassinet is a decent buy at $36—it features a firm mattress with fitted sheet and mesh panels. As the name implies, it folds compact for travel.

Quality is good and our reader feedback has been effusive, with frequent travelers praising the Fold N' Go for its ease of set up and fold down.

FYI: Most bassinets work up to about five months of age, but the BRICA Fold N' Go can only be used for babies who are under three months of age and 15 pounds.

BRICA is part of the Munchkin baby gear brand.

The Best Nursery Dresser

Now that you've got a place for the baby to sleep, where are you going to put baby's clothes? The juvenile trade refers to dressers, armoires, and the like as "case pieces" since they are essentially furniture made out of a large case (pretty inventive, huh?).

As you shop for baby furniture, you'll note a wide variety of dressers—three drawer, four drawer, armoires, combination dresser/changing tables, and more. In case you are new to dresser shopping, let's go over some basics.

7 Things No One Tells You About Buying A Dresser For Your Nursery!

1 FORGET THE PRETTY STAIN. FOCUS ON DRAWER GLIDES. The better made dressers have drawers with glide tracks on BOTH sides of the drawer for a smooth pull. Cheaper dressers have drawers

that simply sit on a track at the bottom center of the drawer. As a result, they don't roll out as smoothly and are prone to coming off the track. Look at the drawer glide itself. Cheaper dressers have simple metal glides. At top right, a drawer with center mount glides.

Under mounted metal drawer glides are better than center mount, but may not be as smooth as ball bearing glides (see right).

The best dressers use elaborate glide mechanisms including ball-bearings or self-closing glides (you push the drawer nearly closed and it automatically/ slowly closes the rest of the way). A few nursery dresser makers use wood-on-wood glides, more commonly seen in adult furniture.

2 LOOK CLOSELY AT THE SIDES OF THE DRAWER. The best furniture makers use "dove-tailed" drawer joints. There are two types of dove-tail drawers: English and French (see pictures at right). Both are acceptable. What's not good? Drawers and drawer fronts that are merely stapled together.

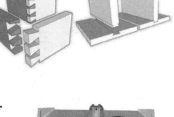

English Dovetail   French Dovetail

3 A THIRD QUALITY INDICA-TOR: CORNER BLOCKS UNDER THE DRAWERS. Use a makeup mirror to look at the underside of the drawer—if there is a small block that braces the corner, that's good. Cheaper dressers omit this feature, which adds to the stability of the drawer.

4 THE BACK OF THE DRESSER HAS QUALITY CLUES. Cheaply-made dressers have a flimsy piece of chipboard stapled to the back of the dresser frame. But if it's a good quality piece of furniture, a dresser back will be a solid (although perhaps only one-quarter inch thick) piece of wood that is screwed to the frame.

5 **MEDIUM DENSITY FIBERBOARD (MDF) VERSUS SOLID WOOD.** The best-made dressers have solid wood tops and drawer fronts (and some have solid wood sides).

Of course, solid wood is expensive. To make dressers more affordable, many furniture makers turn to substitute wood products such as medium density fiberboard (MDF). What is MDF? Basically, MDF is made from wood scraps that are turned into fiber and then glued together to form a solid board.

In addition to being affordable, MDF is easier to sculpt since it lacks knots or wood grain. Hence, you often seen MDF used in modern furniture groupings where a sleek, smooth aesthetic is the goal.

One downside to MDF: the glue or resin that is used to hold it together may contain formaldehyde. Back in 2008, five nursery furniture makers were sued by the state of California for unsafe levels of formaldehyde in their dressers.

Of course, not all glues are high in formaldehyde. Look for furniture manufacturers that are GREENGUARD certified to be low emission.

Our opinion: MDF isn't necessarily good or bad. The more money you spend, however, the more solid should be in that dresser!

6 **SKIP BUYING A SEPARATE CHANGING AREA AND USE A DRESSER.** Most folks look for dressers to do double duty: not only a place to store clothes, but also to change diapers. Basically, you need a changing area of the right height to do this—evaluate your and your spouse's heights to see what you'd need (a lower side-by-side dresser or a taller chest). Then you can purchase a changing pad for your dresser top. Some pads have non-skid bases. Changing table pads typically cost around $20.

7 **NOT RECOMMENDED: COMBINATION CRIB AND DRESSERS.** As the name implies, a combo crib and dresser is a crib with an attached dresser or changing area. This may sound like a good deal, but these combos are a safety risk, in our opinion. The hazard: babies can climb out of them too easily, based on reports to government safety databases we reviewed. Clever babies can get a toe

hold on the railing or dresser drawer and push themselves up to the top of the dresser. From there, nothing good can happen.

The Best Nursery Dressers

We've broken down our picks for best dressers into these categories:

- ◆ Best Dresser (Overall)
- ◆ Best Budget-Friendly Dresser
- ◆ Best Dresser Splurge
- ◆ Best Eco-Friendly Dresser

The Best Nursery Dresser (Overall)

After researching over 80 manufacturers of dressers and other nursery furniture our top pick for best nursery dresser is the **Eco-Chic Baby Clover Five-Drawer Chest** ($550). Eco Chic also makes a great double dresser option for $700.

The Best Nursery Dresser: Eco Chic Baby Clover 5 Drawer Chest The Eco Chic Baby Clover 5-drawer chest is a well-made $550 dresser sold exclusively at Babies R Us. Dresser drawers are dove-tailed and use metal ball-bearing glides for smooth opening. These dressers are also GREENGUARD certified. The only flaw: Eco Chic Baby doesn't use self closing drawers. Otherwise, quality is excellent.

Also Great: Pali Designs Trieste Double Dresser

Pali constructs its dresser drawers from Radiata pine, a northern hardwood, for durability. Drawers have dovetailed fronts and full extension glides for added storage space. The quality of Pali's dressers is excellent, with prices ranging from $700 to $1000; the **Pali Trieste** pictured above is $900.

Best Budget-Friendly Dresser

IKEA's affordable cribs won our best budget-friendly pick, so let's talk about their equally affordable dressers (about $100 to $230). Yes, assembly can be challenging. And these dressers probably won't last until your kid goes to college, but $249 for a double dresser (the **Hemnes eight drawer dresser**, above)? You can't beat that price.

Readers praise IKEA's dressers for their simplicity and value. (One caveat: IKEA dressers were recalled in 2016 for tip-over hazards. Always anchor a dresser to the wall, whether it is from IKEA or any brand for that matter!).

Best Dresser Splurge

If you've got the bankroll, the very best quality in dressers can be found from Canadian nursery furniture maker Natart. A double dresser from Natart typically tops $1000 (example: **Natart's Ithaca five drawer dresser** for $1300) and features top notch construction.

A close runner up to Natart is Romina, with their all solid-wood construction, and best-in-class drawer glides—smooth like butter! But it will cost you: a double dresser from Romina can run $1500 to $1800. The **Romina Cleopatra five drawer chest** , right, is $1575 to $1764.

Best Eco Friendly Dresser

Romina is also our top choice for eco friendly nursery dresser. These dressers are made of solid European beech and tree sap-

based organic glues, then finished with a non-toxic, water based finish (or a Bees Wax organic finish for an up charge).

No need to worry about formaldehyde emissions, since Romina's line is GREENGUARD certified. And Romina makes their furniture in Europe, not Asia. We are impressed with Romina's quality touches—corner blocks, dove tailed drawers and soft-close drawer glides. All this eco-goodness comes at a price, however. The **Imperio six-drawer dresser** (above) runs $1625 to $1820.

The Best Glider Rocker

More than a mere rocking chair, glider rockers feature a ball-bearing system so they glide with little or no effort. They've earned a place in the nursery to help with those long hours of breastfeeding. Many are then repurposed later into a living room.

Here are some shopping tips when looking at rocker gliders.

7 Things No One Tells You About Buying A Glider Rocker!

1 YES, YOU CAN SWAP THE CUSHIONS DOWN THE LINE. Glider rockers are certainly an investment, but there is one plus when you purchase one from a major brand like Dutailier and Shermag: you can order a replacement cushion to replace a stained one or just to change the look. Dutailier has a special part of their site dedicated to replacement cushions. Target sells Shermag replacement cushions online for about $100.

2 BETTER PADDING = HAPPIER PARENT. Sure, there are some affordable $200 gliders out there—and we do like IKEA's version (see later in this section).

But heed this warning: other super bargain glider rockers have skimpy padding. You'll be spending a good amount of time in this chair, from feeding to reading bed time stories and more. Our readers are unanimous: go for the better padding, even if it is another $100 or $200. Try out the chair in person to make sure you are happy before ordering. Your bum will thank you later.

Also worthwhile: padded armrests. If that is an option for the model you are looking at, go for it.

3 WATCH THE WIDTH. Some bargain glider rockers are quite narrow, which might work if you are a small person. But remember you will most likely be using a nursing pillow with your newborn . . . and having the extra width to accommodate this pillow is most helpful!

Trying to follow this advice can be difficult, as many glider rockers do not list their seat width online (product dimensions may be the glider's *box* width, not the chair width). Again, trying chairs out in person is probably the best way to go.

4 **ONE WORD: LOCKS.** Consider a chair with a locking mechanism. Some brands (notably Shermag) have an auto-locking feature; when you stand up, the chair can no longer rock. Very helpful if you have a curious toddler who might end up with pinched fingers or tipping over an unoccupied glider.

5 **FOCUS ON THE CHAIR FIRST, NOT THE FABRIC OR COLOR.** With most glider rocker companies, you can choose from dozens if not hundreds of fabric colors. Hence the first task is not focus on the fabric, but decide on the chair *style*. Certain styles can fit better than others—chairs with deeper backs are better for taller parents. Make sure your feet can comfortably rest on the floor when you are sitting all the way back in a rocker glider. Once you've decided on the best chair style, then consider fabrics and colors.

6 **CLEANABLITY CAN BE POOR.** The Achilles heal of many rocker gliders is cleanability, or lack there of. Most glider rocker cushions lack zip-off covers that are machine washable. Hence, you're only choice is dry cleaning. One solution: you can buy affordable slip covers online for around $100 (Luxe Basics sells their covers on Amazon). If your baby spits up a lot, this may be a wise investment!

7 **DON'T OVERLOOK REGULAR FURNITURE STORES FOR DEALS.** There is no federal law that says you have to buy a glider rocker for your nursery from a store with "baby" in its name! Upholstered rockers that recline are available from a wide variety of stores . . . and adult furniture stores usually have more generous sales than nursery store retailers.

The Best Glider Rockers

Up next, we'll give you our top picks for glider rockers in these categories:

◆ Best Glider Rocker (Overall)
◆ Best Budget-Friendly Glider Rocker
◆ Best Upholstered Glider Rocker

The Best Glider Rocker (Overall)

After comparing 11 different glider rocker brands, we pick the **Dutailier Glider Recline and Ottoman Combo, Platinum Sleigh** ($442 on Amazon, model C2081C693128) as the Best Glider Rocker.

Made in Canada, Dutailier's glider rockers have been one of the most reliable recommendations we've made since we started writing about glider rockers back in 1994.

This model (C2081C693128) has a back that reclines and Dutailier's patented "glide-r-motion" technology that relies on sealed ball bearings for a smooth motion.

At $442, you might be thinking—why spend that much money when you can buy a glider rocker and ottoman combo online for under $200? Three reasons: comfort, quality and durability.

Many of the super bargain glider rockers have cushions that are less than, well, cushiony. Others are too narrow in the seat. As for quality, read the 1-star reviews for the sub-$200 glider rockers. You'll note more than one person said the bargain glider fell apart after one (or there or six) months of use. Or they start to squeak. Our readers concur.

Here's a picture posted to Amazon from a parent who purchased a StorkCraft $200 bargain glider rocker. After nine months of use by a skinny mom and dad, the chair looked like this (right).

That's the difference between those slapped together glider rockers and our pick, Dutailier: you don't have to worry about it falling apart.

In fact, in our experience Dutailier rocker gliders can easily be reused for more than one child . . . and then repurposed to another room in the house down the road.

We have an extended write up on Dutailier on our web site (babybargains.com/best-glider-rockers/), complete with pictures from a recent tour we took of Dutailier's Quebec factory (yes, we paid for all our travel expenses).

The Best Glider Rocker: Dutailier Glider Recline & Ottoman Combo, Platinum Sleigh

This brand sets the standard for quality and comfort in the glider rocker category. This $442 rocker-glider /ottoman has a recline feature, which is major plus.

Best Budget-Friendly Glider Rocker

For sheer value, it is hard to beat **Ikea's POÄNG rocking chair** for $129-$159 (a leather version is $319). A matching, non-rocking footstool is $49.

Made of "layer-glued bent beech", the POÄNG comes in ten different cushion colors with a light brown frame. There is also a darker color frame available (IKEA calls this "medium brown").

The downside? Well, if you guessed "I have to assemble it because it is IKEA," you are correct, sir!

Like most things IKEA sells, you're going to need set aside about an hour to put the POÄNG together.

Also: The POÄNG is a rocker, not a rocker-glider (as we discussed earlier). What's the difference? Well, rocker-gliders have ball bearings to enable them to rock more easily. Rockers are simpler but require more umph—if you have a c-section, it might be easier to use a rocker-glider than the POÄNG.

Despite these minuses, our readers report they are happy with the POÄNG as a stylish, yet affordable option.

Best Upholstered Glider Rocker

If you have the budget for
an upholstered glider rocker,
we like Best Chair's offerings,
most of which are in the $400-
$700 range. The **Best Chair
Jacob**, pictured, is $450 for the
chair and $160 for the ottoman
at JCPenney (seven micro fiber
fabrics are available). Best Chair
is also sold in specialty stores.

Best Chair is an Indiana-based rocking chair maker that
entered the baby biz in 2002, although they trace their roots to
the 1960's. We were very impressed with their quality and offerings. Best specializes in upholstered chairs with over 700 fabric
choices. They also make traditional glider rockers and furniture
for other rooms in the house.

Cool feature: Best offers an optional 10-position glide lock
that makes it easier to get in and out of the chair.

Delivery is four weeks and prices are decent for an all-uphol-
stered look—compare these prices to the $1000+ Pottery Barn
wants for their similar fully upholstered glider rockers.

Besides the Jacob, JCPenney.com sells 10 different Best chair
models, in both fabric or leather.

Best Chair most recently began offering a "bonded" leather
fabric option dubbed PerformaBlend. Bonded leather is made
of leather scraps and costs less than a full leather chair (about
$750 compared to $1000 or more for leather).

Feedback from readers has been mostly positive on Best—a
few complaints centered on Best models sold on JCPenney.com
that had backs that were too short for some taller parents. Most
folks had no problem, however and generally loved Best's overall quality and durability. For taller parents, it might be good to
try out this chair in person before purchasing.

Whew! That was a lot of nursery planning. Next up: let's talk
baby bedding (sheets, blankets and more!). Good news! These
items are much less expensive than furniture!

Chapter 3

BABY BEDDING

Baby Bedding & Decor

Inside this chapter

What are the best crib sheets? Blankets? What the heck is a wearable blanket? We'll answer that one, plus reveal our top picks and a chart with crib bedding brand ratings. Plus, a look at seven things no one tells you about crib sheets!

Baby blankets used to be simple—they were just, well, baby blankets. But like everything today, baby blankets have morphed into a confusing array of choices: wearable blankets, swaddling blankets, receiving blankets and so on.

Before we decipher the word of baby bedding, let's go over some shopping basic when it comes to your kiddo's linens.

7 Things No One Tells You About Buying Crib Bedding!

1 SAY **NO** TO CRIB BUMPERS. Yes, they look cute—but do not use bumpers in your baby's crib, cradle or bassinet.

A landmark investigation by the *Chicago Tribune* back in 2010 detailed a link between crib bumpers and two dozen infant deaths in the past decade. The article ("Hidden Hazard of Crib Bumpers," December 12, 2010) prompted the CPSC to open a review of the safety of crib bumpers. An earlier study by a Washington University pediatri-

cian, Dr. Bradley Thach "concluded that 27 babies' deaths were attributed to bumper pads from 1985 to 2005." This study, however, has been largely ignored by both the industry and the CPSC, although it prompted the American Academy of Pediatrics to discourage parents from using bumpers.

Now we know what you're thinking: "Aren't bumpers a safety thing? What if my baby hits his head on the hard wood slats?" or "What if she gets her arm or leg stuck between the slats?" First, these issues are rare—very few kids are injured by knocking their heads against a crib's slats and even fewer get limbs stuck.

However, there are a couple of bumper *alternatives* if your little baby decides getting a leg stuck in the crib slats is fun: **Wonder Bumpers** and **BreathableBaby Railguard**. Most of these products are either breathable mesh or firm, shock absorbing foam that don't pose a suffocation risk. Again, most folks will not need these bumper alternatives. The best advice is go without any bumpers in the crib at all.

2 SOME CRIB SHEETS WILL SHRINK IN THE WASH—AND THAT'S A BAD THING. Check the labels carefully on the sheet or bedding set you're thinking of buying. If a sheet recommends washing in cold water and line drying, chances are it's going to shrink. And if it shrinks, it won't fit the mattress properly. This is a suffocation hazard if the sheet should come off at one of the corners.

Once you've checked the washing instructions, look for elastic around the bottom of the entire sheet. Cheap sheets only use elastic on the ends.

Here is a list of manufacturers who make their crib sheets with elastic all around the sheet:

American Baby	Circo (Target)	Maddie Boo
BB Basics	Fleece Baby	Bobble Roos
Baby Basics	Garnet Hill	Restoration
Baby Gap	Hoohobbers	Hardware
Carousel	Land of Nod	Sweet Kyla

3 TELL-TALE SIGNS OF GOOD QUALITY CRIB BEDDING.

◆ *If possible, try to buy sheets with a 200 thread count.* Frustratingly, most crib sheets do not label thread count, but here's a clue: hold a sheet up to a light—if you can count the individual threads, that's probably a sheet with a low thread count.

◆ *Ruffles (on crib skirts) should be folded over for double thickness*—not a single thickness ruffle with hemmed edge.

♦ *Designs on bedding should be printed or woven* into the fabric not stamped on (like a screen printed t-shirt).

♦ *Make sure the pieces are sewn with cotton/poly thread,* not nylon, which can melt and break.

♦ *Check for tight, smooth stitching on any appliques.*

4 **NO SOFT BEDDING IN BABY'S CRIB.** This is an extension of the bumper discussion in Tip #1. Studies on Sudden Infant Death Syndrome (SIDS, also known as crib death) have linked SIDS to infants sleeping on fluffy bedding, lambskins, or pillows. A pocket can form around the baby's face if she is placed face down in fluffy bedding, and she can slowly suffocate while breathing in her own carbon dioxide.

The best advice: put your infant on her back when she sleeps. And don't put pillows, comforters or other soft bedding or toys inside a crib.

The Consumer Product Safety Commission now recommends that parents not use ANY soft bedding around, on top of, or under baby. If you want to use a blanket, tuck a very thin blanket under the mattress at one end of the crib to keep it from moving around. The blanket should then only come up to baby's chest. Safest of all: avoid using any blankets in a crib and put baby in a wearable blanket for warmth (see our wearable blankets recommendation later in this chapter).

One reader wrote to tell us about a scary incident in her nursery. She had left a blanket hanging over the side of the crib when she put her son down for a nap. He managed to pull the blanket down and get wrapped up in it, nearly suffocating. Stories like that convince us that putting any soft bedding in or near a crib is risky.

How much bedding is too much? A new father emailed us this question: "With all the waterproof liners, fitted sheets and quick change crib sheets, we're worried that our firm mattress is now becoming soft and squishy. How many layers are safe?"

Good point. We know that some parents figure it is easier to change crib sheets at 2 am if they simply pile on several layers of sheets on the crib mattress. (This way, you simply remove the top wet layer when changing the sheets). While we admire the creative thinking, we suggest NOT doing this.

Our advice: one sheet over a waterproof crib pad is enough. Or use a waterproof SHEET (QuickZip sheet or an Ultimate Crib Sheet; see recommendations coming up) over a mattress (no additional waterproof crib pad needed then). The take-home message: any more than TWO layers on top of a mattress is not advisable!

5 AVOID ELECTRIC BLANKETS AND HEATING PADS. Baby diapers often leak (sorry, fact of life) and an electric blanket or heating pad shouldn't get wet! Also, overheated babies have a higher risk of SIDS. If your baby seems cold, add an extra layer (t-shirt) under her wearable blanket for warmth. Don't turn the thermostat up over 68°, however. A too warm nursery is dangerous.

6 BE CAREFUL NOT TO OVER-SWADDLE. Take care if you are swaddling your baby, you could be wrapping her too tight.

It's fine to wrap your baby's arms snugly but leave the legs loose enough for him to move them around. Experts advise this technique to possibly prevent hip dislocation from spending hours wrapped like a mummy!

And stop swaddling after two months—your baby will need to move around and stretch out after that age.

7 LET'S TALK ABOUT HOW MUCH BEDDING YOU REALLY NEED. Start with three to four fitted sheets. This gives you enough for quick changes without doing laundry every day.

Next you'll want a couple waterproof mattress pads (the second pad is used when pad #1 is in the wash). You don't want your baby's pee to soak into the mattress or its seams.

We also recommend some light blankets. A few for swaddling, a few to throw on the floor to play on.

Additional but not necessary bedding options include dust ruffles and curtains—these are optional decor items. (Never put a curtain near the crib).

You definitely don't need diaper stackers (fancy fabric case for diapers), pillows (can't use them until about age three) and thick baby quilts. Wall hangings might be nice for decor but they aren't necessary.

An optional teething rail should be tightly secured to th crib and ONLY be used for older babies who are standing.

In the end, all you really need are sheets and blankets (or wearable blankets).

The Best Crib Bedding (Overall)

After comparing and testing more than 60 different crib bedding sets and sheets, we pick **Carousel** (babybedding.com) as the best crib bedding you can buy.

Carousel's breadth of options is universally praised by our readers. Yes, you can custom design a look using Carousel's patterns or fabric of your choosing—more on this shortly.

Bonus: you can also buy fabric by the yard from Carousel in case you have a relative that offers to sew you matching accessories for the nursery.

Prices are on the higher side: sheets run $30 each, but let's talk quality: Carousel's sheets are 200 thread count, wash well and have all-around elastic.

Carousel/Baby Bedding Online used to sell its line of bedding exclusively through retail stores at premium prices. Over a decade ago, however, they decided to change to an online sales model online at BabyBedding.com (and through Amazon as well). Smart move.

The site sells all its bedding as separates plus other decor items like matching window valences and lamp shades. Have a desire to outfit a nursery with the colors/logos of your favorite college football team? Yep, Carousel has that too.

What if you want to custom design your baby's bedding? That's Carousel's secret sauce. The site's Nursery Designer tool allows parents to mix and match any of the patterns and colors available, using drop and drag swatches. For example, let's say you plan to get a comforter (not for use in a crib, but for play on a floor). You can pick a fabric for the front then a different fabric for the back. Or another color/pattern for the sheets. Or you might like your sheets to come in two or three different patterns. The crib skirt can also be customized.

Then you'll be able to see the final nursery on line with all the different patterns and colors. When you pick your first pattern, the site will recommend some solids and patterns that go together—but you can pick anything you like. Prices are similar to Carousel's ready made designs.

Bargain tip: check out Carousel's "sale" tab, with clearance and sale items at 30% to 50% off.

Bottom line on Carousel: good designs and great quality.

One minor quibble: Carousel still displays their sets of crib bedding online with bumpers and blankets draped over a crib rail or teether pads tied to a top rail. While it is still legal in most locales to sell items like bumpers, it would be more socially responsible if Carousel didn't merchandise these items that way.

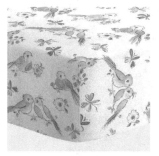

The Best Crib Bedding: Carousel

No, it isn't the cheapest option out there for crib sheets ($30), but Carousel's quality impresses. And the custom design options are unique.

Also Great: Aiden + Anais

Aden + Anais makes sheets in cotton muslin, bamboo rayon, organic cotton and cotton flannel for $22 to $40.

Aden + Anais first came to our attention when we discovered their excellent muslin swaddle blankets. Parents love them, so when they expanded into crib bedding, we were intrigued.

Aden + Anais (A+A) now makes crib sheets, blankets, towel/washcloth sets, changing pads and sleep sacks (called sleeping bags). Their classic crib sheets are made of cotton muslin ($29), organic sheets are certified organically grown cotton muslin ($40) and their bamboo sheets are made of rayon derived from bamboo fiber ($35). Cotton flannel sheets are also available for $23.

Patterns are simple including leaf prints, dots, stars and drag-onflies plus a few solid sheets. A+A don't offer bumpers (yea!), but muslim quilted blankets ("dream blankets") are available in cotton or rayon from $35 to $60 each (never for use in a crib for a baby under one year of age, in our opinion).

What's the feedback from parents? Universally, A+A is praised for super softness and cute patterns. They wash well too, although we hear a few complaints that some items can snag in the wash. This brand is on the expensive side, espe-cially if you choose the organic cotton option. But like anything organic, you have to pay a premium.

Bottom line: if you're looking for super soft, adorable prints, A+A may be the perfect option.

Tips on eco-friendly crib bedding

Like many products sold as organic today, there is no stan-dard for "organic" or natural baby bedding. This leaves it up to bedding manufacturers to determine for themselves what's organic. So, let's review some terms you'll see.

Many organic crib bedding makers claim their items are made from organic cotton. Organic cotton simply means cot-ton that's been grown with a *minimum* amount of toxic pesti-cides or fertilizers. That doesn't mean it is completely free of all pesticides and fertilizers.

Next let's talk sheet dyes. Conventional cribs sheets are dyed with synthetic chemicals—so how are organic bedding companies addressing this issue? Can an organic sheet be col-ored anything other than the natural shade of cotton (that is, an off-white)?

Turns out, the answer is yes. Organic cotton can be grown in a few colors. Yes, that's right, just like you can buy naturally orange or purple cauliflower, cotton can be cultivated in colors. Three colors are available: pink, light brown and green. Another solution: vegetable dyes. Look for manufacturers that sell baby bedding made with low-impact vegetable dyed cotton.

Of course, all this comes for a price: organic crib bedding is often 20% to 35% more expensive than conventional bedding.

Our favorite brands that offer organic crib bedding include Aden + Anais, American Baby and Carousel. FYI: not all of these brands' bedding is organic; only certain designs.

Best Budget-Friendly Crib Bedding

American Baby is one of the most affordable brands offering excellent quality 100% cotton percale and jersey sheets.

Starting at $13 (some on sale for as little as $10) per sheet and going up to $20, American Baby makes separates as well as three- and six-piece sets starting at $30.

American Baby makes waterproof mattress pads, changing pad covers, crib rail covers, mini crib and cradle bedding sets. They even have a few organic cotton options. Colors and patterns are basic.

Bottom line: our readers like American Baby overall and are happy with the quality and price.

Best Quick Change Sheets

The **QuickZip Crib Sheet** is our top pick for best quick change sheet.

What are quick change sheets? As the name implies, these sheets have a zip-off top layer to make changes quicker. You place it on the mattress like any fitted crib sheet, but if your baby's diaper leaks in the middle of the night, you don't have to struggle with removing the entire sheet and replacing it. Simply zip off the top layer and zip on a clean, dry one. Voila! Minimal hassle.

Ok, that convenience comes at a price: the sheets run $40 for the sheet with base and $25 for just the zip-on top. (You buy the $40 set and then a few $25 top sheets).

Also great: **Summer Ultimate Crib Sheet,** which lays on top a regular fitted sheet and is snapped to the crib slats. Just unsnap it and replace it with a clean, dry sheet. It's less expensive than the QuickZip at $32 for two sheets.

What's the difference between the two? Unlike the QuickZip, Summer has a waterproof backing. But we find the QuickZip's zippers easier to use than Summer's snaps.

Best Blankets

There are three types of baby blankets to consider: swaddle, wearable and receiving.

Our top pick for swaddle blanket is the **Aden + Anais classic muslin swaddle**, in a four pack for $50. Excellent quality and a generous size makes swaddling easy for novices. And they come in cute patterns too!

What are wearable blankets? Well, they take the place of the traditional blankets, which have been banished from the crib for safety reasons.

As the name implies, your baby wears this blanket, which zips up for coziness. For wearable blan-

kets, we recommend the **Halo SleepSack**, an all-cotton wearable blanket for $17.50 (prices range from $12 to $30 depending on color).

FYI: Halo makes the SleepSack in different weights, including a lighter muslin for summer and a "winter weight" for, well, winter.

And if you want a traditional receiving blanket, check out **BobbleRoos**. These 100% cotton flannel blankets ($15) are great to have around the house or throw in the diaper bag.

Best Play Yard Sheets

Play yards are handy, but they have one drawback: they only include one sheet. So if your baby's diaper leaks, you'll need a backup play yard sheet or two.

Our pick in this category is **American Baby Company's fitted play yard sheet,** which fits the Graco Pack N Play bassinet/play yard mattress (as well as many other brands). At $10, it is a good deal and is made of organic cotton.

BEDDING RATINGS

Name	Rating	Cost	Organic?
Aden & Anais	A-	$$	◆
Annette Tatum	B	$$$	
Banana Fish	B	$ to $$	
BB Basics Online	B-	$	
Caden Lane	B+	$$$	
California Kids	A	$$	
Carousel	A	$$	
Cotton Tale	A-	$$	◆
Crown Crafts	C+	$ to $$	◆
Dwell	B+	$$	◆
Gerber	D	$	
Glenna Jean	B+	$$	
Hoohobbers	B+	$$$	
Koala Baby	C+	$	
Lambs & Ivy	B+	$	
Land of Nod	B	$$	◆
Living Textiles/Lolli Living	A-	$$	
Maddie Boo	A	$$$	
My Baby Sam	B+	$$	
Pine Creek	A-	$$$	
Pottery Barn	C+	$$	◆
Restoration Hardware	B-	$$ to $$$	◆
Serena & Lily	B+	$$	◆
Skip Hop	A	$$	
Sleeping partners	B	$	◆
Sumersault	A	$	◆
Summer	A	$	◆
Sweet JoJo Designs	B	$ to $$	
Sweet Kyla	A	$$	◆
Target (Circo)	C	$	
TL Care	A-	$	◆
Trend Lab	B-	$ to $$	
Whistle & Wink	B+	$$$	

Key

Cost: Cost of a sheet. $—under $20; $$=$20 to $50; $$$=over $50
Organic: Does the bedding maker offer any organic options? Yes/No. Note: this does not mean that ALL of the maker's offerings are organic.

A quick look at some top crib bedding brands

bedding

Fiber Content	Notes
100% COTTON	Famous for swaddling blankets. Sheets are excellent.
100% COTTON	Pricey, shabby chic vibe.
100% COTTON	MiGi line starts at $90 per set. Adult-like fashions.
100% COTTON	Buy Buy Baby's private label; quality is mixed.
100% COTTON	Modern vintage collections; 230 thread ct sheets.
100% COTTON	Bright, whimsical patterns; most made in California.
100% COTTON	Nursery designer tool online for custom looks
100% COTTON	Whimsical prints, soft pastels. Made in USA.
Mix	Baby-ish designs; sold in major chain stores.
100% COTTON	Stylized prints to match mid-century cribs.
POLY/COTTON	Cute patterns, but poor quality.
100% COTTON	Low price line Sweet Potato features modern looks.
100% COTTON	Made in U.S.; bright designs. Many accessories.
100% COTTON	Sold in BRU, recent quality improvements.
POLY/COTTON	Snoopy, Hello Kitty licensed designs.
100% COTTON	Nice selection of accessories such as lamps.
100% COTTON	Affordable 5-pc sets, designed in Australia.
100% COTTON	Sophisticated looks, accented by silk and linen.
100% COTTON	Affordable, readers love quality and soft fabrics.
100% COTTON	Custom-made or off-the-shelf designs, pricey.
100% COTTON	Peter Rabbit and other themed bedding.
100% COTTON	600 thread count sheets; muted neutral looks.
100% COTTON	Crisp, clean look with color accents.
100% COTTON	Clever no-bumper sheet designs. Wash well.
100% COTTON	Sold as Tadpole Basics in Target.
100% COTTON	Traditional nursery looks; sold in chain stores/online.
100% COTTON	Maker of Ultimate Crib Sheet; separates line.
100% COTTON	9-piece beddings sets offer value; sold online.
100% COTTON	Quality is good; sets can be ordered w/o bumpers
100% COTTON	Low price, low thread counts. Shrinkage issues.
100% COTTON	Affordable basics line sold in Buy Buy Baby
Mix	Sheet are good quality, textured fabrics.
100% COTTON	Vintage looks with embroidery accents.

Fiber Content: Some lines have both all-cotton and poly/cotton blends—these are noted with the word "Mix."

LICENSE TRANSLATOR

Who makes what brand of bedding

A perennial trend in crib bedding is licensed characters— just about every cartoon character imaginable has been licensed to one of the big bedding makers for use in juvenile bedding. But how can tell you tell who makes what? Here is a list of popular licensed characters and their bedding makers. See our web site BabyBargains.com for reviews of the these brands.

LICENSE	IS MADE BY
BABY LOONEY TUNES	CROWN CRAFTS
CARE BEARS	BABY BOOM
CARTER'S INFANT	CROWN CRAFTS
CLASSIC POOH	CROWN CRAFTS
DISNEY BABY	PEM AMERICA
DISNEY BABY	CROWN CRAFTS
DR. SEUSS	TREND LAB
DORA THE EXPLORER	BABY BOOM
EDDIE BAUER	CROWN CRAFTS
FISHER-PRICE	CROWN CRAFTS
HELLO KITTY & FRIENDS	CROWN CRAFTS
JONATHAN ADLER	CROWN CRAFTS
KATHY IRELAND	THANK YOU BABY
LALALOOPSY	CROWN CRAFT
LAURA ASHLEY	PEM AMERICA
NAUTICAKIDS	CROWN CRAFTS
NOJO	CROWN CRAFTS
PADDINGTON BEAR	TREND LAB
PRECIOUS MOMENTS	BABY BOOM
SESAME STREET	CROWN CRAFTS
SNOOPY	LAMBS & IVY
TAGGIES	CROWN CRAFTS
THOMAS AND FRIENDS	BABY BOOM
TOO GOOD BY JENNY	PEM AMERICA
WAMSUTTA	SPRING
WAVERLY BABY	TREND LAB

CHAPTER 4

REALITY LAYETTE

The Reality Layette:
The Best Baby Clothes & Diapers

Inside this chapter

What the heck is a "Onesie"? How many clothes does your baby need? How come such little clothes have such big price tags? We unravel these mysteries in this chapter, plus give our top brand picks for baby clothes. Next, let's talk diapers—how to save and top brands for both disposable and cloth.

Baby Clothes

So you thought all the big-ticket items were taken care of when you bought the crib and other furniture? Ha! It's time to prepare for your baby's "layette," a French word that translated literally means "spending large sums of cash on tiny clothes." But, of course, there are some creative (dare we say, sneaky?) ways of keeping your layette bills down.

At this point, you may be wondering just what does your baby need? Sure you've seen those cute ruffled dresses and sailor suits in department stores—but what does your baby really wear everyday?

Meet the layette, a collection of clothes and accessories that your baby will use daily. While your baby's birthday suit was free, outfitting him in something more "traditional" will cost some bucks. In fact, a recent study estimated that parents spend $13,000 on clothes for a child by the time he or she hits 18 years of age—and that sounds like a conservative estimate to us. Baby clothes translate into a $20 billion business for children's clothing retailers.

7 Things No One Tells You About Buying Baby Clothes

1 IGNORE BABY STORES' RECOMMENDED LISTS. Surprise, many stores load up their recommended baby clothes lists with unnecessary items (baby kimono, anyone?). See our "Baby Bargains" Layette later in this chapter for the real deal.

2 SIZING—YEAH, IT'S CONFUSING. Most baby clothes come in a range of sizes rather than one specific size ("newborn to 3 months" or "3-6 months"). For first time parents buying for a newborn, we recommend you buy "3-6 month" sizes (instead of newborn sizes). Why? Because the average newborn will grow out of "newborn" sizes way too fast. The exception to this rule: preemies and multiples, who tend to be on the small side.

No matter how big or small your newborn, a smart piece of advice: keep all receipts and tags so you can exchange clothes for larger sizes—you may find you're into six-month sizes by the time your baby hits one month old! (Along the same lines, don't wash all those new baby clothes immediately. Wash just a few items for the initial few weeks. Keep all the other items in their original packaging to make returns easier).

3 YOUR BABY WILL OUTGROW CLOTHES MUCH FASTER THAN YOU THINK! Babies double their birth weight by five months . . . and triple it by one year! On average, babies grow ten inches in their first year of life. Given those stats, you can understand why we don't recommend stocking up on "newborn" size clothes.

Also: remember, you can always buy more later if you need them. In fact, this is a good way to make use of those close friends and relatives who stop by and offer to "help" right after you've suffered through 36 hours of hard labor—send them to the store! FYI: our supply list should last for the first month or two of your baby's life.

4 YOUR BABY'S DEVELOPMENT FACTORS INTO CLOTHING. If you're new to this baby thing, you may be wondering how to pair the right clothing with your baby's developmental stage (if you're back for another round, think of this as a refresher). Here's a little primer on ages and stages.

◆ **0-3 months:** Newborns aren't even lifting their heads and they aren't able to do much besides eat, sleep and poop. Stick with sleepers, wearable blankets, and nightgowns for these guys. They don't need overalls or shirts and pants. Look for items sized by weight if possible since 0-3 month sizes can be all over the board.

◆ *3-6 months:* By the end of this stage your little one will be rolling over, sitting up and sleeping somewhat less. Still need those sleepers, but you're probably going to expand the wardrobe to include a few more play clothes. Two new items you will need now: bibs and socks. Depending on your baby's growth, you may find that you're buying nine and 12-month sizes.

◆ *6-12 months:* Finally, your baby is crawling, standing, maybe even cruising. At the end of a year she's likely tried those first tentative steps! Play clothes are a layette mainstay during these months. You'll also need good, no-skid socks that stay on (or very flexible shoes). You may find you're buying into the 18-month sizes.

5 YOU'RE GOING TO SPEND QUALITY TIME WITH YOUR WASHER. You may wonder, if you follow our list, how much laundry will you do? The answer: there is no answer. Factors such as whether you use cloth or disposable diapers (cloth can leak more; hence more laundry) and how much your baby spits up will greatly determine the laundry load. Another factor: breast versus bottle-feeding. Bottle-fed babies have fewer poops (and hence, less laundry from possible leaks). An "average" laundry cycle with our layette list would be every two to three days, assuming breast feeding, disposable diapers and an average amount of spit-up. Hint: if your washing machine is on its last legs, this might be something to upgrade before baby arrives.

6 SECOND-HAND BABY CLOTHES = BIG SAVINGS. Especially when you're talking about infant clothing. After all, infants don't do much damage to their clothes. They aren't playing in puddles, sucking down OtterPops or finger painting yet. So you can bet the wear and tear on used infant clothing is minimal.

Yes, there are national resale chains that specialize in kids clothes—Once Upon a Child (onceuponachild. com) is a reader favorite. But a quick Google search should uncover local stores.

Safety tip: make sure any second-hand clothes you buy don't have hazards like drawstrings or easy-to-detach buttons or bows.

7 ONE SIZE DOES NOT FIT ALL. A six month-size t-shirt is a six-month-size t-shirt, right? Wrong. For some reason, baby clothing companies have yet to synchronize their watches when it comes to sizes. Hence, a clothing item that says "six-month size" from one manufacturer can be just the same dimensions as a "twelve-month size" from another. All this begs the question: how can you avoid widespread confusion? First, open packages to check out actual dimensions. Take your baby along and hold items up to her to gauge whether they'd fit. Second, note whether items are pre-shrunk—you'll probably have to ask (if not, allow for shrinkage). Third, don't key on length from head to foot. Instead, focus on the length from neck to crotch—a common problem is items that seem roomy but are too tight in the crotch. Finally, forget age ranges and pay more attention to labels that specify an infant's size in weight and height, which are much more accurate. To show how widely sizing can vary, check out the following chart. We compared "six-month" t-shirts from six major clothing makers (sold at Babies R Us and Amazon.com) plus two popular web sites, Hanna Andersson, and Baby Gap. Here's what these six-month t-shirts really translated to in terms of a baby's weight and height:

What a six month t-shirt really means

MAKER	WEIGHT	HEIGHT
BABY GAP	17-22 LBS.	27-29"
CARTER'S/OSHKOSH	12.5-16.5 LBS.	24-26.5"
GYMBOREE	17-22 LBS.	25-29"
HANNA ANDERSSON	14-21 LBS.	26-30"
GERBER	16-20 LBS.	26-28"
LITTLE ME	12-16 LBS.	24-27"
LUVABLE FRIENDS	16.5-20.5 LBS.	26.5-28.5"
SPASILK	12-18 LBS.	24-26.5"

Here's another secret from the baby clothing trade: the more expensive the brand, the more roomy the clothes. Conversely, cheap items usually have the skimpiest sizing. What about the old wives' tale that you should just double your baby's age to find the right size (that is, buying twelve-month clothes for a six-month old?). That's bogus—as you can see, sizing is so all over the board that this rule just doesn't work.

The "Baby Bargains" Layette

Let's talk quality when it comes to baby clothes.

First, you want clothing that doesn't shrink. Look at the washing instructions. "Cold water wash/low dryer setting" is your clue that this item has NOT been pre-shrunk. Also, do the instructions tell you to wash with "like colors?" This may be a clue that the color will run. Next check the detailing. Are the seams sewn straight? Are they reinforced, particularly on the diaper area?

Go online and check message boards for posts on different brands. On our boards (Babybargains.com), parents comment frequently on whether a brand shrinks, has plenty of diaper room, falls apart after a few washings, etc. Spend a little time online to get some intel on the best brands—and which ones to avoid.

Now, let's get to the list:

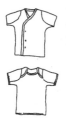

◆ **T-Shirts.** Oh sure, a t-shirt is a t-shirt, right? Not when it comes to baby t-shirts. These t-shirts could have side snaps, snaps at the crotch (also known as infant bodysuits, Onesies, creepers) or over-the-head openings. If you have a child who is allergic to metal snaps (they leave a red ring on the skin), you might want to consider over-the-head t-shirts. (FYI: While some folks refer to Onesies as a generic item, the term Onesie is a registered trademark brand by Gerber.)

By the way, is a t-shirt an outfit or an undergarment? Answer: it's both. In the summer, you'll find Onesies with printed patterns that are intended as outfits. In the winter, most stores just sell white or pastel Onesies, intended as undergarments.

How many? T-shirts usually come in packs of three. Our recommendation is to buy two packages of three (or a total of six shirts) of the side-snap variety. We also suggest buying two packs of over-the-head t-shirts. This way, if your baby does have an allergy to the snaps, you have a backup. Later you'll find the snap-at-the-crotch t-shirts to be most convenient since they don't ride up under clothes.

◆ **Gowns.** These are one-piece gowns with elastic at the bottom. They are used as sleeping garments in most cases. (We'll discuss more pros/cons of gowns later in this chapter.)

How many? This is a toss-up. If you want to experiment, go for one or two of these items. If they work well, you can always go back and get more later.

◆ **Sleepers.** This is the real workhorse of your infant's wardrobe, since babies usually sleep most of the day in the first months. Also known as stretchies, sleepers are most commonly used as pajamas for infants. They have feet, are often made of flame-retardant polyester, and snap up the front. As a side note, we've seen an increase in the numbers of cotton sleepers in recent years. Another related item: cotton long johns for baby. These are similar

Garage & Yard Sales
Nine Tips to Get The Best Bargains

It's an American bargain institution—the garage sale. Sure you can save money on baby clothes online or get a deal at a department store sale. But there's no comparing to the steals you can get at your neighbor's garage sale.

We love getting email from readers who've found great deals at garage sales. How about 25¢ Onesies, a snowsuit for $1, barely used high chairs for $5? But getting the most out of garage sales requires some pre-planning. Here are the insider tips from our readers:

1 CHECK CRAIGSLIST FIRST. Many folks advertise their garage sales a few days before the event—zero in on the ads/posts that mention kids/baby items to keep from wasting time on sales that won't be fruitful.

2 BECOME A GPS NINJA. Plot your route to avoid doubling back, factoring in travel time.

3 START EARLY. The professional bargain hunters get going at the crack of dawn. If you wait until mid-day, all the good stuff will be gone. An even better bet: if you know the family, ask if you can drop by the day before the sale. That way you have a first shot before the competition arrives. One trick: if it's a neighbor, offer to help set-up for the sale. That's a great way to get those "early bird" deals.

4 DO THE "BOX DIVE." Many garage sale hosts will just dump kids clothes into a big box, all jumbled together in different sizes, styles, etc. Figuring out how to get the best picks while three other moms are digging through the same box is a challenge. The best advice: familiarize yourself with the better name brands in this chapter and pluck out the best bets as fast as possible. Then evaluate the clothes away from the melee.

to sleepers, but don't have feet (and hence, may necessitate the use of socks in winter months).

One parent emailed us asking if she was supposed to dress her baby in pants, shirts, etc. or if it was OK to keep her daughter in sleepers all day long. She noted the baby was quite comfortable and happy. Of course, you can use sleepers exclusively for the first few months. We certainly did. As we've said all

5 CONCENTRATE ON "FAMILY AREAS." A mom here in Colorado told us she found garage sales in Boulder (a college town) were mostly students getting rid of stereos, clothes and other junk (sadly, a used beer pong table isn't useful in a nursery). A better bet was nearby Louisville, a suburban bedroom community with lots of growing families.

6 HAGGLE. Prices on big-ticket items (that is, anything over $5) are usually negotiable. Another great tip we read in the newsletter *Cheapskate Monthly*: to test out products, carry a few "C" and "D" batteries with you to garage sales. Why? Some swings, bouncers and other gear use such batteries. Pop in your test batteries to make sure items are in good working order!

7 SMALL BILLS. Take small bills with you to sales—lots of $1's and a few $5's. Why? When negotiating over price, slowly counting out small bills makes the seller feel like they are getting more money. A wad of 20 $1's for a high chair feels like a more substantial offer than a $20 bill.

8 DON'T BUY A USED CRIB OR CAR SEAT. Old cribs may not meet current safety standards. It's also difficult to get replacement parts for obscure brands. Car seats are also a second-hand no-no— you can't be sure it wasn't in an accident, weakening its safety and effectiveness. And watch out for clothing with drawstrings, loose buttons or other safety hazards.

9 BE CREATIVE. See a great stroller but the fabric is dirty? And non-removable so you can't throw it in the washing machine? Take a cue from one dad we interviewed. He takes dirty second-hand strollers or high chairs to a car wash and blasts them with a high-pressure hose! Voila! Clean and useable items are the result. For a small investment, you can rehabilitate a dingy stroller into a showpiece.

along, a comfortable baby is a happy parent!

How many? Because of their heavy use, we recommend parents buy at least four to eight sleepers.

 ◆ ***Blanket Sleepers/wearable blankets.*** These are heavyweight, footed one-piece garments made of polyester. Used often in winter, blanket sleepers usually have a zipper down the front. In recent years, we've also seen quite a few fleece blanket sleepers, their key advantage being a softer fabric and a resistance to pilling.

Another option is a wearable blanket or swaddling blanket. See the previous chapter for our top recommendations. You may want to put a t-shirt on baby and then wrap her up in a swaddling blanket or wearable blanket.

How many? If you live in a cold climate or your baby is born in the winter, you may want to purchase two to four of these items. As an alternative to buying blanket sleepers, you could put a t-shirt on underneath a sleeper or stretchie for extra warmth.

 ◆ ***Coveralls.*** One-piece play outfits, coveralls (also known as rompers) are usually cotton or cotton/poly blends. Small sizes (under 6 months) may have feet, while larger sizes don't.

How many? Since these are really play clothes and small infants don't do a lot of playing, we recommend you only buy two to four coveralls for babies less than four months of age. However, if your child will be going into daycare at an early age, you may need to start with four to six coveralls.

 ◆ ***Booties/socks.*** These are necessary for outfits that don't have feet (like gowns and coveralls). As your child gets older (at about six months), look for the kind of socks that have rubber skids on the bottom (they keep baby from slipping when learning to walk).

How many? Three to four pairs are all you'll need at first, since baby will probably be dressed in footed sleepers most of the time.

◆ ***Sweaters.*** How many? Most parents will find one sweater is plenty (they're nice for holiday picture sessions). Avoid all-white sweaters for obvious reasons!

clothes

◆ **Hats.** Believe it or not, you'll still want a light cap for your baby in the early months of life, even if you live in a hot climate. Babies lose a large amount of heat from their heads, so protecting them with a cap or bonnet is a good idea. And don't expect to go out for a walk in the park without the baby's sun hat either.

How many? A couple of hats would be a good idea—sun hats in summer, warmer caps for winter. We like the safari-style hats best (they have flaps to protect the ears and neck).

◆ **Snowsuit/bunting.** Similar to the type of fabric used for blanket sleepers, buntings also have hoods and covers for the hands. Most buntings are like a sack and don't have leg openings, while snowsuits do. Both versions usually have zippered fronts.

FYI: Snowsuits and buntings should NOT be worn by infants when they ride in a car seat. Why? Thick fabric on these items can compress in an accident, compromising the infant's safety in the seat. So how can you keep your baby warm in an infant car seat? There are car seat covers that fit over the top of the car seat to keep baby warm. Cozy Cover (Cozy-Cover.com, $20), makes a variety of styles and fabrics to protect your child from the cold or the sun.

How many? Only buy one of these if you live in a climate where you need it. Even with a Colorado winter, we got away with layering clothes on our baby, then wrapping him in a blanket for the walk out to a warmed-up car. If you live in a city without a car, you might need two or three snowsuits for those stroller rides to the market.

◆ **Kimonos.** Just like the adult version. Some are zippered sacks with a hood and terry-cloth lining. You use them after a bath.

How many? None. We recommend you pass on the kimonos and instead invest in good quality towels.

◆ **Saque Sets.** Two-piece outfits with a shirt and diaper cover.

How many? Forget buying these as well.

◆ **Bibs.** These come in two versions, believe it or not. The little, tiny bibs are for the baby that occasionally drools. The larger versions are used when you begin feeding her solid foods (at about six months). Don't expect to be able to use the drool bibs later for feedings, unless you plan to change her carrot-stained outfit frequently.

How many? Skip the drool bibs. The exception: if your baby really can't keep dry because he's drooling the equivalent of a bathtub full every day, consider buying a few of these. When baby starts eating solid foods, you'll need at least three or four large bibs. One option: plastic bibs for feeding so you can just sponge them off after a meal.

◆ ***Washcloths and Hooded Towels.*** OK, so these aren't actually clothes, but baby washcloths and hooded towels are a necessity. Why? Because they are small and easier to use . . . plus they're softer than adult towels and washcloths.

How many? At first, you'll probably need only three sets of towels and washcloths (you get one of each per set). But as baby gets older and dirtier, invest in a few more washcloths to spot clean during the day.

◆ ***Receiving Blankets.*** You'll need these small, cotton blankets for all kinds of uses: to swaddle the baby, as a play quilt, or even for an extra layer of warmth on a cold day.

How many? We believe you can never have too many of these blankets, but since you'll probably get a few as gifts, you'll only need to buy two or three yourself. A total of seven to eight is probably optimal.

Baby Clothes to Avoid

◆ ***Clothing that Leads to Diaper Changing Gymnastics.***
It's pretty obvious that some designers of baby clothing have never had children of their own. What else could explain outfits that snap up the back, have super tiny head, leg and arm openings, and snaps in inconvenient places (or worse, no snaps at all)? One mother we spoke with was furious about outfits that have snaps only down one leg, requiring her baby to be a contortionist to get into and out of the outfit.

Our advice: stay away from outfits that don't have easy access to the diaper. Look instead for snaps or zippers down the front of the outfit or on the crotch. If your baby doesn't like having things pulled over his head, look for shirts with wide, stretchie necklines.

◆ ***Shoes for newborns.*** Developmentally, babies don't need shoes until after they become quite proficient at walking (around

11 to 14 months). In fact, it's better for their muscle development to go barefoot or wear socks. While those expensive baby Merrells or Air Jordans might look cute, they're really a supreme waste of money.

Once your baby (now a toddler) masters walking, *then* you need shoes. Here's our thoughts.

First, look for shoes that have the most flexible soles. You'll also want fabrics that breath and stretch, like canvas and leather—stay away from vinyl shoes. The best brands we found were recommended by readers. *Robeez* (robeez.com, a division of Stride Rite) are made of leather, have soft, skid-resistant soles and are machine washable. They start at $24 for a basic pair. Another reader recommended New Zealand-made *Bobux* shoes ($29, bobuxusa.com). These cute leather soft soles "do the trick by staying on extremely well," according to a reader. Finally, we also like *PediPeds* (pedipeds.com). The soft-soled shoes are hand stitched and made of leather. They are sized from 0 to five years and start at $35.

◆ **Drool bibs.** These tiny bibs are intended for small infants who drool all over everything. Or infants who spit-up frequently. Our opinion: they're pretty useless—they're too small to catch much drool or spit-up.

When you do buy bibs, stay away from the ones that tie. Bibs that snap or have Velcro are much easier to get on and off. Another good bet: bibs that go on over the head (and have no snaps or Velcro). Why? Older babies can't pull them off by themselves.

Stay away from the super-size vinyl bibs that cover the arms, since babies who wear them can get too hot and sweaty. However, we do recommend you buy a few regular-style vinyl bibs for travel. You can wash them off much more easily than the standard terry-cloth bibs.

◆ **A toss-up: gowns.** The jury is still out on whether gowns are useful. We thought they were a waste of money, but a parent we interviewed did mention that she used the gowns when her baby had colic (that persistent crying condition; see our other book *Baby 411* for a discussion). She believed that the extra room in the gown made her baby more comfortable. Still others praise gowns for their easy access to diapers, making changes easy, especially in the middle of the night. Finally, parents in hot climates say gowns keep their infants more comfortable. So, you can see there's a wide range of opinions on this item.

The Best Baby Clothes Brands

Walk into any store and you'll see a blizzard of brand names for baby clothes. Which ones stand up to frequent washings? Which ones have snaps that stay snapped? Which are a good value for the dollar? We asked our readers to divide their favorite clothing brands/stores into three categories: best bets, good but not great and skip it.

The Best Bets tend to be clothes that were not only stylish but also held up in the wash. The fabric was usually softer and pilled less. Customer service also comes into play with the best brands. Hanna Andersson is a great example of a company that bends over backwards for their customers. Gymboree, on the other hand, seems to be less satisfactory for many parents, souring them on the brand. Keep in mind, some brands are pricey, so look for sales and second hand deals. Or just point Grandma to these sites!

Good but not Great clothes were pretty good, just not as soft or as stylish as Best Bets. The Skip-It brands were most likely the poorest quality: they shrunk in the wash, pilled up or fell apart. Inconsistent sizing was also a problem with brands like Babies R Us' Koala Kids.

Some of these brands sell direct; others just through retailers.

Best Bets

Baby Gap	(800) GAP-STYLE	babygap.com
Baby Lulu		babylulu.com
Carter's	(770) 961-8722	carters.com
Cozy Toes		cozytoesdesignstudio.com
First Impressions		macys.com
Flap Happy	(800) 234-3527	flaphappy.com
H & M		hm.com
Hanna Andersson		hannaandersson.com
Janie and Jack		janieandjack.com
Kissy Kissy		kissykissyonline.com
Little Me	(800) 533-5497	littleme.com
LL Bean		llbean.com
Boden All Baby		bodenusa.com
Old Navy		oldnavy.com
OshKosh B'Gosh	(800) 692-4674	oshkoshbgosh.com
Sarah's Prints	(888) 477-4687	sarasprints.com
Tea collection		teacollection.com
Wes & Willy		wesandwilly.com
Zutano		zutano.com

Good But Not Great

Children's Place	childrensplace.com
Good Lad of Philadelphia	goodlad.com
Gymboree	gymboree.com
Le Top	letop-usa.com
Target (Little Me, Carter's Just One You, Halo, Circo)	target.com
Walmart (Faded Glory, Carter's Child of Mine)	walmart.com

Skip It: Gerber, Hanes, Koala Kids (Babies R Us), Disney, Carter's Just One Year at Target, George by Walmart

Top Picks For Day Care, Weekends & Special Occasions

What clothing brands are best? Well, there is no one correct answer. An outfit that's perfect for day care (that is, to be trashed in Junior's first painting experiment) is different from an outfit for a weekend outing with friends. And dress-up occasions may require an entirely different set of clothing criteria. Hence, we've divided our clothing brand recommendations into three areas: good (day care), better (weekend wear) and best (special occasions). While some brands make items in two or even three categories, here's how we see it:

Day Care & Play. For everyday comfort (and day-care situations), basic brands like Carter's, Little Me, and OshKosh are your best bets. We also like the basics (when on sale) at Baby Gap (Gap Kids) for day-care wardrobes. For great price to value, take a look at Old Navy and Target.

Weekend Outings. What if you have a miniature golf outing planned with friends? Or a visit to Grandma's house? The brands of better-made casual wear we like best include Baby Gap, Flapdoodles, and Gymboree. Also recommended: Jake and Me, MulberriBush, and Wes and Willy. For online sites, we like the clothes in Hanna Andersson and Boden's All Baby as good brands, especially on sale.

Special Occasion. Yes, holidays and other special occasions call for special outfits. We like Janie and Jack (janieandjack.com), and Wooden Soldier (woodensoldier.com)

The Best Diapers: Cloth vs Disposable?

The great diaper debate still rages on: should you use cloth or disposable? Fans of cloth diapers argue cloth is better for the planet. On the other hand, those disposable diapers are darn convenient—and the choice of 96% of parents in the US.

Considering the average baby will go through 2300 diaper changes in the first year of life, this isn't a moot issue—you'll be dealing with diapers until your baby is three or four years old (the average girl potty trains at 35 months; boys at 39 months). Yes, you read that last sentence right . . . you will be diapering for the next 35 to 39 MONTHS.

Now, in this section, we've decided NOT to rehash all the environmental arguments pro or con for cloth versus disposable. Fire up your web browser and you'll find plenty of diaper debate on parenting sites. Instead, we'll focus here on the FINANCIAL and PRACTICAL impacts of your decision.

Let's look at each option:

◆ **Cloth**. Prior to the 1960's, this was the only diaper option available to parents. Fans of cloth diapering claim that babies experienced less diaper rash and toilet trained faster. From a practical point of view, cloth diapers have improved in design over the years, offering more absorbency and fewer leaks. They aren't perfect, but the advent of diaper covers (no more plastic pants) has helped as well.

Another practical point: laundry. You've got to decide if you will use a cloth diaper service or launder at home. Obviously, the latter requires more effort on your part. Meanwhile, we'll discuss the financial costs of cloth in general at the end of this section.

Final practical point about cloth: most day care centers don't allow them. This may be a sanitation requirement governed by state day care regulators and not a negotiating point. Check with local day care centers or your state board.

◆ **Disposables**. Disposable diapers were first introduced in 1961 and now hold an overwhelming lead over cloth—about 95% of all households that have kids in diapers use disposables. Today's diapers have super-absorbent gels that lower the number of needed diaper changes, especially at night (which helps baby sleep through the night sooner). Even many parents who swear cloth diapers are best often use disposables at night. The downside? All that super-absorbency means babies are in no rush to potty train—they simply don't feel as wet or uncomfortable as babies in cloth diapers.

The jury on diaper rash is still out—disposable diaper users generally don't experience any more diaper rash than cloth diaper users.

Besides the eco-arguments about disposables, there is one other disadvantage—higher trash costs. In many communities, the more trash you put out, the higher the bill.

The financial bottom line: Surprisingly, there is no clear winner when you factor financial costs into the diaper equation.

Cloth diapers may seem cheap at first, but consider the hidden costs. Besides the diapers themselves ($100 for the basic varieties; $200 to $300 for the fancy ones), you also have to buy diaper covers. Like everything you buy with baby, there is a wide cost variation. The cheap stuff (like Dappi covers) will set you back $6 to $7 each.

And you've got to buy several covers in different sizes as your child grows. If you're lucky, you can find diaper covers second-hand for $2 to $4. Of course, some parents find low-cost covers leak and quickly wear out. As a result, they turn to the more expensive covers—a single Mother-Ease cover is $20, for example. Invest in a half dozen of those covers (in various sizes, of course) and you've spent another $300 to $500 (if you buy them new).

What about laundry? Well, washing your own cloth diapers at home may be the most economical way to go, but often folks don't have the time or energy. Instead, some parents use a cloth diaper service. In a recent cost survey of such services across the U.S., we found that the average is about $1000 to $1200 a year. While each service does supply you with diapers (relieving you of that expense), you're still on the hook for the diaper covers. You'll make an average of eight changes a day (more when a baby is newborn, less as they grow older), so be sure you're getting about 60 diapers a week from your service.

Proponents of cloth diapers argue that if you plan to have more than one child, you can reuse those covers, spreading out the cost. You may also not need as many sizes depending on the brands you use and the way your child grows.

So, what's the bottom line cost for cloth diapers? We estimate the total financial damage for cloth diapers (using a cloth diaper service and buying diaper covers) for just the first year is $1100 to $1300.

By contrast, let's take a look at disposables. If you buy disposable diapers from the most expensive source in town (typically, a grocery store), you'd spend about $700 to $800 for the first year. Yet, we've found the best deals are buying in bulk from the discount sources we'll discuss shortly. By shopping at these sources, we figure you'd spend $450 to $550 per year (the lowest figure is for private label diapers, the highest is for brand names).

The bottom line: the cheapest way to go is cloth diapers laundered at home. The next most affordable choice is disposables. Finally, cloth diapers from a diaper service are the most expensive choice.

11 Keys To Saving Money on Diapers

1 **THINK PRICE PER DIAPER.** Stores sell diapers in all sorts of package sizes—always compare diaper prices per diaper, not per box.

2 **BUY IN BULK.** Don't buy those little packs of 20 diapers—look for the 80 or 100 count packs instead. You'll find the price per diaper goes down when you buy larger packs. That's why grocery stores are usually the most expensive place to buy diapers—they sell diapers in smaller packages, with the highest per diaper price. Online discounters often sell packs of more than 200 at even bigger discounts.

3 **GO FOR WAREHOUSE CLUBS.** Sam's (samsclub.com), BJ's (bjs.com) and Costco (costco.com) wholesale clubs sell diapers at incredibly low prices. For example, Costco sells a 192-count package of Huggies Little Snugglers stage 1 for just $37.49 or about 19.5¢ per diaper. We also found great deals on wipes at the wholesale clubs. The downside to these warehouse clubs? You buy a membership to shop at clubs, which runs about $45 to $55 a year. And clubs don't stock the usual sizes of diapers—some carry "size 1-2" diapers, instead of just size 1 or 2. Readers are frustrated with this combined sizing, according to our message boards.

4 **BUY STORE BRANDS.** Many readers tell us they find store brand diapers to be equal to the name brands. And the prices can't be beat—many are 20% to 30% cheaper. Chains like Target, Walmart and Toys R Us/Babies R Us carry in-house diaper brands, as do many grocery stores. Warehouse clubs also carry in store brands: Costco's Kirkland, BJ's Little Bundles and Sam's Club's Member's Mark.

5 CONSIDER TOYS R US. If you don't have a wholesale club nearby, you're bound to be close to a Toys R Us or Babies R Us. And we found them to be a great source for affordable name-brand diapers. The best bet: buy in bulk. You can often buy diapers (both name brand and generic) by the case at Toys R Us, saving you about 20% or more over grocery store prices. Bonus: TRU and BRU often offer in-store coupons for diapers—combine these with manufacturer's coupons for double savings.

6 ONLINE DEALS MAY BEAT IN-STORE PRICES. If you've got Amazon Prime, sign up for Amazon Family (it's free) to get another 20% off "Subscribe & Save" deals on diapers. Not to be outdone, Walmart now offers free two-day shipping on diapers with no membership fee. And Walmart aggressively prices diapers to be completive with Amazon.

7 DON'T BUY DIAPERS IN GROCERY STORES. We compared prices at grocery stores and usually found them to be sky-high. Most were selling diapers in packages that worked out to over 25¢ per diaper. Of course, sales and coupons can lower those prices—some grocery chains aggressively price diapers as a loss leader.

8 COUPONS. Yep, it doesn't take much effort to find high-value coupons for diapers. If you have to make a late-night diaper run to the grocery store, use these to save. We've got diaper coupons on our web site (http://bit.ly/diapercoupons).

9 ASK FOR GIFT CARDS. When friends ask you what you'd like as a shower gift, you can drop hints for gift cards from stores that sell a wide variety of baby items—including diapers and wipes. That way you can get what you really need, instead of cute accessories of marginal value.

10 FOR CLOTH DIAPER USERS, GO FOR INTRODUCTORY OR TRIAL DEALS. Many suppliers have special introductory or trial packages with built-in discounts. Before you invest hundreds of dollars in one brand, give it a test drive first.

11 BUY USED CLOTH DIAPERS. Many of the best brands of cloth diapers last and last and last. So you may see them on eBay or cloth-diaper message boards. Buy them—you can get some brands for as little as a buck or two. As long as you know the quality and age of the diapers you're buying, this tip can really be a money saver.

The Best Diapers

We break down our diaper picks into several categories:

◆ Best Disposable Diaper Overall
◆ Best Budget-Friendly Disposable Diaper
◆ Best Disposable Diaper To Buy at 2am
◆ Best Eco-Friendly Disposable
◆ Best Cloth Diapers

The Best Disposable Diaper

After extensive research into 18 different diaper brands, sur-veying our readers about their diaper favorites and evaluating several diaper leakage lab tests, we pick **Pampers Swaddlers** as the **Best Disposable Diaper**.

Pampers Swaddlers checks all the boxes we look for in a dia-per—great leak protection (as judged by independent tests), excellent reader feedback for overall fit and performance and wide availability with affordable pricing.

Yes, there are some bells and whistles here that you don't see in generic diapers (Pamper's color-changing wetness indicator), but what we care about is performance and fit. On that score, Pampers Swaddlers is excellent.

A box of 216 count Size 1 Pampers Swaddlers runs 17 cents per diaper on Amazon (you can slice that price down another 20%—to 13.6¢—by being a member of Amazon Prime, sign up for the free Amazon Family program and use Subscribe & Save.). Walmart sells the same box for 13.9¢ per diaper.

Pampers does sell a couple of variations on the Swaddlers, including **Swaddlers Sensitive** (for babies with sensitive skin). Those are also excellent diapers, but much more expensive (31¢ a diaper).

The Best Budget-Friendly Disposable Diaper

We conduct rolling price checks on diapers, both online and offline, chain stores and warehouse clubs. We then take the lowest priced diapers and compare them to lab tests for effectiveness.

The winner this year is *Luv's Ultra Leakguards*—on Amazon, these diapers are as low as 8.3 cents—that's for Prime members who do Subscribe & Save and with a $2 off coupon.

FYI: both Amazon and Walmart are engaged in a diaper price war as of press time. In the past, we found generic diapers like Walmart's Parent's Choice and Target's Up & Up to be the least expensive diapers, along with club picks like Costco's Kirkland Supreme diapers. But Kirkland is now 15.6¢ per diaper—and not everyone has a Costco near by.

Fans of Target say their diaper promo sales (buy $125 worth of diapers, get a $20 or $25 gift card) drop prices under 10¢ per diaper for top brands like Huggies. Target's Cartwheel app also regularly features diaper deals.

Of course, a disposable diaper deal that leaks is no bargain. That's why *Luv's Ultra Leakguards* tops our list of bargain choices, based on fit and leak testing. A close second would be *Huggies Snug & Dry* when they are on sale on Amazon or Walmart.

We realize we are talking cents per diaper savings and that may not seem like much. But pennies add up when you're talking about buying 2300 diapers in your baby's first year.

Total annual savings of Luv's Ultra Leakguards at Amazon versus Pampers Swaddlers would be $120+. That's 61% less money on diapers! Heck, just following that one tip paid for this book almost ten times over!

The Best Disposable Diaper to Buy at 2am

As all bargain ninjas know, plans to get the best prices on diapers sometimes run into the 2am diaper emergency. You're out of diapers and the closest diaper source is a drug store. So in a pinch, which drugstore diaper performs the best at a price that won't break the bank?

Walgreens Well Beginnings is our pick for a 2am diaper run. Fit and leakage protection are excellent and the price, surprisingly, is decent—about 14¢ per diaper. No, there aren't any bells and whistles like wetness indicators, but you don't them at 2am!

Best Eco-Friendly Disposable

How is that even possible—to be both eco-friendly and disposable? Our top pick for best eco-friendly disposable, **Bambo Nature**, manages that and more.

Made in Denmark, Bambo Nature backs up its environmental talk with certifications: the diapers are FSC-certified, Nordic Ecolabel and the EU's Ecolabel. Other eco-friendly diapers talk eco-friendliness but rarely back it up with third-party testing.

These diapers tick just about every box for sustainability and eco-friendliness. While we don't have room here for a full run-down, Bambo Nature's web site lays out the features in detail.

Bambo Nature diapers scores at the top for performance—very little leakage, strong absorbency and comfort/fit. Too often we see expensive green diapers that tout their eco credentials but do an average to poor job of stopping leaks.

So what's the catch? Well, if you said price, give yourself bonus points. Like many other eco-baby gear picks, all the environmental goodness will cost you. Even on Amazon in a large box (56 count), size 1 Bambo Nature diapers run about 40¢ each. Ouch.

Another caveat: the sizing of European diapers is a bit different from the USA. Basically, the Bambo Nature diapers run large compared to Pampers or Huggies.

Best Cloth Diaper

Ask ten cloth diaper afficionados for their favorite cloth diapers and you'll probably get 11 different answers! That's because there are so many different options out there it can be confusing. And then there is the learning curve.

So let's cut through the clutter and give you a pick, assuming you are a first-time cloth diaperer and looking for a simple solution: **BumGenius First Year Adjustable All-in-One cloth diaper.**

Also known as the BumGenius Freetime, this diaper is the easiest for first-timer cloth diaperers—as an all-in-one, you don't need to buy separate covers or inserts. Basically, you pop the entire diaper in the wash.

Best of all, the BumGenius adjusts to fit babies from seven to 35 lbs. So what's not to like? Well, the BumGenius must be line-dried, and that can take a while (especially in humid climates). Also: the diaper is a bit bulky. These diapers run $20 on Amazon.

Also Great: Rumparooz One-Size Cloth Diaper

If you consider yourself a more advanced cloth diaper, we would suggest the **Rumparooz One-Size Cloth Pocket Diaper**.

Rumparooz is a one-size diaper that adjusts to fit babies six to 35 lbs. What our readers love about this cloth diaper is Rumparooz's attention to detail and high quality materials. You can customize the absorbency via different liners (the diaper comes with a microfiber "6r soaker" insert). An inner and outer elastic barrier stops nearly all leaks. Overall, excellent quality.

What's not to like? Well, you do have to deal with those inserts, with can be a pain. The Rumparooz is bulky and a few readers complain it doesn't fit toddlers well, despite the claimed 35 lb. weight limit. And they are very pricey: $25 per diaper.

Best Diaper Wipes

Diaper wipes are diaper wipes, right? What's the difference?

Yes, the differences can be subtle and somewhat objective: what seems like a soft wipe to one parent may be sand paper to another.

We extensively survey our vast readership to find the best wipes. In the past few years, we've seen a new crop of eco-friendly wipes join the market. These wipes drop the typical wipe chemicals (disodium phosphates? Phenoxyethanol?) for a mix of more natural ingredients free of chemical perfumes or dyes.

We break down our diaper wipe picks this way:

◆ Best Diaper Wipe (Overall)
◆ Best Eco-Friendly Diaper Wipe

Best Diaper Wipes (Overall)

diaper wipes

Amazon Elements Sensitive Diaper Wipes are our choice for the best diaper wipe. Readers praise these wipes for overall quality and value.

A 480 count box (six packs of 80 wipes each) with Amazon Prime and Subscribe & Save run just 2.1¢ per wipe—that's less than half of the price of name-brands. These wipes come in three versions: scented, unscented and sensitive (which are also unscented).

Also Great: Pampers Sensitive Diaper Wipes

Pampers Sensitive Diaper Wipes also score high with our readers, who like the very soft texture. Compared to Pampers other wipes, these are somewhat thicker and come unscented. The price is about 2.5¢ when bought with Amazon Prime and Subscribe & Save. In stores, these wipes run 2.6¢ to 3¢ wipe.

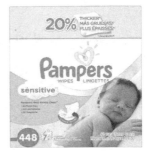

Another bonus: these wipes are so popular, you can typically score coupons to drop the price further.

Costco fans tell us their ***Kirklands Signature Diaper Wipes*** are a winner and we agree—these wipes perform just as well as the name brands at a price (2.2¢) that is hard to beat.

Best Eco-Friendly Diaper Wipe

Babyganics Diaper Wipes is our pick for best eco-friendly diaper wipe. Our readers loved Babyganics for all the things that aren't in these wipes: no parabens, sulfates, dyes or fragrances. Instead, Babyganics substitutes a blend of fruit and vegetable oils. They run 3.7¢ per wipe.

While Babyganics is our top pick here, we should note they didn't work for a sizeable minority of readers who tried them. Critics say they are too thin and didn't clean well. Others were put off by their smell, which one mom compared to "cat saliva." As a dog owner, we can't vouch for that last one, but let's say Babyganics smell is not universally loved.

Also Great: WaterWipes

What if you took out all the chemicals in wipes and just left water? That's the essence of **WaterWipes**, which we would also recommend as an eco-friendly wipe.

As the name implies, these wipes are 99.9% water with the balance being grapefruit seed oil. Readers love their simplicity, especially for babies who've developed rashes from standard wipes.

A few caveats: some of these chemicals in standard wipes keep them from molding. So it doesn't come as a surprise we heard more than a few complaints about molding with WaterWipes—this would be a case were we suggest *not* ordering in bulk. And no wipe warmers. Critics note that a 2016 change to WaterWipes made them smaller and thinner, which dismayed fans. These wipes can also be drippy, irking more than one reader.

Those caveats aside, we still like WaterWipes for folks who desire a simple wipe for babies with super-sensitive skin.

CHAPTER 5

Feeding

Feeding Baby

Inside this chapter

Feeding baby comes with many decisions . . . and it's own array of gear. We'll go over everything from bottles to high chairs, breast pumps to formula plus baby food in this chapter!

The Best Breast Pumps

This category can be confusing, with an array of options that start at $20 and go over $300. Before we get to our picks, let's go over some basic things to learn.

7 Things No One Tells You About Buying a Breast Pump

1 **BREAST PUMP 101 : THE THREE BASIC TYPES OF PUMPS (AND WHAT THEY DO WELL).** Even if you exclusively breastfeed, you probably will find yourself needing to pump an occasional bottle. After all, you might want to go out to dinner without the baby (yes, that is possible). Maybe you'll have an overnight trip for your job or just need to get back to work full or part time. Your partner might even be interested in relieving you of a night feeding (it can happen).

The solution? Pumping milk. Whether you want to pump occasionally or every day, you have a wide range of options. Here's an overview:

◆ *Manual Expression:* OK, technically, this isn't a breast pump in the sense we're talking about. But it is an option. There are several good breastfeeding books that describe how to express milk manually. Most women find that the amount of milk expressed, compared to the time and trouble involved, hardly makes it worth using this method. A few women (we think they are modern miracle workers) can manage to express enough for an occasional bottle; for the majority of women, however, using a breast pump is a more practical alternative. Manual expression is typically used only to relieve engorgement.

◆ *Manual Pumps:* Non-electric, hand-held pumps are operated by squeezing on a handle. While most affordable, manual pumps are generally also the least efficient—you simply can't duplicate your baby's sucking action by hand. Therefore, these pumps are best for moms who only need an occasional bottle or who need to relieve engorgement.

◆ *Mini-Electrics:* These breast pumps (most work either with batteries or an A/C adapter) are designed to express an occasional bottle. Unfortunately, the sucking action is so weak that it often takes twenty minutes per side to express a significant amount of milk. And doing so is not very comfortable. Why is it so slow? Most models only cycle nine to

BREAST PUMPS	Which pump works best in which situation?			
	Manual	Mini-Elec.	Professional	Rental*
Do you need a pump for:				
A missed feeding?	■	◆		
Evening out from baby?	■	◆		
Working part-time.	■	◆		
Occasional use, a few times a week.	■	◆		
Daily use; full-time work			●	●
Premature or hospitalized baby?			●	●
Low milk supply?			●	●
Sore nipples/engorgement?	■		●	●
Latch-on problems or breast infection?			■	●
Drawing out flat or inverted nipples?	■	◆	●	●

Key: ■ = Good ◆ = Better ● = Best
*Rental refers to renting a hospital-grade pump. These can usually be rented on a monthly basis.
Source: Medela.

fifteen times per minute—compare that to a baby who sucks the equivalent of 50 cycles per minute!

◆ *High-End Double Pumps (aka Professional Grade):* The Mercedes of breast pumps—we can't sing the praises of these work horses enough. In just ten to twenty minutes, you can pump both breasts. And high-end double pumps are much more comfortable than mini-electrics. In fact, at first I didn't think a high-end pump I rented was working well because it was so comfortable. The bottom line: there is no better option for working women who want to provide their babies with breast milk.

2 **THAT "FREE" ACA BREAST PUMP MAY NOT WORK BEST FOR YOU.** Yes, as a new mom, you may qualify for a free breast pump with your health insurance, thanks to the Affordable Care Act.

So what's the catch? (You knew there would be a catch.) That "free pump" is determined by your insurance carrier—and that's whatever breast pump they decide to cover. So, they could give you a cheap, underpowered mini-electric . . . or a top-of-the-line professional grade electric pump. In the former case, you may find yourself needing to purchase a breast pump out of pocket.

As of press time, the ACA's political fate is uncertain, so it is unclear how this benefit goes forward, if at all.

3 **IT MAY MAKE MORE SENSE TO RENT THAN BUY.** Rental pumps are what the industry refers to as hospital-grade or piston electric pumps. They are built to withstand continuous use of up to ten times a day for many years. The interior parts are sealed to prevent contamination from one renter to the next.

Compared to purchased pumps, rentals have much more powerful motors and can often empty both breasts in 10 to 15 minutes without hurting breast tissue.

We recommend renting first before buying, just so you can get the hang of it and determine if you really need a breast pump for long-term pumping. They usually rent from $65 to $90 per month, plus the cost of a collection kit.

4 **DON'T PURCHASE A USED PUMP.** We're big proponents of saving money, but somethings you must draw the line at for safety's sake. One is never, ever buy a used professional grade electric pump. Models like Medela's Pump In Style can actually collect milk in the pump mechanism—that can expose your baby to bacteria and pathogens from another mother's breast milk.

So, let's state it clearly: DO NOT PURCHASE A USED BREAST PUMP. The risk of exposing your baby to any pathogens isn't worth the savings. Of course, it is fine to re-use your own breast pump for another child down the road. Just replace the tubing and collection bottles to make sure there are no bacteria left over from previous uses.

5 NEXT DECISION: HOW TO STORE THAT MILK. You have options: plastic bags, plastic bottles and ice cube trays. Plastic bags designed for breast milk storage are the cheapest option— we recommend Lansinoh bread pump bags ($29 for 150 bags or 19¢ per bag). Yes, there is some concern that some nutrients in breast milk can stick to the bags, but they are a safe and convenient option.

If you prefer plastic bottles, Medela makes plastic bottles ($11 for six five-ounce bottles) that are compatible with all their breast pumps.

Milkies Milk Trays is our last recommended storage product. They look like old fashioned ice cube trays, but they include lids to help avoid freezer burn. The cubes come out as long cylinders, perfect for a baby bottle. Cost: $20.

6 WHEN IT COMES TO BREAST PUMPS, DON'T SKIMP ON QUALITY. It's important to buy a pump you can successfully use. Invest in quality, speed and comfort. Yes, you can find a $20 breast pump in a discount store . . . but if it is slow, painful and inefficient, it's no bargain.

7 HIRING A LACTATION CONSULTANT IS A WISE INVESTMENT. Successful breast feeding and pumping is not just about the pump. A lactation consultant (either affiliated with your doctor or with a hospital) can help make sure you're using that pump correctly. It should not hurt! Lactation consultants can help troubleshoot problems, enabling your breastfeeding and pumping to be as successful as possible. We strongly suggest using a lactation consultant's services.

Up next, our picks for best pump (overall), best manual pump and best mini-electric pump.

The Best Breast Pump (Overall)

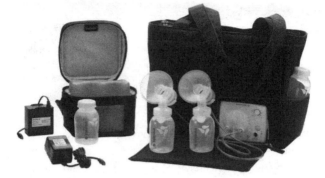

We researched, tested and evaluated 20+ breast pumps before crowning a winner: the **Medela Pump In Style Advanced** ($180) is the best breast pump for moms who need to pump frequently. Fast, easy to use, transportable with three different carry bag options, this pump has been a favorite of our readers and lactation consultants we interviewed for several years.

It's the 800-pound gorilla of the breast pump category—the Medela Pump In Style Advanced is the king of breast pumps, in our opinion. So what's all the fuss about? If you are serious about pumping every day, the Pump In Style (PIS) allows you to carry a high-quality pump with you to work. You can empty both breasts in a short amount of time with great comfort. As a nursing mom, I personally used a previous version of this pump and found it to be comparable in quality to a hospital-grade pump.

The PIS has evolved over the years—the current flagship is called the Advanced, which comes in three flavors: tote bag, backpack or no bag. This no bag version is called the Pump in Style Advanced Starter Set, which is provided by some insurance carriers to comply with the Affordable Care Act. Price: $138.

FYI: All three versions of the Advanced come with the same pump, which features Medela's "2-Phase Expression" technology that mimics the way infants nurse at the breast. At first, infants apparently nurse quickly to simulate let down, then they settle into a deeper, slower sucking action—the Pump In Style Advance simulates this pattern. Fans of Medela love the availability of parts (sold in many retail stores) and Medela's great customer service. Bottom line: we recommend the Pump in Style—it is an excellent pump.

Also Great: Avent Double Electric Comfort Pump

The **Avent Double Electric Comfort Pump** ($200) comes with three flow settings and is much smaller/lighter and less expensive than the Medela Pump In Style Advanced. The design of the flange with a textured massage cushion is impressive. As you might expect, this pump is compatible with Avent's bottles—you can connect them directly to the pump. Not all of our readers are fans—parents have complained to us the pump did not work as well as the Medela Pump In Style Advanced . . . or, worse, it broke after a few months.

Best Manual Breast Pump

Our readers love the **Avent Comfort Manual**, which Avent claims is as efficient as a mini-electric (it takes about eight to ten minutes to empty a breast). That assumes you have the hand strength to pump for 8-10 minutes, of course. Comfort is the focus here: no more hunching forward, the Comfort Manual keeps the milk flowing into the bottle no matter your position.

In a recent refresh Avent added a "soft massage cushion" to the flange that feels soft to the touch and massages the breast for better letdown.

The pump has an ergonomic handle for easy one hand operation. Other great features included easy cleaning (you can pop it in the dishwasher), compatibility with other Avent bottles (it comes with a 4 oz. Avent Natural bottle), and ease of use. Reader feedback is very positive and at this price, it's a real winner.

Flaws but not deal breakers. Avent's Comfort Manual is great, but there are a few caveats. Some are the result of the limitations of manual pumps in general (it takes a while to empty both breasts; not much milk is expressed; manual pumps are physically demanding to work.) A few readers said the Avent Comfort Manual can develop a loud squeak after prolonged use.

Also Great: Medela Harmony manual pump

The **Medela Harmony** is a great runner up in the manual pump category. Similar to the Avent's Comfort Manual, the Harmony has even fewer parts to wash than the Avent and some parents tell us it is easier to assemble. Medela notes the Harmony utilizes "two-phase expression technology" that is supposed to stimulate let down, then slows down to mimic slower, deeper sucking action.

One reader with larger breasts found this pump worked better for her than Avent. The Harmony is also slightly more affordable than the Avent. On the downside, Medela does not recommend using the Harmony every day. It is intended for occasional use only. Some parents complained it lost suction after a while. And Medela includes only one size flange: medium. If you need a different size, you'll have to order this from Medela online and wait for delivery.

Best Mini-Electric Breast Pump

The **Medela Swing** single electric pump ($112) offers Medela's 2-Phase Expression (the same system as Medela's more expensive pumps), which is designed to copy baby's natural sucking rhythm.

The pump has two different modes: first it stimulates letdown and then it simulates baby's normal sucking pattern. Other features include compact size (weighs only 2.5 lbs.), AC adapter or battery power, shoulder/neck strap (so you can move around while pumping), and user controlled comfort settings.

So here's the bottom line on the Swing: it is an excellent pump. Moms applaud this Swing's ease of use and comfort.

The only negative: it's a single pump and hence is best for occasional use. Most negative reviews we heard from parents center on the fact that the Swing didn't work well over time when moms were using it every day. But, again, the Swing is only intended for occasional use. For daily use, check out our pick for best professional grade pump.

Flaws but not deal breakers. The Swing gets mostly great reviews, but we should note some caveats. The Swing is only available as a single pump. Some moms would have liked a double for the speed and convenience.

This pump is only intended for occasional use, not daily use. That means pumping a bottle for a night out with a babysitter, or to relieve engorgement. This disappointed parents who assumed they could use it for daily pumping.

And it's expensive. Parents probably assume this pump is intended for daily use because it is rather expensive compared to other mini electrics.

Also Great: Avent Single Electric Comfort pump

Avent's Single Electric Comfort breast pump ($130- $150) is a credible runner up to the Medela Swing. Like the Avent Comfort Manual, the Single Electric has an angled neck that allows mom to sit up straight and still get milk  into the collection bottle. Avent also added their massage cushion, a feature moms love. But the flange is only available in one size—if it doesn't fit, you'll have to buy another size. Another drawback: some parents complain the Avent Single Electric Comfort pump is rather loud.

More reviews online at BabyBargains.com

We review another 20+ breast pumps on our web site, including brands like Spectra and Dr. Brown's.

The Best Baby Bottle

Nothing is more intimidating upon visiting a baby superstore than the WALL OF BOTTLES. The mere sight has been known to make grown adults cry. Who knew there were so many choices for such a simple item?

Let's break down the basics of baby bottles and then give you our picks.

7 Things No One Tells You About Buying Baby Bottles!

1 **THE NIPPLE IS REALLY MORE IMPORTANT THAN THE BOTTLE.** There are three basic types of baby bottle nipples: orthodontic, flat-topped and bell-shaped.

Which is best? All of them claim to be "closest to mom's breast," but here's our advice. If you're breastfeeding and only intend to give your baby an occasional bottle, these babies tend to do best with bell shaped nipples. With babies who are bottle fed from the get-go, any of the nipple shapes will likely work well.

Orthodontic

2 **NIPPLES HAVE DIFFERENT FLOW RATES.** When you're buying your first nipples/bottles, be sure you're using newborn nipples. This means the hole in the nipple is small, allowing a slow flow. If you use a nipple for older babies, you'll find your newborn gagging and sputtering.

Flat-topped

Some parents find their babies get used to the newborn nipple and never need to change to the nipples for older babies. And you'll only need 2 oz. bottles if you're feeding a newborn—that's the right amount at first.

Bell shaped

3 **BABY BOTTLES DON'T NEED TO BE STERILIZED.** That's right, you can just put baby bottles in the top rack of the dishwasher or wash them by hand in hot, soapy water. There is no proven benefit to sterilizing baby bottles. Hint: get a dishwasher basket to keep bottles and tops in place in your dishwasher.

4 **YOU'LL WANT TO BUY ENOUGH BOTTLES TO GET THROUGH A COUPLE DAYS WITHOUT WASHING.** Who wants to wash bottles the first day you get home from the hospital? If you're bottle feeding baby every two to four hours, that's quite a few bottles—as many as 24 bottles per day! For parents who are breastfeeding, three to six bottles is the max you'll need. Because you don't want to start bottle feeding until breastfeeding is well established (a few weeks, usually), get a couple 4 oz. and a 9 oz. bottles.

5 **WE RECOMMEND SILICONE NIPPLES, NOT LATEX.** Nipples are made of either silicone or latex. Silicone nipples are stronger, last longer, don't have any flavor, are heat resistant and may resist bacteria better than latex, according to our research. Latex is a natural product (and allergenic for some) and is softer than silicone. Bottom line: we like silicone better overall.

6 **THE CAUSE OF LEAKY BABY BOTTLES MAY BE . . YOU!** Before you return that leaky baby bottle to the store, consider how you are tightening the bottle. We see lots of complaints from parents that a particular baby bottle leaks, but when we ask manufacturers about this problem, they point out that parents often over tighten the bottle, which (ironically) can cause leaking.

Some baby bottles also have vents to allow air to escape the bottle and keep baby from swallowing that air leading to colic and discomfort. While the venting is a great idea, it complicates how the bottle is put together, however. Consult the bottle's instructions on assembly (and yes, there are even YouTube videos) especially if you are a first-timer!

7 **LOTS OF LITTLE PARTS = CLEANING FRUSTRATIONS.** Sometimes simpler is better. Baby bottles with lots of gaskets, vent tubes and more, mean you have to clean more small parts. And it's easier to lose those parts in a dishwasher.

Example: Comotomo. A rising star among bottle makers, Korean import Comotomo's baby bottles have *five* separate parts, including a "fastening top ring" and "fastening ring bottom" that sit between the nipple and bottle.

We break down our bottle recommendations into four areas: best bottle (overall), best glass bottle, best bottle warmer and best bottle sterilizer.

Best Baby Bottle (Overall)

After talking to lactation consultants, surveying more than a thousand of our readers and researching dozens of baby bottles, we've chosen **Avent** as the Best Baby Bottle.

Avent gets the nod for its well-designed nipple, which is clinically proven to reduce colic (uncontrollable, extended crying that starts in some babies around one month of age). Avent bottles are perhaps the most popular baby bottles on the market today. Many parents swear by them for being easy to clean (easier than the multi-piece Dr. Brown's bottles). Feedback from readers is excellent.

Avent makes two types of baby bottles: Classic+ and Natural. The big difference between the bottles is their nipples. The Natural is breast-shaped plus it has "Comfort Petals," which are supposed to make the nipple softer and more flexible. The Classic+ has a plain nipple. FYI: you can't use the Natural nipples on the Classic+ bottles or visa versa.

Both bottles use Avent's twin valve, anti-colic system to keep baby from ingesting too much air. And they are both compatible with Avent's breast pump, the Comfort Double (reviewed on our web site). While the Classic+ and the Natural are available in the BPA-free plastic, only the Natural comes in a glass version.

The prices per bottle average around $7 each—the Natural bottles run about $1.50 more than the Classic+. There are also colored bottles (pink or blue) and glass bottles that are bit more in price. Starter sets range from $34 to $40 and include three 4 oz. bottles and two 9 oz. bottles. Avent even offers a gift set that includes their microwave sterilizer for about $50.

Avent bottles are priced in the middle of the pack for baby bottles—if you find them pricey, there is some good news: they go on sale frequently.

Avent bottles are perhaps the most popular baby bottles on

the market today, along with Dr. Brown's.

The biggest complaint about Avent: the measurement markings on the side rub off after a few months of use. This understandably frustrates parents who've shelled out $7 a bottle, only to discover it's now hard to measure out formula and water.

Some readers report trouble with leaking, although this may be because some folks over-tighten the top. (Avent addresses this issue on their web site with graphics on how much to tighten).

Leaks can also occur with the Classic+ bottle if the gasket ring is incorrectly installed. Make sure the blue side is always facing down. And while there is no separate gasket for the Natural bottles, the nipple has to be set into the bottle correctly or it too can leak.

Overall, these complaints are minor compared to the effusive praise the bottles receive from readers. We highly recommend Avent's bottles.

Also Great: Dr. Brown's

Dr. Brown's baby bottles are neck and neck with Avent when it comes to popularity. Dr. Brown's big selling point is its two-piece vent system which keeps air out of the milk or formula, ensuring the nipple never collapses. They claim this type of venting (called "positive-pressure flow") reduces colic, spit-up and gas.

Dr. Brown's makes four types of bottles: the Natural Flow (the flagship), a wide-neck version, a glass model and Options. Their newest bottle, Options is so named because (wait for it) the bottle gives parents the "option to use it with or without the internal vent."

Since colic starts around three weeks of age and ends around three months, we guess Dr. Brown's wanted to give parents of older babies the option of using the bottle without the vent.

Prices start at $4.50 for a 4 oz. Natural Flow bottle or glass, $5 for the Options.

One caveat: Dr. Brown's bottles have more parts than a traditional bottle. Cleaning can a pain.

Best Glass Baby Bottle

Nobody beats **Evenflo's** glass baby bottles, in our opinion. They are very affordable, available in several sizes and quantities and the best choice for folks who don't want plastic. Prices range from $2 to $3.50 per bottle. The more expensive versions

have elasticized plastic sleeves to help avoid breakage if dropped or you can purchase sleeves separately for $6.

Best Bottle Warmer

Avent's Fast Bottle Warmer ($36), which warms a room temperature bottle in about four minutes, is our pick for the best bottle warmer. Parents like it overall, although a few complain it doesn't heat a cold bottle as fast as Avent claims. Another bummer: it doesn't have a timer or auto shut off. On the plus side, Avent's Fast Bottle Warmer does fit baby food jars and all types of baby bottles (not just Avent).

Another good bet is the **Kiinde Kozii Breast Milk & Bottle Warmer** ($52). This warmer accepts frozen breast milk storage bags, liner bottles, plastic bottles, glass bottles and even food containers— any type, any brand. Kiinde's SAFEHeat technology consists of a "circulating bath of warm water" to heat a bottle.

Since the water is heated to only about room temperature (70°F), Kiinde claims to prevents hot spots and allays concerns that boiling water can cause chemicals like BPA to leach out of older bottles. A timer and automatic shutoff means it won't overheat and the water reservoir does not require parents to add water each time it's used.

Feedback on the Kiinde is positive. Most folks like the warmer, say readers—Kiinde's features and quality make it worth the extra investment, in our opinion. A few dissenters note the Kiinde requires regular maintenance (you have to clean the water scale out periodically). And we heard one or two reports of the warmer breaking after just eight or ten weeks. We'd like to see the company step up its customer service on these issues— more than one parent who had a problem said the company wasn't helpful in solving the issue.

FYI: The Kiinde Kozii bottle warmer used to be more expensive, around $70. In recent months, we've noticed the price drifting down to about $50, which definitely makes it more competitive!

Best Bottle Sterilizer

Yes, earlier we pointed out that you don't need a sterilizer—just pop the bottles in the dishwasher; it's safe! But if you still want a sterilizer, we pick the ***Avent Express II Microwave Steam Sterilizer*** as the best bottle sterilizer. This model holds up to four Avent bottles for $20. If you prefer a plug- in sterilizer, the Avent 3-in-1 Electric Steam Sterilizer sterilizes six bottles in six minutes and keeps bottles sterile for up to 24 hours. Like the microwave version, it can also sterilize up to two breast pumps. Cost: $53.

While Avent makes a good sterilizer, we would suggest getting the matching sterilizer for your bottle brand. For example, if you decide to use Born Free bottles, then the Born Free Tru-Clean Bottle Sterilizing System ($56) is a good bet. Why? Sterilizers for one brand can sometimes damage other brand's bottles.

The Best Baby Formula

Baby formula is a $7 billion a year business in the US. But is there any nutritional difference between brands of formula? We'll answer that question and give our picks for best baby formula next.

7 Things No One Tells You About Buying Infant Formula!

1 **GENERIC FORMULA INCLUDES EXACTLY THE SAME NUTRITION AS NAME BRAND FORMULA.** That's right, the federal government mandates that all baby food include the *same* nutritional ingredients. So what's the difference between formulas? Some name brands include additional ingredients to help with digestion, such as pre-biotics. They aren't necessary ingredients, so we recommend trying less expensive generic formulas like Bright Beginnings, Member's Mark (Sam's Club), and Parent's Choice (Walmart). These are all made by PBM Products.

2 **PREMIXED FORMULA WILL COST YOU.** Formula 101: there are three types of formula: powdered, liquid concentrate and ready-to-drink (pre-mixed). Liquid concentrate and ready-to-drink premixed formula is very expensive—50% to 200% more than powdered formula. A word to the wise: start your baby on powdered formula, not liquid concentrate or ready-to-drink. Why? Because babies get used to the texture of whatever they try first (powdered formula tastes different). Start on ready-to-drink formula and baby may refuse powdered formula.

3 **YOUR TODDLER DOESN'T NEED TODDLER FORMULA.** In an attempt to keep parents buying formula way past the time kids need it, some formula manufacturers have created "toddler formulas." These toddler formulas claim to contain more calcium, iron and vitamins, but nutritionists and pediatricians point out that toddlers should be getting most of their nutrition from solid foods, not formula.

Toddlers should ideally only be drinking about two cups of whole milk a day. Whole milk should be served to toddlers between 12 and 24 months of age. At age two, switch to skim or 1% milk. By the way, whole milk is significantly less expensive than formula. No toddler needs "toddler formula" (unless instructed by your pediatrician for a health condition).

FEEDING

4 **FORMULA MAKERS LIKE SIMILAC AND ENFAMIL HAVE FREQUENT BUYER CLUBS YOU CAN JOIN FOR COUPONS AND OTHER FREE-BIES.** Similac's program is called StrongMoms Rewards while Enfamil has Family Beginnings. Of course, there is a trade off for all those freebies—formula companies want your personal info (email address, street address, birth date, etc). But no one said you have to use your main email address. Create another Gmail email address for joining clubs like this.

5 **WHERE YOU SHOP CAN MAKE A DIFFERENCE IN THE PRICE OF FORMULA.** Yes, Amazon sells formula at good prices. And you've probably discovered that chains and warehouse clubs offer great prices on formula as well. But did you realize that some locations of the same chain, say Walmart, offer lower every day prices than other locations in the same town.

Yes, this really happens. One reader stopped by a Walmart location in a different part of her home town and discovered that she was paying $6.61 per can at her local Walmart while this other Walmart location 20 minutes away was selling that same can for $3.68!

6 **YOUR PEDIATRICIAN GETS LOTS OF FREE SAMPLES.** That's right, the formula companies bombard pediatricians with samples and most pediatricians don't have lots of room to store them. Don't be afraid to ask if your doctor has free samples. (But don't start your newborn on ready-to- drink or liquid concentrate formulas, see tip #2 above!).

7 **DON'T FORGET TO FACTOR IN THE COST OF BOTTLED WATER!** What, you say? Don't you just mix tap water with powered formula? No, bottled water is recommend by both the American Academy of Pediatrics and the American Dental Association. That's because tap water can contain *too much* fluoride, which is a problem (discolored teeth).

If your tap water contains .3 ppm or less fluoride, tap water is okay (ask your local water department for fluoride levels). But if fluoride levels are HIGHER than that, you should use bottled water.

And not just any bottled water: purified, demineralized, deionized, distilled or reverse osmosis filtered water is recommended. Also: be sure to boil that bottled water before mixing with powered formula. For a full discussion of formula and how to prepare it, see our Baby 411 book.

Next, our recommendations for best baby formula (overall), best name brand formula and best organic formula.

The Best Baby Formula (Overall)

formula

After comparing and testing over 15 baby formulas, **Walmart's Parent's Choice** infant formula is our top choice for best baby formula.

Parent's Choice is made by PBM Products, a privately owned formula manufacturer based in Georgia. This formula is sold under the Parent's Choice label on formula for sale in Walmart stores.

At 57¢ per ounce, we picked Parent's Choice because it is the least expensive generic cow's milk formula with iron that is available everywhere in the US (excluding membership clubs). Other chains carry PBM-made generic formula (see below for a list), but Parent's Choice is consistently cheaper at Walmart than other stores.

Insider tip: all formula sold in the U.S. must meet the SAME nutritional and safety guidelines mandated by the government. So that expensive name brand formula you see is virtually the same as the affordable store brand generic—same basic ingredients, same nutrition, and so on.

If you belong to a warehouse club, here's some good news: you'll find even cheaper prices on generic formula there. Sam's Club's Members Mark and JB's Berkley & Jenson formulas are also made by PBM Products. Costco is the only generic in-store formula that is not made by PBM; Kirkland Signature is made by Abbott Laboratories. We like Kirkland baby formula as well.

Let's take a look at prices for generic (store-brand) powdered formulas available at chain stores and warehouse stores, from cheapest to most expensive (priced per ounce of dry powder):

Sam's Club Members Mark: 48¢/oz.
Costco Kirkland Signature: 50¢/oz. (made by Abbott Labs)
BJ's Berkley&Jenson: 52¢/oz.
Walmart Parent's Choice: 57¢/oz.
Target Up&Up: 59¢/oz.

Babies R Us/Toys R Us: 62¢/oz.
Kmart Little Ones: 63¢/oz.
CVS Health: 68¢/oz.
Rite Aid Tugaboos: 81¢/oz.
Walgreens Well Beginnings: 86¢/oz.

Wow! You can spend 86¢ per ounce of basic powdered formula
. . . or 48¢ per ounce. Why pay twice as much for the same thing?

Remember that baby formula is very promotional—it goes on
sale all the time. And then there are coupons, which you can find
with a five second Google search. So here's an expert bargain
shopper tip: record the best formula price per ounce in your
phone. Then when you see a "sale", divide the sale price by the
ounces in the container. If it is below your strike price, buy!

Best Name Brand Baby Formula

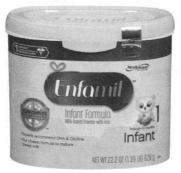

If you prefer a name-brand infant formula, our top pick is
Enfamil. They offer a great club program (Enfamil Family
Beginnings) with freebies and coupons. You'll find Enfamil pretty
much anywhere in a wide variety of options including Gentlease
(for gassy, fussy babies), Reguline (constipation), A.R. (reflux),
ProSobee (soy), and allergy formulas. (Heads up: only use specialized formula as directed by your pediatrician).

Yes, Enfamil also has some non-GMO versions. We found the
least expensive basic, powdered Enfamil runs about $1 to $1.20
per ounce online. Costco had it for 92.6¢ per ounce.

Also great: **Similac** is another name brand we recommend.
Their flagship formula is Similac Advanced. We didn't think it possible, but Similac has even more "specialty" formulas for sensitive
kids, those with allergies and assorted other issues. They also offer
non-GMO versions as well as organic formula.

Best Organic Formula

formula

Earth's Best infant formulas (cows' milk, soy and sensitive) are our top pick for best organic baby formula. Their formulas are certified by the USDA to be organic, do not include corn syrup, and have added pre-biotic fiber.

FYI: Earth's Best does add DHA and ARA plus lutein. What is DHA and ARA? Long-chain fatty acids, DHA and ARA are present in breast milk and thought to aid in cognitive development. In formula, DHA and ARA are synthetically made . . . and that's controversial in some organic parenting circles.

Despite that, we recommend Earth's Best—its' easy to find in grocery stores and online. We've seen it online for as little as 91¢ per ounce.

The Best Baby Food

At the tender age of four to six months, you and your baby will embark on a magical journey to a new place filled with exciting adventures and never-before-seen wonders. Yes, you've entered the SOLID FOOD ZONE.

7 Things No One Tells You About Buying Baby Food!

1 **No matter what brand you buy, all "stage 1" baby food is preservative- and additive-free.** But . . . that doesn't mean they're using organic ingredients. Once you move to later stages, however, many baby food makers start adding extra sugar and salt.

2 You don't have to buy baby food. Just use this . . .

That's right, you can make most baby food at home with a food processor you might already own. Just buy veggies and fruit from your favorite grocery store or farmer's market, steam and mash or puree it. You may need to add a bit of water, but that's it. Voila! Baby food. If you want to buy a food processor, we give you a recommendation later in this chapter.

You may still want to purchase a bit of commercial baby food for those days when you aren't eating at home, however. It's pretty convenient to pop open a pouch or cup and feed baby wherever you are.

After baby has mastered pureed food, you'll want to move up to food with more texture. At this stage, you can start feeding baby what you're eating albeit slightly mashed. A detailed discussion on what to feed baby when is in our sister book, *Baby 411*.

3 Feed from a bowl, not from the packaging (jar, pouch or cup). If you feed from the jar, bacteria from baby's mouth can find its way back to the jar, spoiling the food much more quickly. Also, saliva enzymes begin to break down the food's nutrients. The best strategy: pour the amount of baby food you need into a bowl and feed from there (unless it's the last serving in the jar). Refrigerate unused portions.

4 Buying the best quality food won't break the bank. The average baby eats 600 jars of baby food until they "graduate" to adult foods. Sounds like a lot of money, eh? Well, that only works out to $240 or so in total expenditures (using an average price of 40¢ per jar). Hence, if you go for better-quality food and spend, say, 15% to 20% more, you're only out another $36 to $48. And feeding baby food that tastes more like the real thing makes transitions to adult foods easier.

How about organic baby food? Well, there is no scientific data that shows any health benefit for organic baby food. For most parents, the issue is about exposure to pesticides. Organic foods are certified synthetic pesticide-free, but may still use certain "natural" pesticides and fungicides. See Certifications below for further discussion.

5 **AVOID UNPASTEURIZED MILK, MILK PRODUCTS AND JUICES.** And no honey under age 1. Babies don't have the ability to fight off serious bacterium like e. coli. Avoid these hazards by feeding your child only pasteurized dairy and juice products. Also: steer clear of feeding honey to children under one year of age. Botulism spores can be found in honey— while not harmful to adults and older children, these spores can be fatal to babies under age 1.

6 **SHHHH! BABY APPLESAUCE = ADULT APPLESAUCE.** Lets' take a look at a jar of baby applesauce.

Now here's what adult applesauce looks like.

What's the difference? They basically contain the same thing— applesauce. The only difference: applesauce in a jar with a cute baby on it costs several times more than the adult version. On Amazon, you can buy the Gerber baby applesauce for 20¢ per oz. and the Mott's Applesauce for 8¢ per oz. (One caveat: make sure the regular applesauce is NOT loaded with extra sugar; you can find many examples that don't have that).

One of our key Baby Bargains Commandments is "shop for things without baby in their name." Baby food is a good example!

7 **"NEXT STEP" FOODS FOR OLDER BABIES AND TODDLERS ARE A WASTE OF MONEY.** Baby food makers tout "Graduates" foods for older toddlers, but here's the truth: baby doesn't need it.

Pediatricians note you can start feeding your baby the same food you eat when they reach nine to 12 months of age. When baby is ready to eat pasta, just serve him small bites of the adult stuff. Bottom line: babies should learn to eat the same (hopefully healthy) foods you are eating, with the same spices and flavors.

Baby food certifications: what is organic?

In the US, the USDA oversees the program that certifies food as organic. There is a List of Allowed and Prohibited Substances, which is used by certifying agents (along with a host of other requirements) to certify that food is being organically produced.

Organic is defined by the USDA as "products that have been produced using cultural, biological, and mechanical practices that support the cycling of on-farm resources, promote ecological balance, and conserve biconvexity in accordance with the USDA organic regulations."

"This means that organic operations must maintain or enhance soil and water quality, while also conserving wetlands, woodlands, and wildlife. Synthetic fertilizers, sewage sludge, irradiation, and genetic engineering may not be used."

For many organic shoppers, that last part is their most important reason for buying organic.

Once an agricultural product has been certified, it can then carry the USDA Organic Seal.

In our opinion, the word organic in baby food has been so common-place in recent years that shoppers forget its limitations. When it comes to "organic," we are reminded of a line from one of our favorite movies: "I do not think it means what you think it means." (Yes, that's a *Princess Bride* reference.)

For example, organic does not mean pesticide-free. Pesticides and fungicides can still be used by organic farmers, with around 20 chemicals approved for use on organic farms.

Ironically, sometimes these organic pesticides require high rates of application than synthetic chemicals!

The take home message: reducing your baby's exposure to environmental toxins is a goal for all parents. And organic food is one way to do that—if you can afford it. But realize organic food isn't the be-all, end-all to keeping baby healthy!

The Best Baby Food

We've tasted it so you don't have to! That's right, after sampling more than our fair share of commercial baby food, we recommend **Earth's Best** as the best baby food for your baby.

Earth's Best has been around for over 25 years and it's hard to beat this company for quality and price. Put simply, Earth's best tastes like real food. It's certified organic too. And it can be found nearly everywhere: online, in grocery stores and at chains like Target.

The price is reasonable at about 27¢ per ounce, and they offer occasional coupons. (For comparison, we priced other organic baby food around 40 cents per ounce; non-organic baby food from Gerber is around 20 cents per ounce).

At first, Earth's Best was only available in glass jars, but they've recently added a line of pouches. All in all, the best choice for baby food.

Also Great: Plum Organics

Plum Organics was one of the first baby food companies to come out in pouches, which have since become all the rage. Plug Organics' fans came for the easy-to-pack pouches (no glass jars  that can shatter), but stayed for the quality, organic baby food. JUST Fruit (about 30¢ per oz.) and JUST Veggies (about 50¢ per oz.) are made without additives—just fruit and veggies.

Plum Organics' Second Blends (about 30¢ per oz.) include interesting combinations like blueberry, pear and purple carrot. Stage 3 Meals (about 70¢ per oz.) and Mighty 4 Blends (about

30¢ per oz.) are complete meals in a pouch with "fruits, veggies, protein and grains." Prices vary often according to how many packs you buy. Some veggie options can be more expensive than fruit options.

Parents tell us they like the JUST Fruit and Second Blends best. By the time kids are ready for Stage 3 and Mighty 4, they should really be eating what you're eating (not baby food).

Looking for more baby food brand reviews? Check our web site BabyBargains.com for reviews of eight more baby food brands.

Hints on Making Your Own Baby Food

Making your own baby food is clearly on the rise. In fact, the New York Times reported last year that commercial baby food sales have declined 4% per year since 2005 (measured in volume consumed). Yes, some of that might be because of a decline in births, but the commercial manufacturers of baby food are plenty worried. They're trying to improve sales with new flavors and "sexy" packaging (not our adjective, the Times said that).

Our own pediatrician expert and co-author of Baby 411, Dr. Ari Brown, applauds parents who want to make their own food:

"It's actually preferable to offer food from your table. That way, your baby will get used to your cooking! Yes, you can use seasonings, herbs and spices. Just limit the amount of salt and use iodized salt if you must add it. It's not that hard. Trust me, I'd never make it on 'Top Chef' but even I could make baby food."

So grab a food processor and go for it. We review baby food processors next.

Once you've decided to make baby food, how do you store it so it doesn't spoil? Surprisingly, there are more options for baby food storage than you might think.

First, you need something small. Two to four oz. portions are considered ideal for babies just starting out with solid food. Then you have to decide how to store it. Do you want to freeze or refrigerate extra servings? Do you want to be able to microwave them to bring them up to room temperature? Do you prefer glass to plastic? How about single use or reusable storage? And finally, consider whether you'll need to travel with baby food—some options are easier to take with you than others.

There are three basic choices for baby food storage:

Freezer trays. We know, you're asking, "why can't we just used an ice cube tray?" Good question. You could, but you'll have to remove the baby food blocks once they freeze and store them in a freezer bag to prevent freezer burn. Specialized baby food freezer trays, on the other hand, have a lid that helps avoid freezer burn. These are usually BPA-free silicon trays divided into single, 2 oz. serving with a plastic top. Freezer trays are just for freezing—you pop the serving out of the tray and warm it in a microwave safe bowl or defrost it in the fridge.

Storage sets. No doubt you've been using plastic or glass storage containers with snap-on lids for years. Now they make special sets just for baby food. These containers often have measurements marked on the side of the container, leak-proof lids and stacking storage trays. Individual containers can be defrosted and heated in the microwave. The only issue: if you want to freeze a large batch of baby food, storage sets have a major limitation—you can't remove portions from these sets once they are frozen to put in freezer bags and free them up for more batches.

Feeding pouches. You may have seen commercial baby food in pouches (like Sprout and Ella's) at the grocery store. Now you can buy the pouches yourself and fill them with your own foods. You have two choices with pouches: single use (recyclable) or reusable. The pouches can be frozen (don't overfill, though!) or refrigerated, but not microwaved. Instead, you'll have to warm them in a hot water bath.

So now that you know a bit more about baby food storage, check out our reviews of brands you can buy for your own home made baby food.

Best Baby Food Storage

The **Popfex Silicone Freezer Tray** ($15) is our top pick for best baby food storage. For parents who want to make single serve portions of their own baby food, Popfex makes storage easy.

The Popfex comes with a rigid plastic lid to prevent freezer burn and allow for stacking in your freezer compartment. Portion sizes are 2.3 ounces and they pop out of the flexible silicone tray easily. While it doesn't make as many servings as other trays, the ease of removal and cleaning are pluses. Parents love the Popfex giving it a 94% positive rating on Amazon (that's four and five star ratings).

Also Great: OXO Tot Baby Blocks

OXO Tot Baby Blocks ($10 to $20) is also recommended for baby food storage. Sold in sets of ten with 2 to 4 oz. containers with trays, Baby Blocks have handy measurement markings and can be washed in the dishwasher, warmed in the microwave and frozen as well. One caveat: careful cleaning is needed to make sure food doesn't stick in the seal (or that the seal doesn't pop out). Overall, however, Baby Blocks are a winner for ease of use and durability.

Also Great: Infantino Squeeze Pouches

Infantino Squeeze Pouches ($13 for 50) are our top pick for single-use pouches. While the pouches are a winner, we don't recommend the related Infantino Squeeze Station to fill these pouches—instead get a pastry bag or cupcake injector to fill them.

For reusable pouches, we also recommend the **Squooshi Reusable Food Pouches** ($17 to $20 for eight pouches, pictured). They fill from the bottom and seal with a double zip. The designs are bright and colorful; cleaning is easy (they can be washed in the dishwasher top rack). One complaint: the nozzle can be hard on baby's teeth and gums, so consider using silicone Sip 'n Soft tops made by Choomee; they work with these pouches.

Best Food Processor for Baby Food

Making your own baby food has been trending for the last couple of years, so let's look at some key tools for this task: a food processor, food mill and steamer.

First, some basics about shopping for these kitchen gadgets.

7 Things No One Tells You About Buying A Food Processor for Baby Food!

1 **BABY ONLY EATS PUREED FOODS FOR A SHORT PERIOD OF TIME.** That's about six months or so. After that, your baby (around one year of age) can eat regular adult table food (cut into smaller bites, of course). Hence the utility of a *specialized* baby food processor is limited; a regular food processor will give you more bang for the buck since it can blend, chop and grind things like pastry dough, nuts and cheese.

2 **TO FIGURE OUT THE BEST FOOD PROCESSOR FOR YOUR FAMILY, DECIDE HOW MUCH FOOD YOU WANT TO MAKE.** If you're planning to freeze a month's worth of carrots for your little one, consider a regular food processor. You'll be able to puree from 12 to 20 cups of baby food in a full size processor. Some models have smaller bowls that can be used for fewer servings. If you're only interested in a few day's worth of food, the two to four-cup capacity processors will work just fine. And if a single meal is all you need, consider an affordable manual food mill.

3 **CONSIDER THE SIZE OF YOUR KITCHEN.** Do you have room for another appliance on your counter? If you already have a food processor, don't add to the clutter and expense with a specialty baby food processor. If you have limited counter space and don't already have a processor, here's where a steamer/processor might make more sense. The capacity is small and most steamer/processors aren't as well made as a heavy duty food processor, but one might do the trick and save some space.

4 **IF POSSIBLE, GO LARGE.** If you have the money, you'll find that larger processors are useful for other cooking needs. We make pie crust, puree sauces, mix bread dough and more in our Cuisinart. But if price is a consideration, hand-crank food mills are under $20 and will do the job for the small amount of time you'll be making baby food puree.

baby food

5 GOOD NEWS: FOOD PROCESSORS SHOULD LAST A LONG TIME. Most high end food processor are meant to be workhorses. So if you're buying a food processor to use for more than baby food, spend the money to get good quality. This means a heavy base with a strong motor. That's another reason to stay away from some of the "baby food" processors. They don't have the same high quality motor and rugged construction.

6 COMBINATION PRODUCTS DON'T ALWAYS WORK OUT. Steamer/processors are like a lot of combination products. Most of them don't really do multiple tasks well. Or they break. Cuisinart, for example, makes a baby food steamer/processor. But our reader reviews are rather unimpressive, mainly because the steamer sometimes stops working. That's why our top pick is a processor-only appliance.

7 YOU REALLY DON'T NEED LOTS OF EXTRA BLADES OR ATTACH-MENTS. Basically, you'll be able to do almost anything with the main blade plus the shredding and slicing disks. Yes, some processors have extra blades and attachments that sound cool. But do you really need a french fry cutting disk? Or a special storage box? Stick with the basics and you'll be just fine.

In this section, we review the following baby food tools:

◆ Best Food Processor for Baby Food.
◆ Best Food Mill.
◆ Best Steamer/Processor.

Best Food Processor for Baby Food

We've tested a dozen food processors for making baby food and picked the **Cuisinart Elite Collection 2.0 12-Cup Food Processor** as best food processor.

This model ($165 to $200) is a full-featured food processor with four different blades and disks. It includes a smaller 4-cup bowl, which would be perfect for pureeing smaller amounts of food for baby. Just pull out your veggie steamer basket and a pot, steam your preferred veggies then pop them in the Cuisinart. Ta-dah! you've got pureed baby food.

Some fruits are soft enough that you won't need to cook them first (we're looking at you, bananas). And you can vary the consistency easily by hitting the pulse button a few time for chunks. But the beauty of buying a traditional food processor (rather than a baby food steamer/processor) is you can use it for so much more around the kitchen: pie crust, bread dough, chopping nuts, grating cheese and more.

You may have noticed that there are several "baby food steamer/processors" for sale in cooking stores and online. For the most part, these combo appliances are rather disappointing and don't rate very well with parents. However, we know some folks are still tempted to buy one—so later in this chapter, we have a our recommendation for the best of these steamer/processors as well as the best manual food mill.

Also Great: Cuisinart Chopper/Grinder

Looking for a smaller solution to your baby food making quest? Or just don't want to spend $100+ for a fancy processor? Consider the **Cuisinart 4-Cup Food Chopper**. This is a real workhorse that can not only puree baby's food, but also chop herbs, grind spices and other mundane kitchen tasks. At $58, The Chopper is a great option to consider.

Also Great: KitchenAid Chef's Chopper

Similar to the Cuisinart Chopper, the **KitchenAid Chef's Chopper** has a slightly smaller bowl (3-cup) with an added wet/dry compartment on the lid for adding liquids or dry ingredients while shopping. The price: $43 to $73. Parents did note the KitchenAid is pretty noisy.

Best Food Mill

If you lack space in your kitchen but still want to make your own baby food, consider a food mill like the **OXO Good Grips Food Mill** to help puree baby's food. This hand crank model may look like a blast from the past, but it does the job with just a little elbow grease. At $50, it isn't cheap, but it will last and parents love it. Use it to make mashed potatoes and other purees when you're done with the baby food stage.

Best Baby Food Steamer/Processor

Yes, we think these specialized baby food makers are a waste of money. But . . . we know some folks still want a specialized baby food steamer/processor, especially if a relative is insisting on giving you one as a gift. Our pick is the **Beaba BabyCook**. Although it only has a 3.7-cup capacity, parents love the way this steamer/processor works and cleans up. At $90 to $120, the Beaba is pricey for the short time your baby will eat baby food—but parents tell us they love how easy it is to use and clean.

The Best High Chairs

As soon as baby starts to eat solid food, you'll need this quintessential piece of baby furniture—the high chair. As par for the baby gear biz, you can spend $50 on a high chair . . . or $500. We'll break down what you really need and several crucial safety tips before we get to our picks!

7 Things No One Tells You About Buying A High Chair!

1 **THERE ARE THREE TYPES OF HIGH CHAIRS: BASIC, MULTI-FUNCTION AND MODERN.** Here's the run-down:

◆ *Basic* high chairs are sold in chain stores and aimed at parents on a budget or grandparents looking for a basic chair for occasional visits. These high chairs typically run from $30 to $100 and have few features. You won't find wheels, recline or adjustable height on budget chairs. Most  budget chairs are foldable and come with a wipeable chair pad and single tray. Example: the Cosco Simple Fold (pictured) doesn't have any bells and whistles. It just folds and the tray adjusts. $29 at Walmart.

◆ *Multi-function* high chairs offer deluxe features and will morph into additional seating options as your child grows. Ranging in price from $100 to $250, multi-function chairs feature double trays, seat recline, adjustable height positions, foot rests, machine washable pads  and wheels. More expensive chairs might have toys, designer fabrics and other upgrades. Multi-function means these chairs can often convert to toddler seats that attach to your dining room chair. The Graco Blossom (pictured) accommodates infants, babies just starting to eat solids and toddlers. It also attaches to a regular dining chair. $143 on Amazon.

◆ Priced from $200 to $450, *modern* high chairs sell parents on an aesthetic. To borrow a term from fashion, these high chairs are "statement pieces." Seamless molded seats look futuristic with pops of bright colored pads. They may or may not have wheels, but some have pneumatic lift systems (like a barber's chair). Even though modern chairs are pricey, they oddly omit features seen in lower price models, like double trays, a compact fold, seat recline, etc.

2 SUPRISE! THAT DISHWASHER-SAFE TRAY MAY NOT FIT IN YOUR DISHWASHER. Most high chairs today come with a dishwasher-safe tray or tray insert that may claim to snap off and pop into the dishwasher for clean-up . . . but does it? In our reviews of high chairs, we'll note some models whose dishwasher- safe trays are too big to fit in an actual dishwasher. A word of advice: measure the bottom rack of your dishwasher and take that dimension with you when high chair shopping.

3 THE X-FACTOR FOR ANY HIGH CHAIR: HOW EASY IS IT TO CLEAN? So here's what a baby looks like when eating:

Cute? Yes—but then you have to clean that spaghetti sauce from all those nooks and crannies of a high chair. Not fun.

Here's a tip some first-time parents miss: make sure the high chair you buy has a removable, washable seat cover OR a seat that easily sponges clean. In the latter category, chairs with vinyl trump those made of cloth. Vinyl can be wiped clean, while cloth typically has to be washed. This might be one of those first-time parent traps: seats with cloth covers sure look nicer than those made of vinyl. But the extra effort to machine wash a cloth cover is a pain . . . and some cloth covers can't be thrown in the dryer. That means waiting a day or more for a cover to line dry.

Watch out for seat pads that have ruffles or numerous crevices—these are food magnets and a bear to keep clean. What color cover should you get? Anything but white. Sure that fancy white leatherette high chair looks all shiny and new at the baby store, but it will forever be a cleaning nightmare once you start using it. Darker colors and patters are better.

Of course, keeping a chair clean involves more than just the pad–look at the seat and tray itself. Avoid models with numerous crevices and cracks. Seamless seats and trays are best. FYI: Many high chair trays claim they are dishwasher safe, but have cracks that let water collect inside the tray. This can be a mold hazard, as it is hard to get the tray to properly dry.

4 **YOU DON'T HAVE TO BUY A HIGH CHAIR FOR QUITE A WHILE.** Although you may decide to register for a high chair during your pregnancy, you won't need one for at least four or five months after your baby is born. Why? Babies don't need high chairs until they start eating solid food.

Pediatricians don't recommend starting solids until at least four months of age. And if your baby isn't ready for solids till six months of age, that's still developmentally normal. If you don't have a lot of storage space, don't get a chair before you need it.

5 **ONE WORD: WHEELS!** If you have a small kitchen, you might not need a high chair with wheels, but if you plan to feed baby in the dining room and need to wash up in the kitchen, look for a chair with wheels. That way, you aren't tempted to walk away from your baby with the detachable tray, leaving them unattended. As you'll see in our Safety Alert section below, this can lead to kids escaping the harness and falling. Remember, though, that you want wheels that lock and unlock easily–they should move when you want them to but stay in one place when feeding baby.

6 **SAFETY STANDARDS FOR HIGH CHAIRS ARE VOLUNTARY.** Unlike with cribs and car seats, high chairs only have voluntary safety standards. In Safety Alerts below, we discuss some of the shortcomings of this voluntary system and what you as a parent can do to make your child safer in a high chair.

7 **MULTIPLE TRAYS ARE REALLY HELPFUL DURING CLEAN-UP.** We love high chair trays that come with a tray insert. That way you can clear up most of the mess quickly without releasing the main tray. You may still have to wipe down the main tray a bit, but most of the food will be on the insert.

Safety Alert: High Chairs

Here's the good news about high chair safety: the latest Consumer Product Safety Commission (CPSC) data shows that very few babies die in high chair accidents (a rate of one or less per year). Injuries, however, are another story. In 2015 (the most recent year statistics are available), the CPSC estimates that high chairs were the #4 cause on the list of injuries to children under five requiring an emergency room visit. That number: 11,100 high chair accidents.

In late 2015, the CPSC proposed new mandatory safety standards for high chairs. Currently, high chair safety standards are voluntary; this proposal would make standards mandatory. Within the report, the CPSC analyzed high chair injuries and made recommendations for mandatory rules based on that analysis. As you might guess, many injuries associated with high chairs were caused by falls. Thankfully, there is quite a lot you can do to prevent a fall in your kitchen or dining room:

◆ *Always use the harness.* We like five-point harnesses (like those in a car seat), rather than three-point (waist and crotch), so baby can't wiggle out and stand up. Never remove the tray without also removing your child. We know, it's easy to just pop off the tray and run it over to the sink for a minute, but kids are wily. They can wiggle out of a lot of straps and restraints if left to their own devices. Instead, consider wheeling or carrying (if you can) the high chair to the sink, then take off the tray.

◆ *Passive restraints to avoid submarining under the tray.* Most high chair injuries occur when babies are not strapped into their chairs. Sadly, one to two deaths occur each year when babies "submarine" under the tray. To address these types of accidents, new high chairs now feature a "passive restraint" (a plastic post) under the tray to prevent this. Above, the white submarine restraint is positioned between the legs of the pad:

◆ *Some high chair makers attach this submarine protection to the tray; others have it attached to the seat.* We prefer posts that are attached to the seat (see photo above). Why? If the post is on the tray and the tray is removed, there is a risk a child might be able to squirm out of the safety belts (which is all that would hold them in the chair). If it is attached to the chair, it's always there to help block an active baby. By the way, some wooden high chairs only seem to have a crotch strap—no plastic post. Again, not much is keeping baby safely in the chair. But let us reiterate: even if the high chair has a passive anti-submarine restraint, you STILL must strap in baby with the safety harness with EACH use. This prevents them from climbing out and falling.

◆ *Additional injuries occurred when chair frames or legs broke, seat supports failed and screws came loose* (also a potential choking hazard). Since these problems are caused by manufacturer defects, you may think there isn't much you can do to prevent them. However, we recommend parents carefully read and follow assembly instructions. Consider looking for unboxing videos online to supplement written instructions. And put a reminder in your phone to check screws and bolts once a month to be sure they haven't loosened. If you're considering a used high chair, check the CPSC's web site for any recalls of the chair you're considering and check for missing parts.

◆ *The report also noted some injuries (bruises and lacerations) occurred when children ran into pegs on the back of the chair,* which are used for hanging the tray when not in use. These are meant to be convenient storage, but often are projecting out from the back legs at just the right height for toddlers. If your chair comes with these pegs, we recommend removing them. Or folding the chair and putting it out of harm's way.

◆ Finally, the CPSC high chair report also assessed **high chairs in restaurants**, many of which do not adhere to the volunteer safety standards. For example, the report notes that restaurant high chairs often failed the anti-submarining test (babies can slide through the front openings or the sides and get their heads caught or fall right through to the floor). Stability was also a potential issue. The report was concerned that the narrow profile of many restaurant high chairs might lead to tipping and falling. We are also concerned that many restaurant chairs either don't have harnesses at all or only use three-point harnesses. There are hook-on chairs we recommend for parents who want to provide a safe seat for baby at a restaurant without using the restaurants high chair. See later in this chapter for suggestions.

The Best High Chairs. We break down our high chair recommendations into a few categories: Best High Chair (Overall), Best Modern High Chair, Best Urban/Space-Challenged High Chair, and Best High Chair for Grandma's House. Coming up next!

high chairs

The Best High Chair (Overall)

Our pick for the best high chair is the **Graco Blossom 4-in-1** high chair. We compared and tested 29 other high chair models before settling on the Blossom.

The Graco Blossom takes the crown this year with a modern design and a slew of helpful features. Among the Blossom's best tricks: it converts to a toddler booster chair that straps to a regular kitchen chair for older kiddos.

Reader feedback on this chair has been very positive. Yes, the Blossom is pricey at $128 to $170, but worth it. One bummer: the Blossom doesn't fold away for storage. And the restraint bar for the chair is attached to the tray, not the chair, as we'd prefer. Despite these drawbacks, we recommend the Blossom for its utility and value.

Graco's Blossom 4-in-1 Seating System strikes a modern pose compared to other high chairs, thanks to its L- shaped frame. Graco packed this model with just about every feature you can imagine. And yes, you can use it both as an infant feeding booster and a youth chair simultaneously for two children of different ages. Hence the 4-in-1 functionality.

The Blossom starts as an infant feeding chair. Note how the infant is reclined (above right).

Then a regular high chair (basically the same chair, but not reclined, right).

Next the Blossom turns into a toddler booster that attaches to a kitchen chair (right).

And finally a youth chair which can be used with the toddler booster so you can seat both a preschooler and an older infant/toddler (lower right).

The chair has three recline positions and six height levels, a dishwasher safe tray with insert, adjustable footrest and removable seat back insert. The seat pad is machine washable too.

Flaws but not deal breakers. A couple of items to note that make the Blossom a little less than perfect:

It's pricey. Yes, $128-$170 is a chunk of change (especially compared to the Fisher Price SpaceSaver, which is under $50). But for a traditional high chair, we found the features worth the price.

The Blossom doesn't fold away for storage—so you better like how it looks and have space in your kitchen or dining area. Good news: the Blossom is easy on the eyes.

The anti-submarining bar is attached to the tray—we prefer it attached to the seat. Our advice would be to leave the main tray on when you finish feeding and just remove the tray insert for cleaning.

Also Great: Joovy Nook

Joovy is best known for its strollers, but its **Nook** high chair ($90) is worth a look. This is a straightforward high chair that is simple, does the job and isn't too "baby-ish." The Nook is what the brand bills as a "no nonsense" high chair. You get a dishwasher-safe insert, swing open tray and compact fold. But that's it—it doesn't morph into a toddler chair or a toaster when you're done feeding

baby. No wheels, but there is a five-point harness for safety.

Joovy refreshed the Nook for 2017 (now its called the ***Joovy New Nook***, $120) with better tubing, a squared off seat, travel handle and submarining protection attached to the seat. Now the Nook boasts a larger tray plus three depth adjustments to address the large gap between baby and tray that plagued the original Nook.

The new Nook's tray swings out and the chair can be folded with the tray attached. It still comes with a second tray. The new

high chairs

Nook still has the five point harness, plush seat cushion and compact fold. The chair doesn't come with wheels, but for $120 this is a high chair we can definitely recommend.

FYI: Both the older Nook and the New Nook are still for sale as of this writing; we prefer the New Nook. Not all sites or retailers call out the new versus the old, so check Joovy's site to see pictures of the original Nook and the New Nook to make sure you are getting correct version!

Best Budget-Friendly High Chair

If bare bones is all you need, an **IKEA high chair** the fits the bill. The Antilop high chair costs an astonishing $15 for an metal and plastic chair with anti-submarining bar molded into the seat and three-point safety belt. If you want a tray, that's another $5; a seat pad is $6. So even when tricked out, the Antilop with tray and pad is $26.

IKEA has a second high chair, the Blames, which sells for a mere $60. This mostly wood chair comes with the plastic tray and safety belt at no extra charge.

Both high chairs are clearly designed for older kids (no recline, for example) and don't have five-point safety belts which we prefer. That said, parents generally give the Antilop great reviews, noting it's really easy to clean. If you have multiples, two or three $26 complete Antilops may just be what you need.

Best Modern High Chair

The **Boon Flair** debuted quite a few years back, in 2007, but we still think it's one of the best modern style chairs on the market. The Flair's unique pneumatic lift gives the chair "effortless height adjustment" just like a barber chair.

The seat is seamless, meaning clean up is easy compared to other high chairs and it has a dishwasher-safe tray. The Flair retails for $224 to $250, at the high end, but comparable to other modern-style chairs. The only negatives: the Flair has no recline and the tray is rather small. But overall, this is a great chair you'd be proud to have in your space age kitchen.

Best Urban/Space-Challenged High Chair

Is space tight in your kitchen? The **Fisher-Price Space Saver** ($40-$50) lives up to its name. This model features a full-size tray and three- position recline—plus it converts to a toddler booster. If you are short of space (think New York City apartment), this is a great choice.

Detractors point out that once you strap this thing to a chair, you can't push the chair under the table—hence defeating the space saving concept. We see that point, but still think this is a great solution for urban condos with little space to store a bulky high chair. Reader feedback on the Space Saver is very positive—we recommend it.

Best High Chair for Grandma's House

For grandma's house, a basic **Cosco Simple Fold** ($30-$35) should do the trick. No, it doesn't have the bells and whistle of $100+ chairs, but Grandma doesn't need all that. You get a seat with wipeable seat pad, double tray, 3-position tray adjust and slim fold. This chair doesn't recline, so you can't use it for kids under six months. No, the chair doesn't have wheels, but is easy to clean.

More high chairs on BabyBargains.com. We rate and review 25+ different high chair brands on our mobile-friendly web site, BabyBargains.com. The chart on the next page summaries our online reviews.

HIGH CHAIRS

High chairs, compared

NAME	RATING	PRICE	TRAY HEIGHT	TRAY DEPTH
BABY BJORN	B+	$240	5.5"	5.5"
BABY TREND	C+	$55-$100	8.5	8
BLOOM FRESCO	D	$445-$550	10	8
BOON FLAIR	A	$200-$250	5.5	7
CHICCO POLLY	C+	$130-$170	7.5	7
COSCO SIMPLE FOLD	C+	$32-$60	*	*
EVENFLO QUATORE	B	$130	*	*
FISHER PRICE HEALTHY CARE	A	$105-$150	7.5	6
FISHER PRICE SPACE SAVER	A	$40-$50	7.5	5
GRACO BLOSSOM	A	$145-$190	6	6
GRACO SOUS CHEF	A	$170-$250	*	*
IKEA ANTILOP	C+	$15	*	*
IKEA BLAMES	C+	$60	*	*
INGENUITY TRIO	B	$72-$99	*	*
INGLESINA GUSTO	B-	$120-$150	5.5	8
INGLESINA ZUMA	B-	$275-$300	7.5	7.25
JOVVY NEW NOOK	A-	$115	*	*
MAMAS & PAPAS JUICE	B	$125-$150	7	9.5
NUNA ZAZZ	B	$300	*	*
OXO TOT SPROUT	B-	$200	7	7
OXO TOT SEEDLING	B-	$120	6	7
PEREGO PRIMA PAPPA BEST	C+	$250	8.5	7
PHIL & TEDS HIGHPOD	B-	$200	*	*
SAFETY 1ST ADAPTABLE	C+	$90	*	*
STOKKE TRIPP TRAPP	A-	$250	*	*
SVAN SIGNET	C	$150-$250	*	*

KEY

TRAY HEIGHT: Distance from the seat to the top of the tray. Any measurement under 8" is acceptable. Above 8" is too tall.

DEPTH (tray to seat): Distance from the back of the seat to the tray. 5" to 7" is acceptable.

SUB?: Most high chairs have a special guard to prevent a child from submarining under the tray. Some models attach this to the chair; others to the tray. A better bet: those that attach to the seat. See discussion earlier in this chapter.

Sub?	Pad	Comment
Seat	None	No 5-pt. harness, easy clean, small seat
Seat	Cloth	Pad should be hand-washed, line dried.
Seat	Cloth	Seamless seat, auto height, seat reclines
Seat	Vinyl	Seamless seat; automatic height adjust.
Tray	Vinyl	Hard to clean, difficult to adjust harness
Seat	Vinyl	Lowest price, good for grandma's house.
Seat	Vinyl	4 modes including big kid booster
Seat	Vinyl	One of our top picks; 3 versions.
Seat	Vinyl	Attaches to chair; great for small spaces.
Tray	Vinyl	Converts to toddler booster.
Seat	Vinyl	Seat removes to be an infant soother.
Seat	None	Tray is $5 extra; better for older toddlers.
None	None	No harness; better for older toddlers.
Seat	Vinyl	Transitions from chair to booster, chair
Tray	Vinyl	Easy compact fold; 4 height positions
Seat	Cloth	Seamless seat, mod look, very pricey.
Seat	Vinyl	Larger tray, can fold with tray attached.
Seat	Vinyl	Legs pop off to convert to a chair.
Seat	Foam	"Crumb free" design for easy cleaning.
Tray	Vinyl	Doesn't fold; wood hybrid.
Seat	Vinyl	Plastic/metal, dishwasher safe tray.
Seat	Vinyl	3 versions; many colors, hard to clean.
Tray	Vinyl	Seamless pad, but small tray.
Tray	Cloth	Ultra compact, standing fold.
Seat	Cloth	Baby rail is $70 extra; no tray.
Seat	Cloth	Wood chair morphs into toddler chair

high chairs

Pad: Is the seat made of cloth or vinyl? We prefer vinyl for easier clean up. Cloth seats must be laundered and some can't be thrown in the drier (requiring a long wait for it to line dry). Of course, this feature isn't black and white—some vinyl seats have cloth edging/piping.

* Not applicable or not available. Some of these models were new as of press time, so we didn't have these specs yet.

Best Hook-on Chair

The **Chicco Caddy** ($40) is our top pick as the best hook-on chair for travel and restaurants. We love the compact fold, three point harness and "quick grip" table clamps. The seat pad can be removed, although some parents note it can be difficult to remove the first few time, and it is machine washable.

Like most hook-on chairs, the Caddy only has a three-point harness. Because of this, some parents complain it's too easy for active kids to stand up even with the harness latched, so keep an eye on your child when using this or any other hook-chair.

Similar but with more bells and whistles is the **Chicco 360 Hook On** ($63). The 360's seat rotates so you can more easily put your child in or take her out and comes with a tray. While parents like the rotating seat, some have complained this seat is harder to clean than the Caddy.

FYI: We don't recommend hook-on chairs as replacements for a high chair, although many parents with limited space choose a hook-on chair. Hook-on chairs are best when visiting friends and family or when eating at a restaurant. If you are looking for a full-feature high chair that can be attached to a dining room chair, consider the Fisher-Price Space Saver reviewed in our section on high chairs.

Also Great: Inglesina Fast Table Chair

Although it's a bit more expensive than the Chicco Caddy, we think the **Inglesina Fast Table Chair** ($69), is an excellent second choice. It has a quick flat-fold for travel, a small storage pocket in the back and the cover is removable and hand-washable.

A neat trick: the carry back is sewn to the bottom of the seat so you can never lose it. Inglesina makes a tray accessory for the Fast Table as well. A bit more pricey than the Chicco Caddy, but overall, the parent feedback is excellent.

Best Kitchen Booster With Tray

After comparing and testing more than a dozen different kitchen booster seats, we crown the **Fisher-Price Healthy Care Booster Seat** ($22) as the best kitchen booster.

Fisher Price has a winner here: we liked the snap-off feeding tray that can go into the dishwasher, easy fold and shoulder strap for road trips plus three different height settings. When your child gets older, the tray removes so the seat becomes a basic booster.

The only caveat: the back does not recline, so your baby must be able to sit up on his own to use it safely. (No biggie for most older babies, but we know some folks consider these boosters as high-chair replacements—not a good idea unless your child can sit upright).

Also Great: Summer Infant Deluxe Comfort Folding Booster

The **Summer Infant Deluxe Comfort Folding Booster** is an affordable ($17) booster similar to our top pick, but it adds one nice bonus: a more compact fold for easy transport. No snack tray, but the full-size tray is dishwasher-safe. Be aware: this seat has a 33-pound limit—as a result this one won't work for larger toddlers. (FYI: The Fisher Price Healthy Care booster is good up to 45 lbs.).

Best Kitchen Booster (without tray)

If you're looking for a kitchen booster for an older child who wants to sit at your kitchen table but is too short, then you're looking for a kitchen booster seat without a tray (the trays on other boosters keep your child from reaching the table top). Our top pick in this category is the ***Prince***

Lionheart Soft Booster ($27). Designed for kids three and up, the foam seat includes a rubberized, slip-resistant grip.

Also Great: OXO Tot Perch booster seat

Another good bet in the category of boosters without trays is the ***OXO Tot Perch*** booster seat ($30). It quickly collapses and has a carry handle for travel. Reader feedback on this one has been quite positive.

CHAPTER 6

AROUND THE HOUSE

Around the House: Monitors, Diaper Pails, Safety

Inside this chapter

What's the best bathtub for baby? Which baby monitor let's you stream your nursery online? What's the best—and least stinky—diaper pail? In this chapter, we explore everything for baby that's around the house. From bouncer seats to safety gates, play yards to swings, we've got recommendations. Finally, let's talk safety—we'll give you advice on affordable baby proofing.

The Best Baby Bathtub

Sometimes, it is the simplest products that are the best. Take baby bathtubs—if you look at the offerings in this category, you'll note some baby bathtubs convert from bath tubs to step stools and then, to small compact cars.

Okay, just kidding on the car, but these products are a good example of brand manager overkill—there's even a $65 baby bathtub on the market that features a "calming whirlpool and massaging bubbles." (Summer, we are looking at you).

So let's keep it simple and stick to basic baby bathtubs. In this section, we break our bathtub recommendations into several categories, based on different parent needs:

◆ Best Bathtub (Overall)
◆ Best Folding Bathtub
◆ Best Bath Sling
◆ Best New Bath Gizmo for 2017

The Best Baby Bathtub (Overall)

After comparing and testing more than 20 different baby bathtubs, slings and seats, we picked the **Primo EuroBath** as the best baby bathtub.

The EuroBath is a full size tub intended for use on a kitchen or bathroom counter and will also fit in a full size adult tub. It's one of the biggest baby bathtubs and can accommodate babies up to 24 months. It offers two bathing positions and has molded safety supports to keep baby from slipping under water.

Parents are overwhelmingly enthusiastic about their EuroBath tub, according to our reader feedback. They love the molded supports, the huge size (they can use it up to two years of age),

and its durability. (FYI: if you don't have the room for a tub this size, check out our folding tub recommendation below). And at only $21 (for the white version; up to $43 for colors like blue or pink), the Primo Eurobath won't break the bank.

Also Great: First Years Sure Comfort Deluxe Newborn to Toddler Tub

The **First Years' Sure Comfort Deluxe Newborn to Toddler Tub** is a simple tub which includes a sling and foam pads to better fit a newborn. Use the sling for newborns and then remove as baby grows. Once your child is sitting up, flip the tub from the reclined side to the straight back side and your toddler can use it. Priced at $16, our readers love this tub.

Best Folding Bathtub

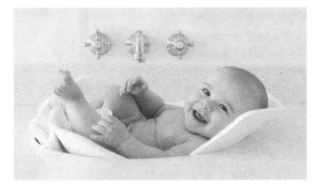

bath

If space is tight, we'd recommend the **Puj Tub** ($45)—a soft, foldable tub designed to fit in a sink. Made of foam, it unfolds when not in use (see lower right) and can hang on the back of a door—perfect if you live in a tiny urban apartment. The only caveat: it doesn't work with all sinks or faucets (an oval sink with a 6.5" depth is best). And it is designed for infants to six month-olds, so this won't work for older babies and toddlers.

Puj also makes a smaller, less-expensive version of the Tub called the **Flyte**, which can be folded for travel ($35). It doesn't get the glowing reviews as the regular Puj Tub. FYI: Safety 1st makes a similar design called the Sink Snuggler for less: $22.

Also Great: Boon Naked Collapsible Baby Bathtub

Boon's modernist take on the baby bathtub is the **Boon Naked**, a folding tub that's also great for the space deprived. The Naked baby bathtub is collapsible with a hook to hang it in the shower

The simple, colorful bathtub has a recline position for newborns. Cost: $50 to $60. It comes in bright teal blue, pink or green.

Best Bath Sling

What's a bath sling? Basically, it's a mesh sling that enables you to give baby a bath in a kitchen sink or larger bathtub.

The **Summer Infant Deluxe Baby Bather** has three reclines and a padded head support. It also folds down so you can store it or take it to Grandma's. Parents like the portability, price ($13) and small size . . . but others complained that it slips around in a big bathtub as there are no rubber grippers on the bottom.

Best New Bath Gizmo

New this year, the **BabyDam** is a unique concept: using suction cups and a seal, it allows parents to decrease the size of their regular bath tub to a size more comfortable for bathing a baby or toddler.

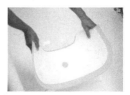

After being sold in Europe, BabyDam is now available in the US. The cost: $40. There is both a European and US/Canada version. Here's how you figure out which size is right for you: If the inside width of your bath tubs is between 22.5 inches & 26.5 inches, go for the BabyDam in US & Canada size. If the inside width of your bath tub is LESS THAN 22.5 inches wide, choose the BabyDam in the European size.

We're looking forward to testing the BabyDam shortly, but early reports are promising.

Potty Seats

Potty seats come in two flavors: floor models and inserts. Inserts are molded (and sometimes padded) seats made for smaller bottoms. They are installed on top of the regular toilet seat. Floor models are traditional self-contained units with a base and seat.

Some potty seats start out as floor models and then the seat can be removed and used as an insert on the regular toilet. Our advice: go for the insert only. Yes, you'll need a step stool for your little one to climb up, but it's much easier to transition to a regular toilet if your child is already using one. And think about how excited your child will be to use the same toilet as his parents (trust us, it is a big deal).

The Best Potty Seat

After comparing and testing dozens of potty seat (and cleaning up a lot of messes!), we picked the **Baby Bjorn Toilet Trainer** as the best potty seat.

The Baby Bjorn is a seat insert that attaches to a full-size toilet seat. It comes equipped with a unique adjustment dial to fit most toilet seats. It also includes an angled splashguard (handy to guide pee into the toilet bowl) and a contoured, molded seat for tushy comfort. Price: $24.

Also Great: Fisher Price Froggy Potty

Floor potties aren't our first choice when toilet training (we prefer toilet inserts), but we know quite a few readers love them. So here's our pick: Fisher-Price makes eight different floor potties for toilet training, but our favorite is the simplest: the **Froggy Potty ($13)**. The seat  has an integrated splash guard, handles on the potty ring, removable bowl and handle on the back for portability. Parents are enthusiastic about the Froggy Potty–their kids love it and it's simple to use and clean.

The Best Diaper Pail

Let's talk diaper pails—there are currently two types on the market: those that use refills (sold by the maker) and those that use kitchen trash bags. Before we get to our picks, here's a quick intro course to diaper pails and how to choose one.

7 Things No One Tells You About Buying A Diaper Pail

1 **THE AVERAGE BABY REQUIRES 2300 DIAPER CHANGES IN HIS OR HER FIRST YEAR.** That's right, 2300 diaper changes. A staggering figure . . . only made more staggering by figuring out what do with the dirty ones once you've changed baby. Yes, we can hear first-time parents raising their hands right now and saying "Duh! They go in the trash!" We'll get to that later.

Why so many? First time parents are inexperienced when it comes to knowing the signs baby needs a change, so they check baby more frequently. Breastfed babies also poop more often than formula fed babies. But you don't get off easy by using formula: formula-fed babies are more "odiferous" than breastfed babies.

2 **DIAPER PAILS VS. REGULAR TRASHCANS: IT'S A STINKY BATTLE.** We've heard from a pretty sizable share of parents who claim they don't need a special diaper pail. A trash can works just fine for them. Maybe they don't have babies eating solids yet or drinking formula, but eventually they'll realize a specialized diaper pail isn't such a bad idea.

Diaper pails often use either deodorizers like baking soda or deodorized plastic liners to keep the stink under control. The effectiveness of such odor control varies widely.

3 **DIAPER BAGS THAT USE REFILL CARTRIDGES OF DEODORIZED PLASTIC CAN GET EXPENSIVE.** Our top choices for diaper pails both use refill cartridges of deodorized plastic to keep down the stink. And the Munchkin pail also releases a shot of baking soda on each diaper for extra deodorizing.

These refill cartridges can really add up. For example, our top choice, the Diaper Dekor Plus refill cartridge holds up to 1160 diapers per cartridge (that means if you have newborn or size one diapers, you might be able to dispose of 1160 diapers before installing a new cartridge). Cost: about $7 per cartridge. But you'll need to use more than one. And likely you won't get 1160 diapers into one cartridge as your baby grows.

So let's say the average per year is four cartridges at $7 each or $28. Then assuming you're changing diapers for three years that's $84. Add in the cost of the Plus itself ($46) and you're talking about $130 for a diaper pail.

4 **YES, DIAPER PAILS THAT USE REGULAR TRASH BAGS ARE CHEAPER, BUT THE TRADE OFF IS THE STINK.** If you choose to go with trash bag liners for your diaper pail, get ready for the smell. They will need to be replaced more frequently. And even if you get odor control kitchen trash bags like Glad OdorShield, there's no guarantee you'll be able to stand the smell after baby starts solid foods. So be aware of the trade off.

5 **SKIP THE ECO-FRIENDLY VERSIONS OF REFILL CARTRIDGES.** Great news for our eco-conscious friends: many diaper pails offer biodegradable refills. Bad news: they may not combat stink as well as the regular kind. We suggest you test out one pack of biodegradable refills rather than invest in several. Biodegradable are slightly more expensive than regular, by the way.

6 **IF YOU'RE WORRIED YOUR CLOTH DIAPERS WILL STINK UP THE NURSERY, LET US PUT YOUR MIND TO REST.** Follow these tips to keep your the nursery from stinking with cloth diapers. Scrape baby's poop from the diaper into the toilet using a flushable wipe. Throw the dirty diaper into a diaper pail. Some parents like to soak cloth diapers in a bleach solution or use a pre-soak product with enzymes (like Shout) that "predigest" the poop. Presoaking will help keep down the odor. Every few days, wash as you would your regular clothes. If you have an older washer, you may need to add bleach during the cleaning process.

7 **AVOID TOXIC DEODORANT DISKS IN YOUR DIAPER PAIL OR KITCHEN TRASH.** Older babies and toddlers are attracted to the oddest things. We recommend you avoid deodorant disks that are stuck onto the lid of the diaper pail or kitchen trash can. You don't want to find your toddler sucking on one!

Next up: our diaper pail recommendations—one for a refill pail and the other no-refills!

The Best Diaper Pail (Refill)

After comparing and testing a wide selection of diaper pails, we selected the ***Diaper Dekor*** brand as our top choice for best diaper pail (refills).

The only serious competition for Playtex's Diaper Genie, here's the skinny on the Diaper Decor's three sizes and how much the hold: Mini ($20, holds 25 diapers), Classic ($30, 40 newborn diapers), Plus ($45, 60 newborn diapers). And each pail has different refills with two options (regular or biodegradable). Refills run about $14.82 for a two-pack that wraps about 1100 diapers. (1100!) Be careful which size refills you buy: the Classic size won't fit in a Plus can.

As you might guess, the Mini is designed for lighter use (grandma's house?) while the bigger Plus version is pitched to folks who want to do less frequent emptying of the pail. The Classic and Plus are available in colors for around $5 more than the white version.

Of all the models, the Plus is most popular—but all the Dekors get generally good marks from readers. No diaper pail can completely seal out the stink and the Dekor's critics (about one in four folks who buy it) say the Diaper Genie works better. But the majority of readers are happy with the Dekor.

As for the refills, the regular ones work better at holding back the stink than the biodegradable, based on reader feedback. Our opinion: the "biodegradable" refills are horrible at blocking odor, the main reason why you'd part with the big bucks to buy one of these pails, right? So stick with the regular refills for the best odor control.

Wipe Warmers: Not Recommended

These $20 gizmos warm wipes to a comfy 90 degrees, so baby isn't surprised by a cold wipe at 2am. While this sounds like a good idea, there have been a series of safety recalls for these devices, which have caused fires, electric shock and other problems. Besides, you can just warm the wipes up in your hands for a few seconds—voila! Warm wipe without spending $20.

Also Great: Munchkin Step Diaper Pail Powered by Arm & Hammer

Our next favorite diaper pail is a mouthful: ***Munchkin Step Diaper Pail Powered by Arm & Hammer*** ($65). Let's just call it the Step.

The Step's lockable pail with deodorized bags really works well at stopping odor. Munchkin added a mechanism to sprinkle odor fighting baking soda on each diaper in the pail to improve the deodorizing power.

Reader feedback on this has been trending positive on this pail. Parents praise the lack of odor, saying it seals better than other brands. And the little shot of baking soda from the refillable cartridge seems to do the job, in our testing. It's also easy to replace the bag and remove the dirty diapers.

Perhaps the biggest complaint we hear from readers is what's called the "squish factor." You have to really push the diaper down to get it into the pail—no fun when it's a really full diaper.

And some enterprising toddlers have easily figured out how to get the door open in the base. Let's not visualize. Let's just move on.

Finally, it does take two hands to open the lid, making for tough going if you have your baby in one hand. Still with all it's faults, Munchkin's Arm & Hammer diaper pail is a great option for odor control.

Best No-Refill Diaper Pail

The ***Ubbi*** steel diaper pail ($70) has a sliding opening with a rubber seal to keep odors in. The reason for the slide? Ubbi told us they think this keeps the smell from wafting out like other diaper pails. And the steel doesn't absorb odors like plastic. Best of all, it uses regular trash bags!

The Ubbi has received positive reviews overall, although it does get some criticism for the sliding opening. We tried it ourselves and thought the slide was a bit sticky, so you may not be able to use it one-handed. Also readers say don't overfill it—the bag can snag on the lid. But it's a lot less expensive than diaper pails that use refills (factoring in refill expense), comes in 15 different colors and patterns . . . and you can really use this as a trash can after baby is out of diapers.

diaper pails

Best Humidifier

We always know when its wintertime here in Colorado—the furnace kicks in and everyone's skin dries out quicker than you can say Mojave Desert. Hence, humidifiers are a way of life here. But even if you live in a more humid climate, running a humidifier in your baby's room in the winter can keep throats, nasal passages and skin from drying out—and make everyone happier.

7 Things No One Tells You About Buying A Humidifier!

1 **THERE ARE TWO BASIC TYPES OF HUMIDIFIERS: EVAPORATIVE AND ULTRASONIC.** Evaporative humidifiers have a wick that soaks up water, then a fan blows the moisture out. These are often the least expensive type, but can be noisy . . . plus the filter must be replaced regularly.

Ultrasonic humidifiers use sound waves to disperse the moisture so there is no fan required. This makes ultrasonics much quieter than evaporative humidifiers. The downside, though, is sometimes they leave a coating of white dust in the room. And they can be quite expensive (that's why our top pick in this category is an evaporative humidifier).

2 **HUMIDIFIERS ALSO COME IN WARM OR COLD MIST.** Warm mist humidifiers use a heating element to warm the water (cold mist do not). While that might sound appealing if you live in a cold climate, we do NOT recommend these humidifiers for baby's room. That's because warm mist humidifiers can overheat the room—and that's a risk factor for Sudden Infant Death Syndrome (SIDS). Also, the hot mist coming out of the humidifier can cause a scalding injury if touched by a wayward toddler.

Warm mist humidifiers require more cleaning and maintenance than cool mist ones. If you are tempted to buy a warm mist humidifier because your nursery is drafty, it would make more sense to buy a separate oil-filled space heater and a cool mist humidifier. That's because a space heater more efficiently heats the room than a warm mist humidifier. (Of course, there is still a safety problem with all space heaters—toddlers can burn themselves on any hot surface. The best long term solution is to have a HVAC specialist see if they can correct the heating/cooling issue in your baby's nursery).

3 DON'T OVERSIZE THE HUMIDIFIER. Humidifiers are rated by gallon output and most will tell you the size room they cover—match this to the size room your baby is in. You don't need a giant humidifier for most bedrooms.

4 HUMIDIFIERS SHOULD BE CLEANED REGULARLY. Humidifiers have detailed cleaning instructions—follow these! If not, you risk mold or mildew build-up in the unit or the shortening of the humidifier's lifespan. See below for one of many online videos on cleaning a humidifier.

5 CONSIDER AN ADJUSTABLE HUMIDISTAT. A humidistat works like a thermostat, setting the humidity at a certain level and turning on or off the humidifier until it reaches that level. This is a nice feature, although it's not completely necessary.

6 SKIP THE VAPORIZER. A vaporizer is a humidifier that lets you disperse medication in your child's room. Generally, this is NOT recommended—that's because pediatricians rarely prescribe medication that needs to be vaporized these days.

7 IF YOU'RE REMODELING, CONSIDER WHOLE HOUSE SOLUTIONS. If you are planning to do any HVAC work on your home, consider installing a whole-house humidifier. These automatically kick in when your furnace runs (or can be controlled by a thermostat). Since they are permanently installed and plumbed to a water line, you never have to refill the humidifier. You do have to change the filter and do some maintenance, but that's typically just once a year. FYI: Honeywell makes a whole house steam humidifier, which is excellent.

humidifiers

The Best Humidifier (Cool Mist)

After comparing and testing more than 20 different humidifiers (and getting plenty wet in the process), we picked a best cool mist humidifier: the **Honeywell HCM-350** for $58.

The Honeywell HCM-350 has a two-gallon tank that is dishwasher safe. It is easy to clean and fill; we also found this model to be one of the quieter evaporative humidifiers on the market. One negative: it is rather large (18" long) and bulky. The HCM-350 also lacks a humidistat—you adjust the amount of output with a fan control knob. Overall, however, an excellent humidifier.

Also Great: Crane's Adorable Ultrasonic Cool Mist Humidifier

Yes, there is truth in advertising: **Crane's Adorable Ultrasonic Cool Mist Humidifier** is, well, adorable. But it actually works well, according to our readers.

Crane has 23 different animal shaped humidifiers as well as a train and Hello Kitty model. Priced at $30 to $50, parents praise the Crane humidifiers for the most part (quiet, easy to fill, easy to clean). But a few dissenters said it stopped working after a couple weeks, the output was too little for larger nurseries and they had problems with leaks. So . . . buy this humidifier from a store or website with an easy return policy just in case.

A few caveats to the Crane: it only has a one gallon tank, so you'll be refilling it more than the Honeywell. And we see some concerns it doesn't disperse the moisture well in a room—adding a small fan might help.

Best Bouncer Seat

Bouncers (also called activity seats) provide a comfy place for baby to hang out while you eat dinner, and the toy bar adds some mild amusement. The most common add-on to these products is a "Magic Fingers" vibration feature—the bouncer basically vibrates, simulating a car ride. Parents who have these bouncers tell us they'd rather have a kidney removed than give up their vibrating bouncer, as it appears the last line of defense in soothing a fussy baby, short of checking into a mental institution.

What features should you look for in a bouncer? Readers say a carrying handle is a big plus. Also: get a neutral fabric pattern, says another parent, since you'll probably be taking lots of photos of baby in this bouncer and neutral works better.

We break down our bouncer recommendations into three categories: Best Bouncer (Overall), Best Budget-Friendly Bouncer and Best Eco Bouncer.

Best Bouncer Seat (Overall)

If you are hoping for a gift in this category, consider registering for the **4Moms' MamaRoo**. Clocking in at a hefty $160 to $249, the MamaRoo's fans love the five unique motions (including car ride, ocean wave, etc.) as well as the built-in nature sounds and the relatively compact footprint. The most recent Mamaroo is Bluetooth-enabled so you control it with a smartphone app. One caveat: it only works to 25 lbs.

The Mamaroo is sold in two flavors—Classic (grey, black) and Plush (colored patterns). The Classic ($160 to $170) is a basic, canvas like fabric. The Plush ($229-$249) has a softer, more velvet like cover. We've evaluated the feel of both versions and think the Classic is fine. If you decide you'd like the more plush fabric later, you can buy an extra pad for $60. (As mentioned above, we like the simple solid patterns better for pictures).

If you think the Mamaroo is overkill, 4Moms offers two scaled down versions: the **RockaRoo** and **BounceRoo**. The RockaRoo ($127) drops the app control, has only one motion (5 speeds), and a smaller footprint than the Mamaroo. The Bounceroo ($80-$100) is portable (fully collapses, 6 lbs.) and has three vibration models; it works on batteries. Between the three, the Mamaroo gets better ratings from our readers than the RockaRoo or BounceRoo.

Best Budget-Friendly Bouncer

The **Fisher Price Infant to Toddler Rocker** ($25-$40) is an affordable bouncer that works up to 40 lbs. (hence the infant to toddler name). It is very lightweight, so it easily moves from room to room, but it doesn't collapse—so its use for travel is limited.

In infant mode, the seat reclines and a toy bar adds musical elements—of course, the key feature is that vibration, which is triggered by a button up front. In toddler mode, the chair sits more upright (and the toy bar is removed). Bottom line: at $25, this simple, affordable bouncer does the job.

Best Eco-Friendly Bouncer

If you want to take an eco-friendly approach to bouncers, the **Baby Bjorn Balance** is our top pick. No sounds, no lights, no batteries—the Balance rocks when you move it.

Yes, it is pricey ($122-$200), but you can use it up to 29 lbs. (most bouncers have 25 lb. weight limits). The Balance has a three position recline and collapses for travel/portability (the Balance weighs 7 lbs).

Readers love the Baby Bjorn Balance's simplicity and design; critics say it is too pricey, as exemplified by the add-on wooden toy bar accessory for $32. We agree on that point, but think the Balance is a good choice for those who want to go green here.

Not Recommended: Fisher-Price Rock N Play

There is one bouncer/rocker we don't recommend: the Fisher-Price Rock 'n Play Sleeper. It's a hybrid between bouncer and bassinet. In a nutshell, we don't recommend it for sleep, which is one of its key functions.

We don't have room here to go into detail, so we wrote a detailed blog post on this product on our web site. See the post "Fisher-Price Rock 'n Play sleeper: Miracle soother . . . or dangerous crutch?" on our website.

The Best Play Yards

The portable play yard has been so popular in recent years that many parents consider it a necessity. Compared to rickety playpens of old, today's play yards fold compactly for portability and offer such handy features as bassinets, wheels and more. First, some shopping tips and then our recommendations.

7 Things No One Tells You About Buying a Play Yard

1 DON'T BUY A SECOND-HAND PLAY YARD OR USE A HAND-ME-DOWN. Many models have been the subject of recalls in recent years. Why? Those same features that make them convenient (the collapsibility to make the play yards "portable") worked too well in the past—some play yards collapsed with babies inside. Others had protruding rivets that caught some babies who wore pacifiers on a string (a BIG no-no, never have your baby wear a pacifier on a string). A slew of injuries and deaths have prompted the recall of ten million playpens over the years. Yes, you can search government recall lists (cpsc.gov) to see if that hand-me-down is recalled, but we'd skip the hassle and just buy new.

2 GO FOR THE BASSINET FEATURE. Some play yards feature bassinet inserts, which can be used for babies under three months of age (always check the weight guidelines). This is a handy feature that we recommend.

3 SKIP THE "NEWBORN NAPPER." Graco has added a newborn napper feature to some of its playpens. This is a separate sleep area designed to "cuddle your baby." You are supposed to use this napper before you use the bassinet feature. Our concern: the napper includes plush fabrics and a head pillow—we consider this an unsafe sleep environment. As we discussed in Chapter 2, Nursery, your baby should always be put down to sleep on his back on a *flat* surface with no soft bedding—the newborn napper is an *inclined* surface with the aforementioned pillow and plush fabrics on the side. Graco also makes a model (the Chadwick) that has non-removeable bumpers on the bassinet. We do not recommend this model play yard for the same reason we don't recommend you use bumpers in a crib.

4 **CHECK THE WEIGHT LIMITS.** Play yards have two weight limits: one for the bassinet and one for the entire play yard (without the bassinet). Graco and most other play yard versions have an overall weight limit of 30 lbs. and height limit of 35". The exception is the Arms Reach Co-Sleeper which tops out at 50 lbs. However, there is more variation in the weight limits for the bassinet attachments. Here are the weight limits for the bassinet attachments on various play yards:

Arms Reach Co-Sleeper	30 lbs.
Graco Pack N Play	15 lbs.
Chicco Lullaby	15 lbs.
Compass Aluminum	18 lbs.
Combi Play Yard	15 lbs.

5 **USEFUL FEATURES: STORAGE AND MORE STORAGE.** You can't have enough storage as a parent, so play yards with side-rail storage, compartments for diapers and the like are most welcome. We also like wheels for mobility and a canopy (if you plan to take the play yard outside or to the beach). If you want a play yard with canopy, look for those models that have "aluminized fabric" canopies—they reflect the sun's heat and UV rays to keep baby cooler.

6 **FEATURES THAT AREN'T WORTH IT: GIZMOS AND TOYS.** Play yard makers like to load up their products with gadgets, lullabies, toys, flashing lights and other bling. You don't need it.

7 **EVEN THOUGH ALL PLAY YARDS PITCH THEMSELVES AS PORTABLE, MOST AREN'T THAT EASY TO TRAVEL WITH.** Yes, most play yards claim they are portable—but the effort it takes to dissemble all the accessories makes it more likely that play pen will stay put. A better bet for portability: go for play yards that are specifically designed for travel. We recommend a travel crib in Chapter 2.

Up next, our recommendations for different types of play yards:

◆ Best Play Yard (Overall)
◆ Best Outdoor Play Yard
◆ Best Play Yard for Multiples

The Best Play Yard (Overall)

The **Graco Pack N Play On the Go** is our pick for best play yard overall. It's simple—bassinet, toy bar and wheels—but gets the job done. And the price? $53.

Graco is the market leader in this category—and given the value and features they offer, that's no surprise. The company offers a dozen models of playpens and each is well designed. Of course, if you want all the toys and gizmos, Graco has models with those features too—but you'll pay $100 to $200 for those versions. One caveat: skip the Graco models with "newborn nappers." As we explained earlier, we don't recommend these for safety reasons.

The Best Play Yard For Outdoors

Planning a beach outing? Soccer game? **Summer Infant Pop N' Play Portable Play Yard** ($48) is the best solution when you need a play yard for outdoors that sets up in seconds. Weighing just 12 lb., the Pop N' Play has a water-resistant floor to keep kiddos dry in wet grass. Readers love the easy set up and overall design—it is about four feet wide and stands 26" tall. A separate $30 canopy that covers the entire play yard is handy at the beach or lake if you are in full sun.

The Best Play Yard for Multiples

Joovy's Room2 Portable Play Yard ($121) has ten square feet of area—twice the size of most standard playpens, giving multiples or toddlers more room to play. No, it doesn't include many other features you see in other playpens (no bassinet, diaper changing area, etc). However, it does what it does well—provide a large, safe area for babies to play. Readers love the easy set-up and heavy weight canvas fabric.

The Best Swings

Soothing a fussy baby has vexed many generations of parents—and the venerable baby swing has been there as a solution for decades.

One of the downsides of swings: they tend to take up a lot of floor space, which can be a challenge if you live in a smaller house or condo. Our top recommend swing when assembled is three feet wide and three feet long.

Fans of swings say they are worth their weight in gold for soothing baby, no matter how much floor space they use. Critics point out that not all babies like swings—so this might be a good product to pick up second hand if you come across one on Craigslist or a garage sale.

Swings have morphed over the years, as bouncers like the **4Mom's Mamaroo** (reviewed earlier) have taken on swing-like functions. Both bouncers and swings typically have 25 lb. weight limits, so there is no advantage of one over the other, except for space issues.

The Best Swing (Overall)

Fisher-Price has swings down to a science. The **Fisher-Price Snugabunny Cradle 'n Swing** ($105) allows for both side-to-side and front-back motion, three seat positions and a plush seat. There are six speeds, eight musical tunes and two-position seat recline. FYI: Fisher Price  makes many different versions of this swing in prices that range from $100 to $160— the difference is typically fashion. The **Fisher-Price Papasan Cradle Swing** ($127) is also a reader favorite.

The Best Portable Swing

Comfort & Harmony Cozy Kingdom Portable Swing ($51) is a six-speed portable swing with removable head support. Even though this swing is portable, it lacks a carry handle (doh!). Comfort & Harmony is part of the Kids II brand empire. Since this swing folds away, it is a good bet for grandma's house.

Best Video Baby Monitor

For her first nine months, your baby is tethered to you via the umbilical cord. After that, it's the baby monitor that becomes your surrogate umbilical cord—enabling you to work in the garden, wander about the house, and do many things that other, childless human beings do, while still keeping tabs on a sleeping baby. Hence, this is a pretty important piece of equipment you'll use every day—a good one will make your life easier . . . and a bad one will be a never-ending source of irritation.

A quick safety tip for monitors: always keep the cord at least three feet away from your baby's crib. Cords from cameras/monitors are a strangulation hazard.

Major caveat to our recommendations: ANY baby monitor, even those that earn our highest ratings, can have problems with static, poor reception or interference. The best advice: keep your receipt and buy a monitor from a store with a good return policy. It might be trial and error to find one that works for you.

7 Things No One Tells You About Buying A Video Baby Monitor!

1 **THERE ARE THREE BASIC TYPES OF VIDEO MONITORS OUT THERE: FIXED, PTZ AND STREAMING.** Fixed monitors have a camera that is, well, fixed and is the most economical choice. PTZ stands for point/tilt/zoom, where a camera can move and tilt: some parents prefer PTZ monitors since they can scan a room for a wayward baby or toddler. Finally, streaming baby monitors can send a video signal over the internet, so grandparents and relatives can see the baby's nursery. Each type has its trade-offs—most streaming monitors are fixed. And most PTZ monitors can be pricey.

2 **SOME CAMERAS HAVE BETTER NIGHT VISION THAN OTHERS.** One of the key times you use a monitor is at night—or to see in a darkened room, while baby is sleeping. To help make visible pictures, cameras use night vision—basically a series of LED lights that bathe a nursery in infrared light. The goal isn't to have a super-crisp picture to see your baby's facial expressions. You just want to see if baby is sleeping. Or playing. Or standing up crying, etc. Of course, weak night vision that doesn't let you even see if your baby is sleeping or sitting up is a problem. And night vision is often limited in distance—you can't put the camera ten feet away from the crib and expect to see clearly in the dark.

3 BATTERY LIFE SUCKS FOR MOST VIDEO MONITORS. That's because portable video screens are power hogs. Expect to plug in the monitor for over-night monitoring— that's because most monitors only last two to four hours on battery power.

4 DON'T EXPECT HDTV-QUALITY PICTURES FROM MOST BABY MONITORS. Many video baby monitors have tiny screens (2.4" to 3.5") and low resolution pictures (640 x 280 pixels). This is a far cry from an HD, but remember the purpose of a monitor is to see what's going on in the nursery, not to count the freckles on your baby's cute little face (no matter how tempting).

5 VOICE-ON-EXCHANGE (VOX) MODE: GOOD OR EVIL? Vox is an optional setting on many monitors that only turns on the screen when baby makes a sound above a preset level. This is helpful to conserve battery.

Folks either love or hate VOX—fans love not having to hear every peep or squeak from baby. Critics say VOX mode can falsely trigger, awakening sleep-deprived parents when there isn't a problem in the nursery. Good news: monitors with VOX have a switch to toggle it off if you hate it.

6 THE Z IN PTZ CAMERAS STANDS FOR ZOOM. And some cameras offer this feature to let you zoom in on a particular area in the nursery. Be aware that most cameras have a digital zoom. This means the pixels in the camera are enlarged when you zoom. As a result, the picture becomes grainy. Hence, the zoom feature is less helpful than you'd think.

7 STREAMING: YES OR NO? The latest trend in baby monitors are those that can stream a picture online—so you can check baby while you are at work. Or a grandparent can see the nursery.

This type of monitor can be tricky to set up, as it requires a secure connection to the internet. Depending on your internet router, these monitors can work fabulously . . . or not at all. Later in this chapter, we'll recommend a streaming baby monitor that is easy to set up.

In this next section, we recommend video baby monitors in two categories:

◆ Best Video Monitor, PTZ
◆ Best Video Monitor, Streaming

Best Video Baby Monitor, PTZ

After researching and reviewing 16 different video monitor brands, we pick the **Infant Optics DXR-8** as the Best Video Baby Monitor.

The Infant Optics DXR-8 features a crisp (but not HD) 3.5" screen, two-way talk and interchangeable lenses, which is unique among baby monitors.

Infant Optics debuted its first baby monitor in 2012 (the fixed camera DXR-5). The PTZ monitor (DXR-8) debuted in 2014. As of this writing, Infant Optics only has these two models. They aren't sold in stores—just online.

Their best-selling model is the DXR-8—this $165 unit has pan/tilt/zoom and interchangeable lenses (the normal and zoom lenses come in the box; wide angle is sold separately). The swappable lenses are unique and you might think, at first blush, what is the point? Why would you need to swap the normal angle lens with a zoom?

After playing around with this monitor for while, the most obvious answer is ease of installation. Depending on the configuration of your nursery, your only option may be to put the camera on a dresser across from the crib—then the normal lens might do. But if you mount the camera on a wall above the crib, the zoom lens might be better. (Always make sure cords are at least three feet from the crib).

Most folks repurpose a baby monitor later to monitor a toddler's room or play area—then the wide angle lens ($10, sold separately) might be the better bet. Of course, interchangeable lens means you might also lose the lenses (at least, that's what would happen to us)— but you can buy replacements from Infant Optics' web site.

Beyond the standard intercom and temperature sensor features (common on many monitors in this price point), we also liked the Infant Optics screen off, audio-only mode which is most useful during over night hours. Infant Optics estimates the battery life at six hours (when the screen is turned on)—our research says that is relatively accurate. Obviously, it would make most sense to have the parent monitor plugged in (instead of using battery power) overnight, but the audio-only mode should get you through the night on a fully charged battery if you forget.

One nice feature: you can recharge the lithium-ion battery in the parent unit with any USB plug—computer, USB power cube, etc.

Need to monitor twins? Or quads? The Infant Optics DXR-8 lets you link up to four cameras to a single display, which will then cycle through the additional cameras every 12 seconds.

Night vision on the DXR-8 is impressive: here's how it looks compared to the Samsung SEW3043W (on left). The DXR-8 had an overall crisper and brighter picture when using night vision:

How's the range? The Infant Optics DXR-8 uses 2.4 Ghz technology—that provides secure transmission (the parent unit is paired with the camera) to prevent eavesdropping. The company claims a range of 700 feet line of sight. Real world tests indicate it works well in two or even three story homes, with few dropouts, say readers.

Flaws but not deal breakers. To Infant Optics credit, the company has tweaked the monitor over the years to address user complaints. Example: there used to be an audible beep when the monitor went into sleep mode or low battery—that obviously drove folks crazy at 2am. So Infant Optics enabled these beep alerts to be toggled off in the menu settings for units shipped after March 2015.

Here are the other key complaints:

No VOX. Voice-activation mode (VOX) turns on the video screen when a certain level of sound is detected. This is a relatively common feature on baby monitors today, but Infant Optics omits it. We should point out that the DXR-8 does have an audio-only night mode (described above) . . . but that means the audio is on all the time, not triggered by noise.

Somewhat bulky parent unit. Compared to the parent units of competitors like Summer or Samsung, the Infant Optics parent unit is kind of chunky. Here's what it looks like from behind (it ain't no iPhone).

Which brings us to flaw #2: notice the back of the parent unit has a stand but **no belt clip**. Hence carrying this unit around requires you to keep it in a pocket—and a large one at that.

No remaining battery life percentage indicator. Summer has a this feature; Infant Optics just has an icon indicating battery life, but a percentage remaining would be more helpful.

Smallish screen, no HD. Competitors like the Samsung BrightVIEW are rolling out five inch parent unit screens. And actual 720p HD resolution. By contrast the Infant Optics DXR-8 is old school at 640 x 480 resolution.

Of course, HD cameras are more expensive (that Samsung unit is $230—35% more than the DXR-8). And most of our readers found the lower rez on the 3.5" screen to be adequate enough to do the job. Plus there is the trade-off in battery life—the higher the resolution and bigger the screen, the less battery time you get—the Samsung BrightVIEW is about only four hours versus six hours for the DXR-8.

Less than stellar audio. One thing Infant Optics could do is beef up the audio quality of the DXR-8. We found the sound to be kind of tinny, especially compared to Samsung and Motorola's offerings. Again, most readers tell us the DXR-8 was adequate to do the job . . . but that is somewhat underwhelming for a $170 monitor. On the plus side, we found the video signal from the Infant Optics unit to be better than Samsung (see the night vision comparison above).

No online streaming. The Infant Optics DXR-8 only can send a signal to the parent unit—it can't stream video online to be viewed by a smartphone. Read our pick for the best streaming baby monitor below.

Also Great: VTech VM343

The **VTech VM343** ($150) has
one of the better parent units
(4.3) with a crisp (but not HD)
picture. There is a two- talk feature, but the battery life is
shorter than our top pick
above (two to three hours ver-
sus the Infant Optics' six hours). Good quality overall.

Best Video Baby Monitor, Streaming

Would you like your baby's grandma to watch
your baby's nursery live? Then you need a camera that can stream video over the internet.
While that sounds simple, this category of camera can be tricky to set up. The best bet here is
Nest Cam, a simple, fixed $200 HD camera with
a 60 second set-up. You can view your baby's
nursery via the Nest web site or via an iPhone or Android app.

The down-side: there is no parent display unit, so you'll have
to re-purpose an old iPhone or iPod Touch to be a viewer. The
promise of streaming video of your baby over the internet sounds
like the perfect marriage of tech and cute, but the reality of getting this to work isn't pretty. Cameras that stream online video
(called IP or network cams) are challenging to set up—getting one
to work with your router requires a master's degree in geek.
Once you pass that hurdle, where do you store the video?

Software to store camera footage and stream it online is
another tech headache. Enter Nest cam, now part of the Nest
smart thermostat family (which in turn, is owned by Google—naturally). Inspired by the founder's quest to figure out which one
of his neighbor's dogs was making a deposit on his lawn, Nest
does all the heavy lifting— streaming the video online and storing
clips in the cloud. Nest made viewing easy, via a browser or app.

Nest Cam's major pitch is for home monitoring. Yet, in the last
couple of years we have seen a convergence of the baby video
monitor market and home security cameras. Many parents are
realizing that affordable home security cameras can be used to
securely stream video from a baby's nursery with quality that sur-
passes so-called baby monitors . . . at a cheaper price to boot.

Quick and easy set-up is Nest Cam's secret sauce—they promise a 60 second set-up and that's pretty much what we found in our testing. No special software is needed and the Nest Cam works on a Mac or PC. Apps are available for iOS and Android devices.

FYI: The most recent Nest cam debuted in mid 2015. Compared to the previous model, the latest Nest Cam features a more narrow shape and magnetic base. Nest Cam has a 130° field of vision and improved night vision and audio quality. You still get an HD picture (1080p) that is crisp and clear.

Nest can send you a mobile alert if it detects movement or sound in your baby's nursery. You can also record video to Nest's cloud web site (called Nest Aware)—but this incurs a monthly fee ($100 a year for ten days of video history, $300 per year for 30 days of storage—there is a free option for three hours of storage). Of course, you don't have to record the video (it's free to monitor the feed online or via a smartphone. And email/mobile alerts are also free).

The Nest Aware subscription has some interesting features—you can set up "activity zones" in your video feed to get alerts for just motion happening in your baby's crib, for example. (You draw these zones in the settings on the Nest web site via a desktop computer). You can also directly share clips to Facebook, YouTube or download to your computer. One slight bummer: you can't share clips from your smartphone or tablet, only a computer. Nest uses a special low bandwidth technology (H.264) to avoid hogging your WiFi bandwidth—but a Nest can easily use up to 60 GB of internet bandwidth during a month's time especially when used in HD mode (that's because it streams video 24/7). That could be a problem if you are on a metered internet plan.

Parent feedback on the Nest cam is excellent—it does live up to the promise of easy set-up. Of course, there are always a few trade-offs: depending on your router speed, there can be a 3-5 second delay between the sound in your baby's nursery and what you hear on your smartphone. Hence, there might be an echo-like effect (baby cries and then 3 seconds later, you hear it on the app). And of course if you plan to use a Nest for night-time monitoring, you'll need to dedicate a device to keep the app open (a retired iPhone or iPod touch would be a good bet).

Finally, we saw a few reports of Nest Cams that dropped their connection (and needed to be manually reset every week or so). We purchased the previous version of the Nest cam to demo here at the home office and are generally impressed—it probably is the easiest to set up webcam we've seen.

Out of the box, you connect the camera to the USB port on your computer (Mac or PC). Then double click on the "Setup" icon and the installation program launches. The camera can be set up wirelessly using an iPad, iPhone or Android device. The set-up program is very easy to follow, even for the tech-challenged. You create a Nest account and then connect it to your WiFi (yes, you'll need your WiFi password). The Nest Cam automatically senses the WiFi networks in your home. Download the apps to your smartphone or tablet and you are good to go.

BABY MONITORS	A quick look at baby video monitor features	

BRAND	MODEL	PRICE
DLINK	WI-FI BABY CAMERA	$40-$155
FOSCOM	F19821P	$65
GARMIN	babyCAM	$200-$350
IBABY	M6	$180
INFANT OPTICS	DXR-5	$99
	DXR-8	$170
LEVANA	ALEXA	$130
	WILLOW	$230
	ARIA	$190
MOTOROLA	MBP36S	$159
NEST	NEST CAM	$200
PHILIPS	DIGITAL VIDEO MONITOR	$130
	AVENT UGROW	$200
SAMSUNG	BRIGHTVIEW	$200
	SIMPLEVIEW	$170
SUMMER	BABYTOUCH DIGITAL	$ 60
	PANORAMA	$170
	WIDE VIEW 2.0	$150
VTECH	SAFE & SOUND VM343	$180
	SAFE & SOUND VM981	$200
	SAFE & SOUND VM311	$75
WITHINGS	THE HOME	$154

Flaws but not deal breakers. Nest cam isn't a perfect solution as a baby monitor. Here are some flaws:

Parent unit, or lack there of. The lack of a dedicated parent unit is probably the biggest problem with Nest Cam. Even if you have an old iPhone or iPod Touch lying around, using this unit as a parent monitor has issues. The biggest: battery drain. Streaming HD video basically requires the iPhone to be plugged in for overnight monitoring. There also isn't a voice-activated mode or way to turn off the screen and still listen to the audio with the Dropcam app—once you put the screen to

---

✔= Yes

PTZ: Point/tilt/zoom feature.

MONITOR: Included display monitor. Models without a monitor are intended to stream to a smartphone or tablet.

STREAM: Can the monitor stream video online?

PTZ	MONITOR	STREAM	OUR RATING
OPTIONAL		✔	C-
✔		✔	D
	✔		C-
✔		✔	D
	✔		A
✔	✔		A
	✔		C
✔	✔		C
✔	✔		C
✔	✔		F
		✔	A
	✔		B
	✔	✔	B
✔	✔		B-
	✔		B-
✔	✔		C-
✔	✔	✔	C-
✔	✔		C-
✔	✔		B
	✔	✔	B
	✔		B
		✔	D

monitors

sleep, it will cut the audio as well. One tip: turn down the screen brightness of your iPhone (in settings) during the night.

The strength of your WiFi signal can be an issue for the Nest Cam. The closer your router is to the camera, the better. That could be an issue if your router is in a basement and the nursery is on the second floor of your home.

Signal dropouts. While using the Nest app or streaming the video to a browser, we notice occasionally the signal can drop out. We'd say this happens more watching the video feed on WiFi on a smartphone, but occasionally a browser video feed (connected via Ethernet) can drop as well. When the signal drops, the app searches for a second or two and then reconnects.

Signal booster may be needed. If your WiFi router is a long distance from the nursery, you may need to buy a repeater-this can add another $30 to $50.

Expensive cloud storage. The cloud storage feature is nice but expensive (adding another $100 a year if you want to store the last ten days worth of videos).

More on BabyBargains.com

We review 15 baby video monitor brands on our web site, including Summer, Levana and Motorola.

Best Audio Baby Monitor

Sure, they are old school but for many parents, audio baby monitors are just the ticket. That's because even with no scientific training, you as a new parent will be able to discern your baby's cries (*I'm hungry!* sounds different from *I'm sick!*). No HD video picture necessary.

Bonus: audio monitors cost a fraction of video monitors. Here's our shopping advice.

7 Things No One Tells You About Buying An Audio Monitor!

1 HACKING ALERT: SOME AUDIO MONITORS ARE VULNERABLE TO EAVESDROPPING. You may have seen stories over the last few years about strangers being able to hack into baby monitors. Pretty creepy, we know. But remember this: an audio monitor is made up of a transmitter (the base unit in baby's room) and a receiver (kept in your room). Yes, you are basically putting a microphone in your baby's room. Anyone with another baby monitor on the same frequency could pick up conversations and sounds on your baby monitor.

The take home message: many baby monitors do not encrypt their transmission. Therefore the best advice is to remember that your house (or at least your baby's room) is bugged. If you want to protect your privacy, don't have any sensitive conversations within earshot of the baby monitor. You never know who might be listening. It is wise to turn OFF the baby monitor when baby isn't in the room.

So are there any monitors that are private? Until recently, the answer was no. But there is good news: several models feature "digital" (DECT) technology—their signals can't be intercepted, unlike older analog monitors. Both monitors we recommend use DECT.

2 BABY MONITORS EAT BATTERIES. Most baby monitors have the option of running on batteries or regular current (by plugging it into a wall outlet). Our advice: use the wall outlet as often as possible. Batteries don't last long—as little as eight to ten hours with continual use.

Another idea: you can buy another AC adapter for $10 or less—you can leave one AC adapter in your bedroom and have another one available in a different part of the house. (Warning: make sure you get the correct AC adapter for your monitor, in terms of voltage and polarity. Otherwise you can fry the monitor. One tip: get a universal adapter like the Velleman PSSMV1USA, $14.50.)

By the way, when shopping for an audio monitor, consider buying a model with a low battery indicator. Without that feature, your monitor could die with no warning (and you wondered why baby was so quiet!). Only a handful of monitors have low battery indicators. Both models we recommend on this page have low battery alerts.

3 INTERFERENCE ISSUES CAN HAMPER YOUR BABY MONITOR, thanks to all the gadgets in your house: WiFi routers, cell phones and other electronics.

Let's talk baby monitor frequencies and interference (geek alert: fun terms like megahertz will be used in the next paragraph).

Baby Monitor 101: the higher the frequency, the longer the range of the monitor. Basic baby monitors work on the 49 MHz frequency—these will work for a few hundred feet. Step up to a 900 MHz monitor and you can double the distance the monitor will work (some makers claim up to 1000 feet). Finally, there are baby monitors that work on the 2.4 GHz frequency, where you can pick up your baby in Brazil. Okay, not that far, but you get the idea. Of course, "range" estimates are just that—your real-life range will probably be much less than what's touted on the box.

Now here's the rub: Wi-Fi networks and cordless phones can often interfere with your baby monitor.

Wi-Fi routers work on the 2.4 GHz band—yep, the same frequency used by some baby audio monitors. FYI: Baby VIDEO monitors work on either the 900 MHz or 2.4 GHz frequencies and can have the same interference issues as audio monitors. Even if your router doesn't cause a problem, you neighbor's ten year old Linksys router may.

As we mentioned earlier, newer digital or DECT monitors, which work in the 1.9 GHz range, are a solution to many interference troubles. Since very few other electronics operate on this band, DECT monitors are virtually interference-free and work at even longer range than 2.4 GHz monitors. (Both of our recommended audio baby monitors are DECT).

So, to sum up, here is our advice: always keep the receipt. Baby monitors have one of the biggest complaint rates of all products we review.

We suspect all the electronic equipment in people's homes today (cell phones, Wi-Fi routers, large-screen TVs the size of a Sony Jumbotron), not to mention all the interference sources near your home (cell phone towers, etc.) must account for some of the problems folks have with baby monitors. Common complaints include static, lack of range, buzzing and worse—and those problems can happen with a baby monitor in any price range.

4 OUT OF RANGE INDICATORS ARE HELPFUL. If you plan to wander from the house and visit your garden, you may want to go for a monitor that warns you when you've strayed too far from its transmitter. Some models have a visual out of range indicator, while others beep at you. Of course, even if your monitor doesn't offer this feature, you'll probably realize when you're out of range—the background noise you hear in your home will disappear from the receiver.

5 **INTERCOMS ARE A NICE FEATURE TO CONSIDER.** More and more baby monitors are adding intercom features, enabling two-way talk between the transmitter and receiver.

Why is that helpful? Let's say you're breastfeeding your baby in the nursery. You're thirsty . . . or hungry or any of a hundred things. Wouldn't it be nice to buzz your partner to bring you a glass of water. Or perhaps your baby is alone in the room and awake, but you don't want to run in immediately to sooth her. You could talk to your baby on the intercom or sing a song, which might help her settle down.

6 **AUDIO BABY MONITORS ARE A SIGNIFICANT SAVINGS OVER VIDEO MONITORS.** At $50, an audio baby monitor is such a deal compared to a video monitor, which typically are $100+. And you don't have to see a picture of a crying baby to realize you'll need to check up on your child–you just need to hear it.

Video baby monitors are a gadget . . . fun, but not necessary for most folks. Think of video monitors as a pacifier for parents, especially nervous first-timers (we know, we were there too!). In most cases, however, a simple audio monitor will do the trick. Experienced parents will tell you that you don't need to see a picture of baby to know someone needs attention! You'll soon recognize your baby's cries just with the audio alone. Trust us.

7 **SKIP THE FRILLS.** You don't need a temperature gauge on your audio baby monitor— besides they aren't very accurate. A basic room thermometer/hygrometer (which monitors temp and humidity) costs less than $10 and will be far more accurate than your baby monitor. Just as you want a nursery at a comfortable temp (not too warm or too cool), you also should monitor humidity. The ideal range is about 40%.

Same goes for a nightlight—it isn't necessary to spend extra for a baby monitor with night light. Simple night lights with dawn to dusk sensors run $12 for four night lights (that's only $3 each), like the one pictured above.

The Best Audio Baby Monitor

After researching and reviewing ten different baby audio monitor brands for quality (can you hear me now?) and durability, we pick the **VTech Safe & Sound Digital Audio Monitor** as the best audio baby monitor.

VTech's affordable Safe & Sound Digital Audio Monitor DM221 ($30 single, $50 double) has 6.0 DECT technology for a secure, interference-free signal. This monitor is loaded with features (intercom, vibrating sound alert, rechargeable batteries with low battery alert and more). It is the best of the audio bunch, in our opinion. Range is rated to 1000 feet (your mileage may vary).

VTech is probably best-known for their cordless phones and interactive toys. In recents years, they entered the baby monitoring market with well received audio and video models.

Parent feedback has been very positive—it's clear VTech's successful track record in cordless phones is a major help here with the technology. The few criticisms we heard from parents centered on the range being less than the stated 1000 feet (that's probably a given for most monitors, sorry to say).

VTech claims 18 hour battery life for this unit, which sounds like a stretch since most folks say it barely lasts a night. For night-time monitoring, we'd suggest leaving this unit plugged in, instead of running off batteries.

While we recommend this monitor, we should note we have received occasional reports from readers about defective VTech units. One reader said the quality of the monitor was excellent, but the battery on his unit would not hold a charge. Others report monitors that don't link properly. As with all monitors, we'd recommend purchasing this unit from a store or site that has a decent return policy just in case.

Also Great: Philips Avent SCD560/10

The ***Philips Avent SCD560/10*** ($94)
features DECT digital technology to stop
interference and eavesdropping. The
SCD510 also has rechargeable batteries,
out-of-range indicator and intercom feature. There is also a low battery alert.

The only bummer: it doesn't have a double receiver option.
Quality is very good.

Our readers universally praise this model. But the high price
(three times that of the top pick above) tempers our praise.

Smart Baby Monitors: Not Ready for Prime Time

New "smart monitors" that watch your baby's vital signs have
debuted to some fanfare in recent years. These wearables
(socks, t-shirts, diaper sensors) monitor baby and are connected
to smartphones. If baby's biometrics (pulse rate, respiration,
blood oxygen, etc.) drop below a certain level, an alarm goes
off on your smartphone.

So which one should you get? None of the above. A 2017
review of these gadgets in the *Journal of the American Medical
Association* found no scientific evidence they work.

"These devices are marketed aggressively to parents of
healthy babies, promising peace of mind about their child's car-
diorespiratory health," pediatrician Dr. Christopher P. Bonafide,
with the Children's Hospital of Philadelphia, told the
Consumerist web site. "But there is no evidence that these consumer infant physiological monitors are life-saving or even accurate, and these products may cause unnecessary fear, uncertain-
ty and self-doubt in parents."

That's right—instead of giving parents piece of mind, smart
monitors most likely cause a myriad of false alarms that make
parenting even more stressful than it already is.

Bottom line: save your money and skip the smart monitors.

Safety: The Best Gates & More Safety Advice

Your baby's safety is Job #1 as a parent. So let's take a look at baby proofing your home.

7 Things No One Tells You About Buying A Safety Gate and Other Safety Tips!

1 **DON'T WAIT UNTIL YOUR BABY "ALMOST" DOES SOMETHING DANGEROUS BEFORE YOU BABY PROOF YOUR HOME.** Babies grow up so fast! In the blink of an eye your bundle of joy is calmly sitting in the middle of the living room sucking her fingers (or a toy, whatever). Next thing you know, she's scaling furniture and trying to make a run for it out an open door.

Of course, every baby is different, so let's talk typical milestones. Let's review how fast your baby will grow:

Rolls over: 2 to 4.5 months.
Stands holding onto something: 5 to 10 months.
Walks holding on to furniture (cruisers): 7.5 to 12.5 months.
Walks alone: 11 to 14.5 months

Yes, you read correctly: before you know it, your baby is standing, cruising and walking. And Murphy's Law of baby safety says your baby's attraction to anything is directly proportional to how dangerous it is.

So get down on your hands and knees and crawl through your home just like your baby will. Check for hazards like hanging lamp cords, blind cords, open electrical sockets, easy to climb items, anything you can think of that will attract babies. Then baby proof them all! See our top safety must haves later in this chapter.

2 **IF YOU'RE CONFUSED ABOUT WHICH TYPE OF SAFETY GATES YOU NEED, YOU'RE NOT ALONE.** Yes, there are several types of safety gates on the market. Pressure safety gates are the most common. These gates are sized slightly larger than a door or stair opening and then squeezed into the space using a spring to create pressure. The problem? They can be pushed over, especially by a large toddler or pet. This makes a pressure gate at the top of the stairs a no-no.

To solve the stair dilemma, we recommend hard-mounted gates at the top of staircases. These have a frame that is permanently attached to the walls or stair banisters with screws. Then there is a swinging gate with a parent activated latch so you can get up or down the stairs.

Of course, one size doesn't fit all when it comes to safety gates. Options to consider are swinging openings on pressure gates, taller gates, wider gates or extensions for wide openings, and new fabrications such as wood and wood/metal combinations.

Yes, all the extras cost money; a basic wood or plastic pressure gate to seal off a dining room sells for as little as $10, while a hard mounted stair gate with stained wood and black metal spindles runs nearly $80. Extra wide gates can be over $100.

3 **DON'T OVERLOOK THE BOTTOM OF THE STAIRS.** That's right, you'll need a gate for the bottom of your stairs too. We recommend you place the bottom gate two steps up from the landing. Why? This way your baby can practice climbing stairs, with little chance of injury.

4 **MAKE SURE THE HARD-MOUNTED GATE HAS A STOP PIN FOR SAFETY.** A stop pin keeps the gate from swinging over open stairs. Our choice for best safety gate, the KidCo Safeway, has this feature.

5 **GATES ARE FOR MORE THAN STAIRS.** Gates and barriers are important to keep kids out of fireplaces, pet rooms and laundry rooms, to name a few. And don't forget window barriers. You can still have fresh air without worrying your baby will fall out the window if you use window guards. Don't worry— we'll give you recommendations for all this shortly.

6 **IF YOU'RE RENTING, STILL USE THE HARD MOUNTED GATES.** I know what you're thinking: my landlord is going to kill me if I attach a hard mounted gate on my stairs. We understand, but this is for your baby's safety. Patching walls and wood is actually simple; you can find simple how to videos on YouTube.

7 **UP NEXT, LET'S REVIEW OUR TOP 11 SAFETY MUST-HAVES FOR YOUR HOME.**

safety gates

Top 11 Safety Must Haves

To sum up, here's our list of top safety items to have for your home (in no particular order).

◆ *Fire extinguishers* rated "ABC," for any type of fire.

◆ *Outlet covers.*

◆ *Baby monitor*—unless your house or apartment is very small, and you don't think it will be useful.

◆ *Smoke alarms.* The best smoke alarms have two systems for detecting fires—a photoelectric sensor for early detection of smoldering fires and a dual chamber ionization sensor for early detection of flaming fires. An example of this is the First Alert "Double Sensor" ($25 to $60). We'd recommend one smoke alarm for every bedroom, plus main hallways, basement and living rooms. And don't forget to replace the batteries twice a year. Both smoke alarms and carbon monoxide detectors can be found in warehouse clubs like Sam's and Costco at low prices or in Home Depot or Lowes home improvement stores.

◆ *Carbon monoxide detectors.* These special detectors sniff out dangerous carbon monoxide (CO) gas, which can result from a malfunctioning furnace. Put one CO detector in your baby's room and another in the main hallway of your home.

◆ *Cabinet and drawer locks.* For cabinets and drawers containing harmful cleaning supplies or utensils like knives, these are an essential investment. For playtime, designate at least one unsecured cabinet or drawer as "safe" and stock it with items safe for baby.

◆ *Spout cover for tub.*

◆ *Bath thermometer or anti-scald device.*

◆ *Toilet locks*—so your baby doesn't visit the Tidy Bowl Man. One of the best we've seen in years is KidCo's toilet lock ($18), an award-winning gizmo that does the trick. Check their web site at kidcoinc.com for a store that carries it.

◆ *Baby gates.* Recommendations are coming up next!

◆ *Furniture wall straps.* Since 2000, over 100 deaths have been caused by TV's and furniture tipping over onto kids. We recommend you anchor all your large furniture to the wall, especially shelves and dressers in baby's room. Once your child becomes a climber, she'll climb anything, so be prepared.

The Best Safety Gate for Stairs

After researching and reviewing over 20 safety gates, we pick the ***KidCo Safeway Gate*** ($43) as the best safety gate for hard mounting to the top of the stairs or anywhere you want to block baby's access.

The gate comes in a few different versions: straight ($43 to $45, available in black or white metal) as well as angled to fit all types of stairs. The angled version is a bit more expensive and comes in metal ($53, black or white), wood ($73, three color options) or wood and steel ($73 to $78, three wood colors, black steel bars).

These gates work on openings from 24 3/4" to 42.5". If you have an extra wide opening, KidCo also offers an extension for angled gates–you can buy a 10" extension for $26. The gate has one hand operation for adults plus quick release hardware if you need to remove the barrier completely. One key quality feature: a stop pin that prevent the gate from swinging out over the stairs. Plus there is no bottom threshold to trip on (as with many pressure mount gates). The gate can also be easily removed if needed.

Reader feedback on this gate is very positive, with fans loving the ease of installation and small footprint (when open, it doesn't restrict the stairway).

Yes, KidCo also makes pressure mount gates of similar quality, which can be used for gate off areas other than stairs.

safety gates

The Best Pressure Safety Gate

While we prefer hard-mounted gates for areas like stairs, pressure mounts gates do have a purpose—they are best at blocking access to rooms that may have baby hazards (like a laundry room).

For this, we would recommend the ***Regalo Easy Step Walk Thru Gate*** pressure gate.

This gate has a one-hand opening for adults with an additional safety lock and fits in doorways between 29″ and 39″ wide. Made of steel, it comes in white and includes a 6″ extension kit. For added strength, they include additional wall suction cups. The Easy Step is priced at $32 for the 30″ tall version. We judged the build and overall quality of Regalo's pressure gates to be the best on the market.

Other versions are available including an extra tall model (41″). Regalo also sells extensions of 4″, 6″, 12″ and 24″. While the gate is popular, some parents note it's easy to mis-install it, then wrongly conclude it's defective. Folks we interviewed recommend reading the directions carefully before trying to install it. Once they got the hang of the install, readers said they loved the gate.

Also Great: Evenflo's Soft and Wide Gate

Evenflo's Soft and Wide Gate ($40) is 20″ tall and expands from 38″ to 60″ wide—perfect for funky openings you need to gate. Mesh lets baby see through the gate. However, this gate isn't designed to be set-up and removed frequently, in our opinion—it is better to set it up and have the adults walk over it to access the non-baby zone.

Best Play Yard Gate

This style of gate is designed to keep baby in, not out of an area. Set up in a hexagon (or octagon), play yard gates are best for babies who aren't walking but in the cute "sitting there and crawling phase." Once a baby can stand, they may be able to exert enough pressure to push over a play yard gate.

The North States Superyard XT Gate Play Yard is our pick as the best play yard gate. It is an expandable panel system (six, $53; or eight panels, $101) that is 26″ high and provides a play area of 18.5 square feet. A two-panel extension kit ($30) provides even more area.

Some readers tell us they use this to protect large Christmas trees from toddlers. Yes, it is all plastic, but it is durable enough to corral babies who are crawling. A few parents say it is hard to open and close the gate (the hinges are tight), but overall, readers give this play yard solution a thumbs up.

Best Fireplace Hearth Gate

A fireplace is an obvious place baby doesn't need to visit—but how do you protect it? **KidCo's Auto Close HearthGate**

safety gates

($136) is pricey but does the trick, in our testing. It is 29.95" tall and works on hearths six feet wide by two feet deep; extensions are available for bigger openings. The HearthGate also includes a walk-through gate that closes automatically.

Best Window Guard

An often over-looked area of baby proofing, window guards are important if you open windows for fresh air.

Here's the best window guard we found in our research: **Guardian Angel**. The company sells affordable metal window guards that fit just about any type of window ($76 for a four-bar gate that can extend from 35-58). Guardian Angel window gates are hardware mounted.

Yes, these are a must for low windows your toddler can access or if you live in a high-rise condo building. Remember babies can climb furniture and access windows you think are safe— keep them locked or install a window guard.

Also Great: KidCo Mesh Window Guard

KidCo's Mesh Window Guard ($32) is a good choice in case you don't want metal bars over your windows.

Great for travel: the **Super Stopper** from Parent Units ($15, below) is a simple device that suctions on a window, preventing it from opening too far to let a toddler out. Perfect for grandma's house or that Airbnb rental.

The Best Baby Thermometer: Rectal

We know what you're thinking—really? Yes, the recommended way to take a baby's (under one year of age) temperature is with a rectal thermometer. Welcome to parenthood.

Let's consult our sister book, *Baby 411* for more on this:

"Most parents cringe just thinking about this task. Are you cringing? Don't. Babies really don't mind. It does not hurt or make them feel like you've invaded their space. In fact, it's a good trick to make them poop. But I digress.

Rectal temperatures are the most accurate way to check a human's body temperature. And for infants under three months of age, one tenth of a degree will make the difference between whether you stay at home in your nice warm bed or head out for an evening of fun at your local emergency room.

If you call the doctor at 2 am and tell her that your six week old has a fever, the first thing she will ask is, "How did you take the temperature?" If you took it any way other than rectally, we make you get a rectal thermometer and call us back. Invest in one now—digital rectal thermometers cost $10 to $20.

FYI: after one year of age, there is more flexibility about how to take your child's temperature. Trendy products on the market for toddler temperatures include a pacifier thermometer, ear thermometer, temporal artery scanners, and plastic skin stickers. Using an oral thermometer in the armpit is also okay. None of these are as accurate as a rectal temperature. But after a year of age, the actual degree of fever is much less important to making a management plan for your child. That is, a child with 101 or 103 is managed based on the other symptoms they have in addition to the fever."

So which one to get? After comparing and testing more than 15 different thermometers, we picked the **Vicks Baby Rectal Thermometer** ($11) as the best rectal thermometer for babies. It is easy to use and designed with a short probe to make sure it isn't inserted too far.

The Vicks Baby Rectal Thermometer is intended only for use as a rectal thermometer. It reads out the temp in only ten seconds, making it impressively fast. Readers tell us this thermometer is also very accurate when compared with a hospital grade thermometer and at $11, it's affordable.

Best Baby Thermometer: Oral & Underarm

The **Veridian Healthcare's VTemp Digital Thermometer** ($5) is both affordable and accurate. It takes oral, underarm and rectal temps.

In case you skipped this discussion earlier, we only recommend using oral or underarm thermometers after one year of age. Because fever in babies under one year can be significantly more dangerous than in babies over one, pediatricians prefer parents use a rectal thermometer for the most accurate reading.

After one year of age, any temperature (taken orally or underarm) of over 100° F should be considered a fever reported to your child's doctor.

Best High Tech Baby Thermometer

If you'd like to track your baby's temperature on a phone app, the **Kinsa Smart Thermometer** ($15) does just that—the thermometer plugs into your headphone port on your iOS or Android phone. Since it is powered by your phone, there are no batteries to replace.

We found the Kinsa to be accurate and the app well designed. If your child has multiple illnesses (or you have more than one baby), the app helps keep track of all that, including medications. Accuracy on the Kinsa is excellent.

A few caveats: yes, the Kinsa now works with the latest iPhone (7) even though it lacks that headphone jack—but you have to follow rather specific install instructions on their web site. The Kinsa is easier to set up with earlier iPhones (versions 4 to 6).

Also: the Kinsa app only works in the United States (sorry, Canada and the UK).

Next: let's talk car seats for your little one!

CHAPTER 7

CAR SEATS

Car Seats: Picking the right child safety seat

Inside this chapter

What's the best car seat for your baby? What is the difference between an infant, convertible or booster seat? We'll discuss these answers, as well as detailed recommendations for each car seat type!

Let's talk child passenger safety—it's come a long way! Here's what car seat safety looked like in the 1960's:

Yes, that is basically a toddler with a pillow lying flat on an auto seat with a lap seat belt. What could go wrong?

Early car seats were just a way to corral babies from wandering around the vehicle—any straps/belts were minimal. While strollers have been around for centuries, it wasn't until 1978 that the first law was passed to mandate car seat use (trivia note: Tennessee was the first state to require usage).

Despite rapid advances in car seat technology, motor vehicle accidents still injure 121,000 kids under age 12 each year (National Center for Injury Prevention and Control, Centers for Disease Control and Prevention, August 2016). And the government estimates 59% of car seats are not used correctly (NHTSA, 2015 study).

So our goal in this chapter is to help you pick out the best car seat to keep your new baby safe. A key point to remember: the best seat for your child is the one that correctly fits your child's weight and size—and can be correctly installed in your vehicle. Even the most expensive car seats ($500!) are dangerous if they aren't installed correctly . . . or are the wrong size for your baby.

Let's start at the beginning: infant car seats.

The Best Infant Car Seats

The Great Wall of Car Seats at your local baby store sure looks intimidating. Car seat 101: there are three basic types of car seats: infant, convertible and booster. In this section, we're focusing on infant car seats.

7 Things No One Tells You About Buying an Infant Car Seat

1 YOUR BABY MIGHT OUTGROW THAT INFANT SEAT LONG BEFORE THEY HIT THE WEIGHT LIMIT. That's because infants grow so fast, they may out grow the seat by height long before weight. Bottom line: don't fret if you don't get the infant seat with the biggest weight limit—we generally recommend a seat with a 30 or 35 pound limit. A seat with a 22 lb. limit is also ok, if your newborn will be average in size at birth.

Even though your baby may outgrow their infant car seat early, that doesn't end rear-facing car seat use. The American Academy of Pediatrics recommends keeping your baby rear facing till two years of age (or as long as possible). While you can use a convertible car seat for both rear and forward facing installation, infant car seats are designed especially for babies and only babies. They often have features (newborn inserts and reclining bases) that fit small ones best. Which leads us to tip #2:

2 THE SAFEST INFANT CAR SEAT IS THE ONE THAT FITS YOUR CAR AND YOUR BABY PLUS IS THE SIMPLEST TO INSTALL CORRECTLY. Unfortunately, surveys reveal that as many as 59% of car seats are not used correctly. Either they are mis-installed or mis-adjusted. So a car seat that is EASY TO USE is safer than one that isn't, in our opinion. A key feature to look at: how easy is it to adjust and tighten the harness as baby grows? We tend to favor no rethread harnesses, enabling you to change the HEIGHT of the harness without rethreading the belts.

3 **CURVE BALL: STROLLER COMPATIBILITY.** Ever since the first "travel system" (stroller + infant car seat = travel system) debuted in the mid 90's, the calculus of an infant car seat purchase included this question: which strollers is that car seat compatible with? Sure, Brand X's infant car seats work with Brand X strollers. But then Brand Y strollers adds an adapter for Brand X infant car seat. And now things just got more complex.

Bottom line: some infant car seats are more cross compatible than others. The biggest infant car seat sellers, Graco and Chicco, probably have the most compatability. On the upper end, Maxi Cosi works with most upper-end strollers. (And Maxi Cosi uses the same adapters as Nuna and Cybex. Oy!).

Other infant car seats have much more limited compatibility. Example: the UPPAbaby Mesa infant seat works with the UPPAbaby Cruz and Vista strollers . . . and that's about it. So you better like the UPPAbaby stroller line if you are going with the UPPAbaby Mesa infant car seat. See our web page for a run-down of infant car seat adapters.

4 **NECESSARY FEATURE: SIDE IMPACT PROTECTION.** Nearly one in four (24%) car crashes are side impact—and these can be deadly for children in the back seat. Of all child fatalities in car crashes, side impact crashes account for 32% of deaths. Protecting a child's head is crucial to surviving a side impact crash, as that is the most vulnerable area to injury.

FYI: First, understand that there is no federal safety standard for side impact protection. Seats are tested in FRONT crashes only. Some manufacturers test for side impact protection, but there is no way to verify claims that one seat outdoes another on side impact protection. The government has proposed a side impact test standard, but as of this writing, there is no date yet for the start of such testing.

Of course, all infant seats provide some side impact protection—those that go the extra mile have extra cushions near the baby's head (example: Graco's Safety Surround, Safety 1st's Air Protect) to distribute energy away. Some makers (Cybex) use a telescoping arm on the side of the car seat to add further protection.

Again, there is no current standard to judge these claims. Note: the safest place for your child's car seat is in the middle of the back seat. The middle of the back seat is farther away from a side impact collision than an outboard position and therefore safer. Picking a vehicle with rear-curtain air bags is also helpful—most newer model cars offer these type of air bags.

infant car seats

5 **NICE IF YOU CAN AFFORD IT: ANTI-REBOUND BARS.** Some of the more expensive infant car seats feature anti-rebound bars. As the name implies, this keeps the seat from rebounding and hitting the back of the vehicle seat in an accident. Anti-rebound bars aren't required in the US and seats that don't have them still must meet minimum crash test standards. We'll probably see more of these bars in the future, but for now they are only seen in the priciest seats.

Is an anti-rebound bar a must? No—seats without them are still safe. The anti-rebound bar just adds an ADDITIONAL layer of safety. If you can afford a seat with an anti-rebound bar like the Maxi-Cosi Mico Max 30 (pictured), great. If not, don't sweat it.

6 **ALSO NICE IF YOU CAN AFFORD IT: LOAD LEGS.** More common on European car seats than seen in North America, "load legs" are metal bars that extend from an infant car seat to the floor of the vehicle. In a collision, these legs absorb energy and keep an infant seat from rotating backwards.

As of this writing, only a handful of car seats in the U.S. have this feature. Example: the Nuna Pipa, Cybex Aton2/AtonQ/Aton Cloud Q and the GB Asana 35 DLX/AP.

If you have a long commute and do a lot of highway driving, an infant seat with a load leg may make sense.

7 **NICE BUT NOT NECESSARY: PREMIUM LATCH CONNECTORS.** LATCH stands for Lower Anchors and Tethers for Children. LATCH is built into all vehicles manufactured since September 2002 and is a universal way to attach a car seat to a vehicle without using the vehicle belt. Note: LATCH isn't safer to use than the auto safety belt—it's just an alternative method.

Infant car seats come with two LATCH connectors, which attach to anchors in the seat back. The least expensive infant car seats have basic LATCH connectors that are hooks (bottom). The more expensive options have "premium" LATCH connectors, which have push buttons (top). Some folks think push button versions are easier to attach to the anchor. Are they nice to have? Yes. Necessary? No. If you plan to frequently move your car seat between vehicles, premium LATCH may be worth it.

The Best Infant Car Seat (Overall)

After researching and reviewing 34 different infant car seats, we pick the ***Chicco KeyFit 30*** ($200 on Amazon) as the best infant car seat.

Crash protection for the Chicco KeyFit 30 is excellent, with added side impact protection making a difference.

The KeyFit gets high scores from our readers on ease of use—installation is a snap and adjusting the harness is easy. The seat also features EPS foam and a newborn insert.

The KeyFit 30 scores an astonishing 90% approval rating on Amazon (4 and 5 star reviews), with those reviews verified as legit via FakeSpot. (Few infant seats have ratings above even 80%, much less 90%).

The downsides? The seat lacks a no-rethread harness and the canopy coverage is somewhat skimpy.

FYI: Chicco makes four versions of the KeyFit—one that works to 22 lbs. (called the KeyFit, $180) and three that go to 30 lbs. (the KeyFit 30, KeyFit 30 Zip and KeyFit 30 Magic.) Here's a quick overview of the three 30 lb. limit versions:

◆ ***The Chicco KeyFit 30 ($200).*** The basic version described above.
◆ ***The Chicco KeyFit 30 Zip ($230).*** Adds a quick-remove machine-washable seat pad, a zip-off canopy, zip on visor and zip-around boot. These are nice add-ons if you can afford the upgrade; the boot especially is welcome if you have a winter baby or live in a cold climate.
◆ ***The Chicco KeyFit 30 Magic ($220).*** Basically the same as the Zip but without the zippers. The Magic has upgraded fabrics over the Zip, even though it is ten bucks less.

infant car seats

In 2017, Chicco debuted a new version of the KeyFit: the Fit2 ($280). The Fit2's unique feature is a base that has two stages: a reclined version for infants and a toddler position that sits more upright, so the seat can be used up to age two (35 lbs.). Also new: an anti-rebound bar and a seven-position no rethread harness.

Between all these versions, we like the base model Chicco KeyFit 30 best . . . unless you live in Chicago and have a January birth. Then by all means, go for the Magic or Zip with the boot! If money is tight, the 22 lb. version (KeyFit, $180) would be ok if you know your child will be around normal birth weight—keep in mind they will likely outgrow that infant seat sooner than those with the 30 lb. limit seats. FYI: the same base works with either the 22 lb. or the 30 lb. carriers.

We do like the Fit2, based on our initial evaluation. Given Chicco's track record, we expect this seat to be an excellent option, but it is so new as of press time that we have little parent feedback yet.

Whichever version you choose, all Chicco KeyFits boast a nice list of features: a seat lined with EPS foam for improved side impact protection, thick seat padding, multi-position canopy and comfort grip handle.

Chicco hired a former Graco engineer (who worked on the SnugRide) to design the KeyFit and it shows in the details . . . the base has a "single-pull" LATCH adjustment, a spring-loaded, leveling foot to account for uneven back seats and even a smooth underside to keep from damaging your back seat upholstery.

As you'd expect from Chicco, the fashion of this seat has a hint of Italian flair and there is even a newborn insert to better fit smaller newborns and preemies.

Our readers have been very positive about the KeyFit's ease of use, lauding the no-twist, easy-to-adjust straps, the ability to leave the handle in the "up" position when driving (most seats require it to be lowered), and overall ease of installation.

Flaws but not deal breakers. Well, no seat is perfect. Here are our quibbles with the KeyFit 30:

◆ The KeyFit carrier weighs 9.4 lbs., a tad heavier than other similar seats. It takes two hands to release/rotate the handle on the seat.
◆ The sunshade has its share of critics. Some readers tell us they think it is too small and doesn't offer enough cover-

age (even with the extended visor that tucks away when not in use). When you fold the canopy back, it sometimes is hard to reach the handle to release the car seat from the base—especially if you drive a smaller vehicle where the front seats are close.

◆ A few readers also report the fabric doesn't breathe, so the seat can get hot.

The Chicco's stroller compatibility used to be an issue, but given the soaring sales of the KeyFit, more brands now offer adapters that fit the seat. Still, it might be wise to check to see if the stroller brand you want has a specific adapter for the KeyFit . . . a few smaller stroller brands still don't.

Also Great: Britax B-SAFE 35 Elite

The **Britax B-SAFE 35 Elite** is also a good pick, especially if you are a fan of Britax strollers (which naturally work with the B-SAFE without any additional adapters). Price: $200, about the same as Chicco KeyFit 30.

FYI: There are currently two different versions of the B-SAFE— the B-SAFE 35 and B-SAFE 35 Elite. (The original B- SAFE that worked to 30 lbs. is now discontinued).

Both the B-SAFE 35 ($168) and 35 Elite ($200) work to 35 lbs. However, the two models are quite distinct so here's the rundown.

The big headline on the B-SAFE 35 is Britax's improved crash protection (which Britax calls SafeCell, a system seen on its convertible seats). The seat features a deep shell that is lined with EPP foam for additional protection in side impact crashes. The basic B-SAFE 35 has two crotch strap positions and four harness heights (sorry, you have to rethread the harness to change the harness height on the B-SAFE 35 model).

One of the B-SAFE's key features is a "removable comfort pillow" that better fits smaller newborns and preemies (as small as four pounds). The adjustable base has five positions and built-in lock-offs to help with belt installation. You also get premium LATCH connectors and an excellent oversized canopy.

How is the B-SAFE 35 Elite different? This models adds additional side impact protection and a no-rethread harness (Quick-Adjust). The Elite also has an easier to remove cover for cleaning (hand washing only, unfortunately).

Flaws but not deal breakers. So what's not to like about the B-SAFE seats? We've seen scattered reports from parents who say their babies outgrew their B-SAFE's too quickly . . . the deep and narrow seat was too tight for bigger babies. We wonder if the seat criticisms are the flip side of the enhanced side impact protection—Britax's B-SAFE 35 Elite looks more narrow because it is deeper than comparable seats and the head wings (side impact protection) make it look narrower. But here are the specs: the 35 Elite is 16" deep (compare that to the Chicco KeyFit's 14.5" depth) and 9" wide (versus Chicco's 9.75").

So, yes, the Britax seat is 7.6% narrower than the KeyFit, but visually it seems more confining than the specs indicate. Yes, we can see how babies that are at the top of the weight/height chart might outgrow the seat well before they hit 35 pounds. But that's probably the exception.

Other negatives: the B-SAFE seats lack anti-rebound bars or load legs seen on other premium seats (the Cybex Aton, for example). And the carriers are heavy—the Elite version is slightly over 11 lbs.; the base model is just under 11 lbs.

Another complaint: the 35 Elite harness buckle always seems to fall back into the seat when you are putting a baby in. This isn't fun, since you have to fish out the buckle underneath a baby's bum every time you use it! Again, we think the deeper seat depth plays a role here. (Britax could add buckle holders on the side of the seat to remedy this issue; that would be a nice future improvement).

Despite these complaints, real world feedback on the B-SAFE has been generally positive. Most parents praise the seat as easy to install and use; the quality is excellent.

One major consideration for this seat: stroller compatibility. If you are getting a Britax stroller, then the B-SAFE would be a no-brainer. As for compatibility with other strollers, well, that's going to be hit and miss (mostly miss). Fewer strollers are compatible with Britax's infant seat, compared with Graco and Chicco.

Best Budget-Friendly Infant Car Seat

The $160 **Graco SnugRide Click Connect 35 LX** is part of the best-selling SnugRide family that has earned high scores from our readers for ease of use and overall quality.

Another major plus for the Snugride family: wide stroller compatibility, as most brands have Graco SnugRide adapters.

Heads up: there are SIX different versions of the SnugRide—this pick is specifically for the model Graco SnugRide Click Connect 35 LX. We like this model in particular because it adds a no rethread harness and seat belt lock-offs (which make for a tighter installation).

At $160, we think it is a great value for all these features. Most seats with a no rethread harness are over $200 and many approach $300.

FYI: Target sells an exclusive version of this seat with added side impact protection: it is called the Graco SnugRide 35 LX with Safety Surround. It is a Target exclusive for $200.

Also Great: Safety 1st Onboard 35 Air

The **Safety 1st Onboard 35 Air** is also a good bet a budget-friendly infant car seat. Running $116 to $180, this seat would make a great option for a second car. The Onboard comes with a newborn insert (works with preemies down to 4 lbs.), is lined with EPP foam  and has four harness height positions plus an adjustable base. Safety 1st's Air Protect cushions provide additional side impact

infant car seats

crash protection.

We should note that there are versions of the Onboard 35 that are less expensive and omit the belt-locks and Air Protect side impact protection. That's why we recommend the version above with the "Air" moniker.

While this seat has a huge base that can make it a problem for small car owners, overall it's a good seat. The features you get for the price are impressive.

One downside for the Safety 1st Onboard 35 Air—stroller compatibility is limited, mostly to the brand's own family of strollers. Fewer stroller brands have Safety 1st adapters compared with other seats like the Graco.

Best Infant Car Seat For Urban Parents

If you live in the urban core of a city, your criteria for an infant seat is probably different from those who live in the suburbs.

First, you may or may not have a car. That means your infant seat will have to belted into an Uber or taxi, requiring quick installation most likely without a base.

Urban parents are more likely to use their stroller to do everyday shopping, requiring an infant car seat to work natively with the stroller for the newborn months. (If you heavy are user of mass transit, we'd suggest also looking at our baby carrier section on this site—it is easier to navigate stairs down to a subway with a carrier than a stroller/infant car seat).

So here's our pick: the excellent if pricey ***Cybex Aton 2*** ($300).

The Cybex Aton 2 is the new improved version of the original Aton with an anti-rebound load leg (optional) and added side impact protection. And it does all that at an astonishingly light weight of only 8.8 lbs! (Other infant car seats can tip the scales at 11+ pounds. That may not sound like a lot, but if you are carrying an infant seat up or down stairs to your condo/apartment, you'd notice it).

The Aton2 is also compatible with most Maxi Cosi stroller adapters. That's important because most upper-end strollers with additional weather protection favored by urban parents only offer Maxi Cosi adapters (sorry Graco fans, there's often no adapter for you).

For urban parents who don't have a car but might be taking Uber or Lyft a lot, the Aton2 is easy to belt in without a base.

So what's the downside: it ain't cheap at $300 (Amazon has it at $250 as of this writing). But if you are lugging your baby around Manhattan or other urban area, it's a great, lightweight option.

The anti-rebound load leg on the base helps the Aton 2 with additional crash protection, as it protects the seat from rebounding in an accident.

If the Aton 2 isn't available, the similar Aton Q ($350-$400) is also a good bet.

What's the difference between the 2 and the Q? The Q includes a new, bigger canopy and top-of-the-line fabrics and padding.

The Q also features an enhancement to the Linear Side Impact Protection first introduced on the Aton 2. The Q now has a telescoping side impact bar for additional crash protection—yes, that is a Cybex first. The bar telescopes off the top of the carrier in whichever direction you need protection.

The Aton Q also has a no rethread harness (not available on the Aton 1 or 2) and will fit any Aton base. Yes, it is quite pricey at $350-$400. FYI: the weight of Aton Q is slightly more than the Aton 2.

More on BabyBargains.com

On our free web site, we've got reviews of 30+ infant car seats, from Maxi Cosi to UPPAbaby.

We've been rating and reviewing infant car seats since 1994. In addition to hands on inspections of infant car seats, we have also visited manufacturer facilities and met with safety regulators—and when we travel, we pay for all expenses out of own pocket. We look to our reader feedback to give us a real world perspective on car seats—our message board on car seats has 23,000 (!) threads. We also evaluate consumer reviews posted on sites like Babies R Us and Amazon.

infant car seats

INFANT SEATS

The following is a selection of better known infant car seats and how they compare on features:

MAKER	MODEL	PRICE	WEIGHT/ HEIGHT LIMITS
BABY JOGGER	CITY GO	$230	35 LBS./32" *
BABY TREND	FLEX-LOC	$70-$110	30 LBS/30"
BRITAX	B-SAFE 35	$170-$210	30 LBS./32"
	B-SAFE 35 ELITE	$200	35 LBS./32"
CHICCO	KEYFIT 30	$200	30 LBS./30"
	FIT2	$280	35 LBS./35"
CYBEX	ATON 1/2/Q/CLOUD Q	$250-$300	32 LBS./30"
EVENFLO	EMBRACE	$85-$150	35 LBS./30"
	PLATINUM LITEMAX	$150	35 LBS./32"
GB	ASANA35 DLX	$195	35 LBS./32"
GRACO	SNUGRIDE 35LX	$150-$190	32 LBS./35"
HAUCK	PROSAFE 35	$200	35 LBS./32"
MAXI COSI	MICO 30	$200	30 LBS./32"
	MICO MAX 30	$250	30 LBS./32"
	PREZI	$290	30 LBS./29"
MUV	KUSSEN	$260	32 LBS./
NUNA	PIPA	$300	32 LBS./32"
PEG PEREGO	PRIMO VIAGGIO 4.35	$300	35 LBS./30"
	PRIMO VIAGGIO 30-30	$200-$290	30 LBS./30"
PHIL & TEDS	ALPHA	$200	35 LBS/32"
RECARO	PERFORMANCE COUPE	$250	35 LBS./32"
SAFETY 1ST	ONBOARD 35 AIR	$110-$160	35 LBS./32"
SIMPLE PAR.	DOONA	$500	35 LBS./32"
UPPA BABY	MESA	$300	35 LBS./32"
URBINI	SONTI	$70-$90	35 LBS./32"

KEY

SIDE IMPACT: Does the seat have side-impact protection?
FOAM TYPE: Does the seat have a EPS or EPP foam (or none at all)? This is for crash protection; EPP foam is softer (more comfortable) than EPS.
LOAD LEG.: Does the seat have a load leg for additional crash protection?
CARRIER WEIGHT: This is the weight of the carrier only (not the base).

SIDE IMPACT	LOAD LEG	ANTI-REBOUND	BASE WIDTH	CARRIER WEIGHT	OUR RATING
◆			17.5"	10.4 LBS.	B+
			16.4	9.4	D
◆			17.5	9.8	A
◆			17.75	11.5	A
◆			17	9.4	A
◆			17	11.3	NOT YET
◆	◆	◆(ATON 2)	15	8.8	A-
			18	7.0	D+
◆			17.75	8.7	NOT YET
◆	◆		17.5	9.2	A-
			15	10.1	A
◆			14.5	10.4	B-
			16	8.7	A-
◆		◆	16	8.7	A-
◆		◆	17	11.6	C+
◆		◆	17.1	12.4	D
◆	◆		12.5	8.6	B-
◆		◆	15.5	11.1	A
◆			17.25	11.1	B+
			14.0	8.3	B
◆			15.5	9.8	D
◆			15	9.0	B
	◆	◆	15	15.5	B
◆			14.25	10.5	A-
			15.3	7.3	NOT YET

The Best Convertible Car Seat

Convertible car seats can be used for both infants and older children (most seats go up to 40 lbs., but newer models top out at 65, 70 and even 80 lbs.)—infants ride rear facing; older kids over two years of age ride facing forward. Unlike infant seats, however, most convertibles do not have snap-in bases.

So, does it make more sense to buy one car seat (that is a convertible, which you will have to buy anyway) and just skip the infant car seat? There is considerable debate on this subject. Some safety advocates think convertible car seats are safer, pointing to crash test results that show convertible seats do a better job protecting babies than infant setas. That stands to reason since convertible seats are bigger (taller, wider) than infant car seats.

Others deride infant car seats for their overuse outside of a car (as a place for baby to nap), speculating that such babies are at risk for SIDS (Sudden Infant Death Syndrome, discussed in Chapter 2). That theory has been largely debunked, but there remain concerns about flat head syndrome (Positional Plagiocephaly) and neck tightness (Torticollis) when an infant seat is overused.

On the other side of the debate are advocates who say infant car seats fit newborns better—most are designed to accommodate a smaller body and baby travels in a semi-reclined position, which supports an infant's head and neck. Yes, some convertible seats recline—but the degree of recline can be affected by the angle of your vehicle's seat back.

Convenience is another issue for parents: an infant car seat is more than just a car seat—it's also an infant carrier when detached from its base. Big deal, you might say? Well, since newborns spend much of their time sleeping (and often fall asleep in the car), this is a big deal. By detaching the carrier from the auto base, you don't have to wake the baby when you leave the car. Use a convertible car seat, and you'll have to unbuckle the baby and move her into another type of carrier or stroller (and most likely wake her in the process).

Bottom line: there is no correct answer. Yes, you can skip the infant seat and go to a convertible from birth. But using an infant car seat correctly is just as safe, in our opinion.

Remember: babies should be REAR FACING until they reach two years of age, regardless of weight. If your child outgrows his infant car seat before one year of age, be sure to use a convertible seat in rear facing mode for as long as possible, given the seat's rear-facing weight/height limits.

7 Things No One Tells You About Buying A Convertible Car Seat!

1 PRO TIP: HOW EASY IS IT TO REMOVE THE COVER FOR WASHING? Yes, all car seats come out of the box looking fabulous. But any experienced parent will tell you how things can get ugly there in the back seat: spit up, juice spills and diaper blow outs. (Let's not visualize. Let's just move on). So then what? You have to remove the cover for cleaning.

That sounds simple, but the truth is some covers remove (and go back on) much easier than others. The best have zip-off or "easy remove" covers. Not so good: seats with multiple loops, snaps and other attachments.

Also: check to see if the cover is machine washable and dryable? Can you remove and wash the harness?

2 SOME RECLINES ARE EASIER THAN OTHERS. Most convertible seats recline for napping babies, but how EASY is it to recline? Remember that when a convertible seat is REAR-FAC-ING, a lever on the front of the seat will be jammed up against the back seat.

3 TWISTY STRAPS: THE PAIN THAT KEEPS ON GIVING. Better quality car seats have thicker straps that don't twist. The result: it's easier to get a child in and out of a seat. Cheaper seats have cheaper webbing that can be a nightmare— "twisty straps" are a key reason why parents hate their car seats. Our top picks avoid the twisty strap issue.

4 GIVE A SECOND LOOK AT THAT HARNESS BUCKLE. For obvious safety reasons, the harness buckle (which holds the two shoulder straps in place) shouldn't be too easy to unclip. Only an adult should be able to do it. But each car seat brand takes a different approach to this critical piece of safety gear. When shopping, take a second to open and close the buckle yourself. Think about any caregivers who might be buckling in baby (grandparents may have less strength, etc).

Hint: "puzzle" or compound buckles can be particularly vexing! As implied by the name, a puzzle buckle must be put together in a particular order to latch—which can be darn near impossible with gloves on in the winter. These buckles tend to be seen more on lower-price seats.

convertible car seats

5 **THE SUN IS NOT ALWAYS YOUR CAR SEAT'S FRIEND.** That plush, black velour car seat cover may look stunning out of the box, but when installed in a car that sits in the hot summer sun . . . you've got a recipe for Sweaty Baby Syndrome. If you have a choice between a dark color and one that is somewhat lighter, we'd go for the latter.

Another related issue: some car seats have exposed metal buckles and hardware. In the hot sun, these buckles can get toasty and possibly burn a child. Pro tip: look for a seat that has buckle clips or holders that keep metal away from direct sun.

6 **CONVERTIBLE DOES NOT NECESSARILY EQUAL PORTABLE.** Convertible car seats vary widely in weight, with some as low as 8 lbs. (Cosco Scenera Next) and others topping 34 lbs. (Clek Foonf, for example). Note that both seats pass federal crash test standard for safety.

While you shouldn't base your entire convertible car seat decision on weight, it may be an important factor for some parents. If you live an urban city center and don't own a car, then you'll need a lightweight seat when using Uber or a cab (see above for our convertible car seats for urban parents). If you see yourself moving a convertible seat between multiple vehicles on a frequent basis, buying a 30 lb.+ seat may have you cursing that decision for years.

7 **THERE IS NO CRASH TEST STANDARD FOR SIDE IMPACT PROTECTION—YET!** As you car seat shop, you'll see lots of seats promoting "side impact protection" with various headrests, cushions and gadgets. But remember this: as of this writing, there is NO federal side impact safety standard that car seat makers are required to pass.

Hence, we have little information to verify which seats are best at protecting children from side impact crashes. (Manufacturers do their own internal side impact crash testing, but aren't required to share those results with the public).

We should note that there is a PROPOSED side impact car seat safety standard that was published way back in 2014. But that rule isn't final yet as of press time and it isn't clear when that will take effect. Follow us on Facebook (facebook.com/babybargains) for the latest updates.

Up next, our recommendations for convertible car seats. We will recommend seats in three categories: best convertible seat (overall), best budget-friendly convertible seat and best convertible seat for urban parents.

The Best Convertible Car Seat (Overall)

After researching and reviewing 50+ different convertible car seats, we pick the ***Britax Boulevard ClickTight*** ($285) as the best convertible car seat.

The Britax Boulevard comes in three versions, ClickTight ($304); ClickTight ARB ($328) and the G4 ($264); more on the differences in a minute. All versions enable a child to ride rear-facing to 40 lbs. and forward facing to 65 with the five-point harness. The Boulevard features a no rethread harness, side-impact protection and excellent ease of use.

The most recent Boulevards feature "ClickTight" technology—the seat pops open for an easier belt installation. The result is a rock solid install. Crash protection is also excellent—the new anti-rebound bar (ClickTight ARB model) adds another layer of safety to keep the seat from rebounding in a collision. Although the price tips the scales at $300, the Boulevard ClickTight is worth it. Our own reader reviews on this seat are quite positive and the Boulevard scores an impressive 83% approval rating on Amazon (4 and 5-star reviews).

Britax is the king of convertible car seats and the Britax Boulevard is their flagship model. There are two major headlines for the Boulevard: the new ClickTight base and added side impact protection. Let's take a look at the ClickTight base—this new feature allows for ease of installation, thanks

to a seat base that pops open to help with belt installations.

The other major feature for the Boulevard (versus the less expensive Britax Marathon) is enhanced side impact protection. This takes the form of deep side walls and a head cushion.

Additional key features include a quick-adjust (no rethread) harness that moves both the harness and headrest in 14 positions. The Boulevard has seven recline positions plus an automatic level indicator helps guide the correct angle for the seat. Thanks to its wide distribution, you can find the Boulevard sold in many stores and online. That means you can often snag one on sale. One tip: watch for discontinued patterns, which can sell for 20% to 30% less. All in all, we found the Britax Boulevard very easy to install. Helpfully, Britax has an extensive series of installation videos for the Boulevard.

The difference between Boulevard ClickTight, ClickTight ARB and the G4. As we mentioned above, there are now three Boulevards on the market: the ClickTight, ARB and the G4. All three seats feature "SafeCell" technology which lowers the seat's center of gravity and makes it safer in a crash.

As you might have guessed, the G4 models do NOT have the ClickTight bases (discussed above). Other differences between the ClickTight and G4 version (besides the base): the G4 has ten harness positions versus 14 for the ClickTight; the G4 has only three recline positions versus seven for the ClickTight. The G4 lacks a level indicator.

Released in 2016, Britax now has a third version of the Boulevard: the ***ARB*** ($307). That stands for anti-rebound bar. This padded steel bar keeps the seat from rebounding in a front-end crash. Britax claims safety testing showed anti-rebound bars reduced seat rebound by 40% and helped stabilize the seat even in side-impact and rear-end crashes. FYI: the ARB model is identical to the Britax Boulevard ClickTight, the only difference is the added anti-rebound bar. What if you have a Britax Boulevard ClickTight and want to add the anti-rebound bar? Yes, you can—Britax is selling the anti-rebound bar as an accessory for $40.

Flaws but not deal breakers. So, what's not to like about the Boulevard? Well, first, this is a big and heavy seat. The Boulevard's bulk (23.5" height; 23" in depth) may make it hard to fit into smaller vehicles, especially rear-facing. And the seat's weight (about 30 lbs.) probably makes this a no go for carpools.

There isn't much leg room when the Boulevard is in rear-facing mode and a child is near the limits of the seat (40 lbs.). This will depend on the slope of your backseat, but just an FYI.

We also see a few customer online reviews that claim the un-installation from LATCH for this seat can be difficult. If you have your heart set on using LATCH, this might not be the best seat if you plan to frequently install and uninstall it.

Best Budget-Friendly Convertible Car Seat

For a decent, no-frills car seat, we recommend the **Cosco Scenera Next**. Yes, it lacks the whiz bang features of newer models, but this seat is the quiet, unsung hero of car seats. That's because it retails for $38 at Walmart—yes, you read that right: $38. This seat's low price makes the Scenera perfect for that little-used second car or Grandma's vehicle.

The Scenera is a basic, bare-bones convertible that works to 40 lbs. and is easy to install. With the prices of some car seats pushing $400, it's nice to know you can find a decent seat for less than 50 bucks.

The Cosco Scenera has been around for many years. The current model has a new narrow profile (17″ wide).

Here are some of the features we like about this seat:

◆ Machine washable pad—it's amazing more seats don't allow you to throw the pad in the washing machine. As any experienced parent will tell you, just about anything can happen in a car seat. Kudos to Cosco for this.

◆ Comes fully assembled. Five harness slots—the top one is only 13″, however.

◆ Light weight—at just 8 lbs., the Cosco Scenera Next is among the lightest convertible seats on the market. And a good choice for airline travel.

◆ A zillion color choices. The Scenera has many fabric choices, so you aren't locked into just one or two colors.

convertible car seats

Flaws but not deal breakers. Perhaps the biggest concern we have with the Cosco Scenera is the lack of side impact protection. In such a crash, a child could make contact with the vehicle door—especially if your vehicle does NOT have side-curtain air bags in the rear seats. We would suggest only installing this seat in the center of the back seat (instead of the outboard positions).

As for ease of use, the Scenera earned just two stars from the NHTSA's Ease of Use Ranking, with rear facing installation holding the seat's rating down.

Along those lines, keep this in mind: in order to install the Scenera with the proper recline in rear-facing mode, you may have to use a rolled-up towel or pool noodle to get the proper angle. This depends in your vehicle (those with deep sloping back seats are more of an issue when installing the Scenera). Using these aids is perfectly safe, by the way.

Critics note the lack of padding or fancy fabric; the Scenera also lacks an infant insert, which means the smallest newborns may not fit well in the seat. And the top harness slot is only 13", so it is doubtful a kid will hit the 40 lb. weight limit before outgrowing this seat by height.

Also: the Scenera lacks EPS or EPP foam for additional crash protection. This is helpful in a side impact collision to prevent injury to a child. Despite this omission, *Consumer Reports* still gave this seat "better" marks in crash protection overall in their most recent crash tests. We deem the lack of foam an acceptable trade-off for a seat that will only get occasional use in grandma's car or a secondary vehicle.

A final negative: the Scenera shell edges can be rough. Without a seat protector (a thin towel will do), your car's upholstery may get scratched or damaged when using the Scenera.

Despite these flaws, we still think the Cosco Scenera Next is a good, basic seat for secondary use. Fans love the Scenera for airplane travel, where the seat's light weight is much appreciated.

Best Convertible Car Seat For Urban Parents

Parents who live in an urban city center have always faced an unique car seat challenge: when you have to rely on Uber, Lyft or a cab to get from point A to point B, what do you do with a baby who's outgrown an infant car seat? What convertible seat is both light in weight and quick to install?

We suggest the **Combi Coccoro** ($240 at Buy Buy Baby). First it is lightweight—14 lbs. That's 10-15 lbs less than other convertible seats. Nonetheless, the Coccoro has scored well in crash tests.

We found the Coccoro very easy and quick to install—which is important when the meter is running. Bonus: you can even install the Coccoro with your child buckled in the seat.

What happens when you arrive at the local park or shopping district? If you need to stroll around a bit, we suggest a **Go-Go Babyz Travelmate** ($81). Strap your Combi Coccoro into this contraption and voila! You have an adhoc stroller which functions like a rollerboard suitcase. (Go-Go even has a specific install guide for the Coccoro).

Obviously, this isn't designed for long outings like a regular stroller, since there isn't any storage or other comfort features. But the telescoping handle is nice. If you need to roll a convertible seat through an airport, the Travelmate is perfect.

One drawback to the Combi Coccoro—the seat has a puzzle buckle, one of the most dreaded car seat features we discussed earlier. The puzzle buckle's separate tongue pieces must be held together before they can be fastened into the buckle. Before you shell out the bucks for this seat, play with the buckle in a store to make sure this won't drive you nuts.

Looking at convertible seat you don't see mentioned here? On BabyBargains.com, we have reviews of 40+ more convertibles!

convertible car seats

CAR SEATS

CONVERTIBLE SEATS	The following is a selection of popular convertible car seats and how they compare on features:		WEIGHT LIMITS (IN LBS.)	
MAKER	MODEL	PRICE	REAR	FORWARD
BABY TREND	PROtect	$125-$180	40 LBS.	65 LBS.
BRITAX	ADVOCATE	$336-$410	40	65
	BOULEVARD CT	$296	40 LBS.	65 LBS.
	MARATHON CT	$264	40	65
CHICCO	NEXTFIT	$300	40	65
CLEK	FLLO	$380-$500	50	65
	FOONF	$450-$500	50	65
COMBI	COCCORO	$200-$235	33	40
COSCO	APT 40 RF/50	$45-$60	40	40/50
	SCENERA NEXT	$39-$60	40	40
DIONO	OLYMPIA	$210	45	70
	PACIFICA	$238-$270	50	90
	RADIAN RXT	$250-$287	45	80/120
EDDIE BAUER	XRS 65	$130	40	65
EVENFLO	SURERIDE	$90-$100	40	65
	SYMPHONY	$165-$230	40	65/110
	TITAN	$85-$100	40	65
	TRIUMPH	$135-$160	40	65
GRACO	4EVER	$300	40	65/120
	CONTENDER 65	$119-$140	40	65
	EXTEND2FIT	$200	50	65
	MILESTONE	$229	40	65/100
MAXI COSI	PRIA 85	$300	40	85
	VELLO 65	$184-$230	40	65
NUNA	RAVA	$450	50	65
PEG PEREGO	PRIMO VIAGGIO SIP	$350	45	70
RECARO	PRORIDE	$220	40	65
SAFETY 1ST	CHART AIR 65	$119	40	65
	COMPLETE AIR 65	$126-$152	40	65
	CONTINUUM	$130-$150	40	50/80
	GROW & GO EX	$150	40	65/100

RATING	COMMENT
NOT YET	HEADREST POPS OFF FOR BETTER FIT IN SMALLER VEHICLES.
A-	SAME AS BOULEVARD, BUT ADDED SIDE IMPACT PROTECTION
A	7 RECLINE POSITIONS; ENHANCED SIDE IMPACT PROTECTION
A	BASIC SIDE IMPACT PROTECTION; NO-RETHREAD HARNESS
A	NO RETHREAD HARNESS; 9 RECLINE POSITIONS.
B	LACK OF SEAT PADDING, CAN'T USE UNTIL 14 LBS.
B	VERY PRICEY, BULKY, LACK OF SEAT PADDING.
B	COMPACT SEAT WEIGHS JUST 14 LBS.
B-	AFFORDABLE BUT NO SEAT RECLINE. WIDE BASE.
B+	SIMPLE SEAT, GREAT FOR AIR TRAVEL OR GRANDPARENTS.
C+	CONVERTS TO BOOSTER; NARROW WIDTH, LATCH TRICKY.
B-	MEMORY FOAM, NARROW WIDTH.
B-	SEAT FOLDS UP; SIDE IMPACT PROTECTION
B-	LIMITED RECLINE, SMALL PROFILE FITS IN SMALLER VEHICLES.
C	VERY SHORT HARNESS, LIGHTWEIGHT. AFFORDABLE.
B+	EASY TO INSTALL WITH LATCH; SMOOTH HARNESS ADJUSTER
B+	GREAT FOR GRANDMA'S CAR OR 2ND VEHICLE.
C	NO RETHREAD HARNESS BUT HUGE SEAT WIDTH
A-	6 RECLINE POS; SIDE IMPACT PROTECT; NO-RETHREAD
C	THERE ARE BETTER ARE GRACO SEATS THAN THIS.
A-	ONE OF THE HIGHEST REAR-FACING LIMITS ON MARKET.
A-	LIKE THE 4EVER BUT DOESN'T HAVE BACKLESS BOOSTER MODE
B+	85 LB HARNESS LIMIT IS UNIQUE; MACHINE WASHABLE PAD
B	NO RETHREAD HARNESS, LEAST EXPENSIVE MAXI COSI.
NOT YET	SIDE IMPACT PROTECTION, EXTENDED REAR-FACING USE.
A	SIDE IMPACT PROTECTION, ADJUSTABLE HEADREST.
F	NOT RECOMMENDED BECAUSE OF CRASH TEST CONCERNS.
B	SIDE IMPACT PROTECTION AT LOW PRICE.
B	SIDE IMPACT PROTECTION, NO RETHREAD HARNESS.
B	CONVERTS TO BOOSTER; MACHINE WASH/DRY PAD.
A	QUICKFIT HARNESS ADJUSTS HARNESS & HEADREST.

convertible car seats

The Best Booster Car Seats

Welcome to the third and final stage of car seats: the booster. Your child needs a booster seat when he outgrows his convertible seat. This happens when he exceeds the weight limit or when he is too tall for the harness (his shoulders are taller than the top slots in the seat). For most children, this happens around ages three to six (it varies depending on the convertible seat).

So what is a booster? This is one of the more confusing categories of car seats. Boosters started out as a way to boost a child to correctly sit in an auto safety belt.

In recent years, a new type of booster (harnessed boosters) blurred the lines between harnessed seats (like infant and convertible seats) and traditional belt-positioning boosters. These 3-in-1 or 4-in-1 seats morph as your child gets older: first in the harness, then with the auto safety belt and so on.

We'll discuss more about these different categories shortly.

A key point to remember: any child from 40 to 80 lbs. and less than 4'9" (generally, kids age four to eight) should be restrained in a booster seat. And in most states, booster seat use is mandated by law.

Our general rule: you should keep your child in a harnessed car seat as long as possible.

7 Things No One Tells You About Buying a Booster Car Seat!

1 BOOSTER SEATS COME IN FOUR DIFFERENT FLAVORS:

◆ *Harnessed boosters:* As discussed above, harnessed boosters morph from a forward-facing harnessed seat to a high-back belt-positioning booster (and in some case) to a backless booster.

With the five-point harness, boosters can generally be used up to 65, 80 or 90 lbs. Then the harness is removed, and the seat can be used as a belt-positioning booster, usually to 80 or 100 lbs.

Our top recommendation in this section is for a harnessed booster. The take-home message: we recommend a harnessed booster as the safest option to transport a toddler. Keep your child in the harness as long as possible (given seat weight/height limits).

◆ *High back boosters (HBB)*: Belt-positioning boosters come in two flavors: high back boosters and backless boosters. High back boosters have often been called "kid's captain's chairs," which they kind of resemble. They are designed to be simple, but provide vital safety features for children who've outgrown a harnessed seats.

These boosters properly position the lap belt on a child's strong hip bones, rather than letting it ride up on the soft internal organs. And they provide correct positioning of the shoulder belt, so the child can comfortably wear it and get critical upper body support.

The high back also protects the child's head from whiplash if there are no head restraints in the vehicle, and the high back may also give some side sleeping support. ALL of these boosters require a lap and shoulder belt. FYI: Some high back boosters convert into backless boosters for older kids.

◆ *Backless boosters:* These belt-positioning boosters work the same way as high back boosters—they just don't have a back.

Safety-wise, these can be a bit better than a high back booster, since the child sits against the vehicle seat. They do the same job positioning the lap belt, and usually include some sort of strap to adjust the shoulder belt. But they don't provide head support if you have low seat backs, and they don't give any side or sleeping support.

On the other hand, they are often popular with older kids, since they can be quite inconspicuous.

◆ *Special Needs Seats:* There are a few seats on the market now that don't really fit into any category. One is the Britax Traveler Plus, which is designed for special needs kids up to 105 lbs.

2 **WHEN IS YOUR CHILD READY FOR THE AUTO SAFETY BELT?** Some states allow children as young as six to legally ride in an auto safety belt (that is, booster seat use isn't required). But there is the law—and the law of physics. Numerous peer-reviewed safety studies show that continued booster seat use is the safest course . . . until a child can SAFELY use an auto safety belt. When is that?

When a child is over 4'9" and can sit with his or her back straight against the back seat cushion (with knees bent over the seat's edge), then he or she can go with just the auto's safety belt. Still have doubts? Try this Five-Step Test from Safety Belt Safe, USA:

◆   Does the child sit all the way back against the auto seat?
◆   Do the child's knees bend comfortably at the edge of the seat?
◆   Does the belt cross the shoulder between neck and arm?
◆   Is the lap belt as low as possible, touching the thighs?
◆   Can the child stay seated like this for the whole trip?

If you answered no to any of these questions, your child needs a booster seat, and will probably be more comfortable in one too.

booster car seats

3 **USING A BOOSTER SEAT TOO SOON CAN BE DANGEROUS.** You'll note that some harnessed boosters have starting weight limits as young as 20 lbs.—that could be as young as a six month aged baby! But remember this: all boosters are forward-facing. And the current recommendation by safety experts is to keep your child REAR-FACING until age 2 or longer. So even though you could use a forward- facing harnessed booster for a one year old, we wouldn't recommend it.

Also: don't abandon the harness too soon. Yes, you could switch to a belt-positioning booster as soon as four years (or 40 lbs.). Our advice: don't. Keep your child in that harness as long as you can (that's why our top recommended seats in this section have top harness limits of 80 and 90 lbs.).

4 **YOUR CAR'S OWNER'S MANUAL IS AN IMPORTANT RESOURCE.** Sure, you probably haven't look at it since you purchased the vehicle. But most auto manuals have detailed advice about car seat use. And that comes in especially handy when you start using a booster. That's because some boosters can use LATCH— but your vehicle may prohibit this use when the weight of your seat plus your child exceed a certain limit.

5 **SITTING IN A BELT-POSITIONING BOOSTER REQUIRES MATURITY.** Yes, we recommend using a harness as long as possible—but we are also the parents of two kids. And we remember the pleas from a toddler who didn't want to sit in a "baby seat" (that is, the harness). The challenge: to use a belt-positioning booster, a child must be mature enough to understand the iron clad rule: you NEVER wiggle out from under the belt when the car is in motion. Some kids are ready for this and others need more time in a harness!

6 **ONLY USE CARDBOARD CUPS IN BOOSTER SEAT CUP HOLDERS.** You'll note that many booster seats come with cup or juice box holders. These are a great convenience, but most car seat makers only recommend putting cardboard cups or juice boxes in these holders. Why? In a collision anything heavier than a cardboard juice box or cup can become a dangerous projectile.

7 **THERE ISN'T ONE NATIONAL STANDARD FOR HOW LONG YOUR CHILD SHOULD BE IN A BOOSTER SEAT.** Booster seat use is regulated on a state-by-state basis, at least when we're talking about how long kids must remain in a booster. Some states have an age limit, some a weight and/or height limit. If you're unsure about the rules in your state, check your state Department of Motor Vehicles' web site.

Best Booster Car Seat (Overall)

After researching and reviewing 51 different booster car seats, we pick the **Graco Nautilus 80 Elite** ($170) as the best booster car seat.

Graco makes the best-selling harnessed booster seat on the market and it's easy to see why—the Graco's Nautilus 80 Elite works with a five-point harness to 80 lbs. and then converts to a high back booster (120 lbs.) and even a backless booster for older kids (a feature the Britax Frontier does not have). Here's what the seat looks like as a backless booster (right).

The harness is a big plus if you have a toddler who has outgrown his convertible seat, but wish to keep him in the harness for a while longer (the 80 lb. limit should fit most six year olds).

The Nautilus' other features include over molded armrests (with side storage), three-position recline and decent padding. The seat is lined with EPS foam.The seat has enhanced side impact protection, an adjustable headrest and belt lock-offs, making it one of the most popular seats in this category.

So what is the Nautilus Elite's biggest selling point? Price: the basic Nautilus is 30% less than the Britax Frontier (see Also Great below) . . . and that's nothing to sneeze at. As for reader feedback, the Graco Nautilus earns positive marks from readers for its overall ease of use. The IIHS ranks the Nautilus as a Best Bet when used in highback mode; the Britax Frontier earns the same rating.

booster car seats

A quick side note. Graco sells several different Nautiluses. Here is a quick review of the current line-up:

◆ The base model is the Nautilus 65 (aka Nautilus 3-in-1, $149).

◆ The Nautilus 65 LX ($169) has upgraded fabrics and buckle pockets to hold the harness when not in use; 120 lb. limit as booster seat.

◆ The Nautilus with Safety Surround Protection features additional, enhanced side impact protections. It is a Target exclusive for $162.

◆ Finally, we have the Nautilus 80 Elite, which is the seat we are focusing on for this review.

Flaws but not deal breakers. The Graco Nautilus 80 Elite isn't perfect. Some readers tell us it is too snug to fit larger kids. In those cases, the roomier Britax Frontier Clicktight might be a better bet.

The Nautilus 80 Elite also must be assembled, which includes several steps such as "Pull elastic loop on the seat pad through the vehicle belt guide on side of seat and attach to hook as shown. Repeat on other side." Compare that to Britax where the seat basically comes out of the box ready to use.

We're not saying the Nautilus 80 Elite is as fun to assemble as IKEA furniture, but we noted more than a few readers who said assembling Graco boosters had them swearing like a pirate. So just a heads up.

Who else likes it. About 79% of our readers gave this seat a four or five star review. The Insurance Institute for Highway Safety gave the previous version of this seat (dubbed the Argos 80 Elite) a "Best Bet." (The Nautilus 80 Elite is basically the same seat, new name).

Also Great: Britax Frontier ClickTight

The **Britax Frontier ClickTight** may be pricey ($255), but it does offer features other seats don't have—it works up to 90 lbs. with a five-point harness.

The Frontier aims for a market similar to the Graco Nautilus—after your child outgrows the five-point harness, the seat morphs into a belt-positioning booster to 120 lbs. The Frontier is designed for kids at least two years old who have outgrown their convertible seats but aren't mature enough to sit in a belt-positioning booster.

Britax has steadily improved this seat over the years (the most recent version on the market is the G1.1). Overall weight and height limits have moved higher and there are a series of small enhancements (example: the cup holders are inset in the seat, rather than stick out from the side, etc.). The Frontier 90 also has:

◆ A ClickTight seatbelt installation system. This system automatically tightens and tensions the seat belt—no more locking clips or concerns about LATCH seat limits. Here's how it works:

| ① Squeeze the Release with Two Fingers to Open | ② Thread and Connect the Vehicle Seat Belt | ③ Click it Closed! |

◆ SafeCell crash protection in base. Seen in Britax's other models, this system absorbs energy in a crash.

◆ Higher top harness adjustment. The top harness slot is now 20.5 , which is the tallest in the industry. That will keep kids from outgrowing the seat in harness mode too soon. Other small improvements to the seat include a better recline feature and now the harness hides away when you convert the seat to booster mode (before it had to be removed completely).

Reader feedback on the Frontier has been positive. Ease of installation is one plus, according to parents, as well as the high weight limits and plush padding.

In the most recent booster seat ratings from the Insurance Institute for Highway Safety (IIHS), the Frontier improved its ratings from a Check Fit to a Best Bet. One point about this: this rating is for the booster mode only (not the harness mode).

FYI: If you want additional side impact protection, there is a special version of the Frontier 90 with Side Impact Cushion Technology (SICT). This model, the **Pinnacle 90,** runs $292 (pictured at right).

Flaws but not deal breakers. Are there any negatives to this seat? Well, this is definitely a big, bulky seat. Carrying it through an airport isn't going to be fun (the Frontier is certified for use in an airplane, but only with its five-point harness—not as a booster).

The Frontier is 19.5″ wide—that means fitting three across in a carpool won't be easy for most vehicles. Also: the Frontier has limited recline settings and that might be a negative for some.

The price of the Frontier 90 is perhaps its biggest draw-back—the similar Graco Nautilus is about HALF the price. Even when discounted from the $330 sticker price, the Frontier's $255 street price is substantially more than the Nautilus. And the Graco Nautilus has an extra use as a backless booster (the Frontier only works as a belt-positioning high back booster).

Bargain tip: Buying last year's fashion is a good way to save. Car seat makers like Britax often leave their seats the same from year to year, but change out the fashion. Last year's fashions usually are discounted. How to find them? Check all the colors of a seat on sites like Amazon—more often than not, a few colors will be less expensive than others!

Who else likes it. User reviews for the seat on Amazon indicate "90% like it," meaning 90% of Amazon reviewers give it a four or five star rating. That's rare—even well loved seats don't exceed 80% combined for four and five-star seats.

The Insurance Institute for Highway Safety awarded this seat a Best Bet in high back mode.

Best Budget-Friendly Booster Car Seat

What's the best harnessed booster for under $100? The **Evenflo Maestro** is our pick—it has a five-point harness that can be used up to 50 pounds. After a child outgrows the harness, the Maestro becomes a belt-positioning booster up to 100 lbs. Best of all, the Maestro is just $79.

The Maestro has performed better than Evenflo's other boosters, which are showing their age. The Insurance Institute for Highway Safety gives the seat a Best Bet rating and it earned four out of five stars for ease of use.

Reader feedback has been mostly positive. Fans cite the LATCH attachments, upfront harness adjustment and two crotch positions.

On the other hand, critics note the harness must be re-threaded when you need to change the height and you have to disassemble the seat to clean the pad. But those are the trade-offs for the sub $100 price.

Bottom line: this is a better effort than Evenflo's other boosters and it is affordable . . . with harnessed boosters soaring to $300 and beyond, it's a pleasant surprise to find a seat that is both well designed and under $100.

Best Booster Car Seat For Urban Parents

You live in an urban city center and need to take Uber/Lyft or a taxi with a toddler that's outgrown a convertible seat. What's the best solution? We have three:

1 ***Uber's in-house car seat.*** If you live in New York City, Philadelphia or Washington DC, Uber offers a professionally installed car seat (the IMMI Go) for a $10 surcharge. A few caveats: your child must be at least 12 months old, 22 lbs. and 31 inches in height. Use the promo code CARSEATNYC10 to get your first car seat ride surcharge for free. Apologies in advance for parents of multiples: there is just one car seat per vehicle. There is an online FAQ on how this program works.

2 ***The BumbleBum*** ($26) is an affordable, inflatable booster that is perfect for carpools or taxis. The Bumblebum's small size makes it perfect when you need to fit three toddlers in one back seat. One caveat: this booster probably isn't the most comfortable for long commutes or road trips. Note to urban parents looking for a lightweight option for Uber and Lyft: The BumbleBum weighs just over one pound.

3 ***The Safety 1st Boostapak*** ($100). It's a booster! And a backpack! The Boostapak works from 40 to 80 lbs. and even includes a storage compartment for a toddler's stuff. Here's what the Boostapak looks like when folded up.

More Booster Seat Recommendations

We believe the safest place for your toddler and young child is in a harnessed booster seat, like the ones recommended earlier in this section.

Yes, there are two other booster seat types—belt-positioning high back boosters and backless boosters. These are for older children who've outgrown harnessed seats. (Note that our top recommended harnessed booster converts into a belt-positioning and backless booster).

So when would you need to purchase just a belt-positioning or backless booster? Well, let's assume you are in a minor car accident and decide to replace your first booster. But now your child is six years old and has outgrown the harness limit. Then you'd go for one of these seats.

Best Belt-Positioning Booster

The **Graco TurboBooster** ($50) is the best belt-positioning booster on the market today. It packs a good number of features into an affordable package: height-adjustable headrest, open belt loop design, armrests, back recline, cup holders and more. If you can afford the upgrade, the **Graco TurboBooster With Safety Surround** ($80) has additional side impact protection in the form of beefed up headrest and torso cushions.

Runner up: The **Britax Parkway SGL** ($128) gets excellent marks from readers for ease of use and safety—you get LATCH connectors and an impressive 120 lb. weight limit.

Bonus: this seat has Slide Guard (SG)—it keeps a child from submarining out of the seat in a crash.

booster car seats

Best Backless Booster

The best backless boosters on the market are the **Graco TurboBooster backless** ($27, pictured above) and the **Evenflo Amp** ($28). Both are affordable and easy to use boosters for older kids who don't need a high back booster.

The Graco backless option works from (roughly) ages four to ten (40 lbs. to 110 lbs.). Again, even though you could use this seat for kids as young as four, we'd suggest a harnessed seat until your child is beyond 80 lbs. or as long as possible.

How we picked recommended car seats

We evaluated car seats with hands on inspections, checking seats for ease of use (installation and adjusting the seat). We also gather significant reader feedback, tracking seats on quality and durability. Besides interviewing parents, we also talk with car seat "techs," certified child passenger safety technicians who install hundreds if not thousands of seats at safety check points nationwide.

We've been rating and reviewing car seats since 1994. During that time, we have also visited manufacturer facilities and watched car seat crash tests. While we don't personally crash test seats, we compare our reader feedback with crash tests done by organizations like the National Highway Traffic Safety Administration and *Consumer Reports*.

We also look at third-party evaluations of seats by groups like the Insurance Institute for Highway Safety (IIHS), which focuses on booster car seats.

Looking at a booster seat in a store you don't see mentioned here? We have 50+ more booster seats reviewed on our web page at BabyBargains.com.

CHAPTER 8

STROLLERS AND MORE

Strollers & Diaper Bags

Inside this chapter

Where to begin? Strollers seem overwhelming—
what do you really need? We'll give you the low
down on finding the right stroller to match your lifestyle.
Then check out our specific stroller picks, from a budget-
friendly lightweight stroller to a fully-outfitted multi-function
model. Finally, let's talk diaper bags—which are best?

We like the British slang for strollers: pushchairs. That perfectly
describes what we call strollers . . . baby chairs with wheels that
you push. Simple!

Then you arrive at the baby superstore and look at the stroller
section. "Section" doesn't quite describe it. It's Strollermageddon.

Strollers range from $20 up to $1700. And the brands! At last
count, we figure there are 54 separate stroller brands sold in North
America. With names you've never heard of. Where to start?

That's why we are here. We've spent 20+ years researching,
testing and writing about baby strollers. All the while not taking
a single dime from the brands we review or recommend.

Before we get to our specific recommendations, let's start
with some stroller basics. The goal is to match the right stroller
to your lifestyle.

7 Things No One Tells You About Buying A Stroller

1 **WHAT'S YOUR STROLLER LIFESTYLE?** Before you fall you in love
with a designer stroller, ask yourself HOW you will be using
a stroller. Yes, you.

Think of strollers as tools—the wrong tool for a job isn't going to help, no matter how shiny it is. It's the same for strollers.

Because we all live in different environs and want to go varied places, the key to stroller happiness is to understand how different stroller options fit your lifestyle. Hence, the perfect stroller for hiking in Colorado isn't the right one for a simple spin around a mall in Atlanta.

Climate plays another factor—in the Northeast, strollers have to be winterized to handle the cold and snow. Meanwhile, in Southern California, full canopies are helpful for shading baby's eyes from late afternoon sunshine.

2 THE PERFECT STROLLER DOESN'T EXIST.

Your stroller needs will change over time. Babies/toddlers use strollers from birth to age four and sometimes beyond. The perfect stroller for a newborn isn't necessarily great for a toddler—although some strollers make a valiant effort at bridging the years.

And what if you add a second child in the mix?

The take-home message: no one stroller can meet all these needs. Most parents end up with more than one stroller. Let's review over the stroller landscape.

3 THERE ARE SIX TYPES OF STROLLERS ON THE MARKET...

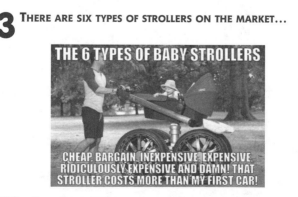

THE 6 TYPES OF BABY STROLLERS

CHEAP, BARGAIN, INEXPENSIVE, EXPENSIVE, RIDICULOUSLY EXPENSIVE AND DAMN! THAT STROLLER COSTS MORE THAN MY FIRST CAR!

We kid. Here are the six basic styles of strollers: umbrella/lightweight strollers, full-size strollers, multi-function strollers, jogging (or sport) strollers, all-terrain strollers and travel systems. Here's a quick look see:

◆ *Umbrella/lightweight strollers* are generally under 20 lbs. in weight. Some feature two handles and a long, narrow fold (like an umbrella; hence the name!). Most umbrellas strollers are very cheap ($20 to $40), although some upper end manufacturers have spruced them up to sell for $100 to $300 (UPPAbaby and Peg Perego have "luxury" umbrella strollers). Premium lightweight strollers boast features like extendible canopies, storage baskets, and high quality wheels. Prices range from $150 to $300. Because seat recline can be limited, many umbrella/lightweight strollers are designed for kids six months old and older.

◆ *Full-size strollers* used to be called carriages or prams. These strollers are more like a bed on wheels with a seat that reclines to nearly flat and can be enclosed like a bassinet for newborns. All that stroller goodness comes at a price: hefty weight, as much as 30lbs. As a result, getting a full-size stroller in and out of the vehicle trunk can be a challenge. Entry level full-size strollers start at $200, but these can top $1000. In recent years, full-size strollers have fallen out of favor, replaced by . . .

◆ *Multi-function strollers* work from infant to toddler with either an infant car seat adapter or bassinet accessory for newborns. Some multi-functions are even expandable into a double stroller with a second seat attachment. Expect to pay $300 to $1000 for multi-function options (accessories like second seats are almost always an additional cost). This stroller type has increased in popularity in recent years, as more parents have kids that are close in age.

◆ *Jogging strollers* feature air-filled, bicycle-style tires and lightweight frames perfect for jogging or brisk walks on rough roads. The best strollers for running have a fixed front wheel for stability. Jogging stroller with lightweight aluminum frames usually run $300 and up although there are some cheaper, steel framed options on the market too.

◆ *All-terrain strollers* are eclipsing jogging strollers for all but the most devoted runner. In fact, they often look like joggers but have a swivel front wheel. Big tires take to hiking trails better than typical stroller wheels, but these strollers are bulky and heavy. And expensive: they can run more than $400 for popular brands.

◆ *Travel systems* combine a stroller and infant car seat which snaps into the stroller. Typically sold at discount and big-box stores, travel systems are aimed at first-time parents and gift givers. Most feature basic infant car seats and full-size strollers at prices that range from $200 to $300. Travel systems have waned in popularity in recent years as more lightweight strollers have added infant car seat compatibility/adapters.

4 **BEWARE THESE COMMON STROLLER SAFETY HAZARDS.** Just because a stroller is on the shelves at the Baby Megastore doesn't mean it is safe. 12,000 babies each year are injured by strollers, according to the most recent government safety data.
Here are our top safety tips:

◆ *Never hang bags from the stroller handle.* Yes, it is tempting to hang that diaper bag or purse off your stroller handles. The danger: your stroller can tip backwards—and even if your child is in the five-point harness, injuries can still happen. Solution: put that purse in your stroller's storage basket. Or use a backpack diaper bag.

◆ *Don't leave your baby unattended* while sleeping in a stroller. Newborns, infants and toddlers all move around when they're sleeping. Injuries have occurred when babies creep down to the strap openings, so keep an eye on them. Or take a baby out of a stroller and put them in a full-size crib for naps.

◆ *Don't trust your stroller's brakes.* The best stroller models have brakes on two wheels rather than one. But even if a stroller has the best brakes on the planet, never leave a stroller unattended on an incline with your baby inside.

◆ *Follow the weight limits.* Forty pounds is typically the maximum for most strollers.

◆ *Jogging strollers are best for babies over one year of age.* Pediatric experts tell us the neck muscles of infants under one year of age can't take the bumps of jogging or walking on rough terrain.

◆ *Fold and unfold your stroller away from your baby.* The opening/closing mechanisms of a stroller can be a pinching hazard, so don't open or close your stroller with baby nearby. Graco recalled over 5 million strollers in 2014 for just such hazards.

5 **THE SECRET TO A SMART STROLLER TEST DRIVE: ADD WEIGHT.** Don't test drive that stroller empty. Take a backpack and put in about 20 lbs. worth of books. Stick that in the stroller seat and you'll see how that stroller actually steers/handles with a baby. And yes, practice folding and unfolding the stroller with the backpack in your arms!

6 **WHAT STROLLER FEATURES REALLY MATTER . . . FOR BABIES.** The Dreaded Wall of Strollers—more than one parent-to-be has been reduced to tears staring at a baby store's mind-boggling display of 37 stroller models. So let's break down what's REALLY important when stroller shopping for baby:

◆ *Reclining seat.* If you plan to use this stroller from birth, the seat must fully recline. That's because babies can't comfortably ride in a sitting position until around six months. And most newborns spend their time sleeping—seat recline is a necessity.

◆ *Extended canopy.* There are three types of stroller canopies: skimpy, extended and fully enclosing. Skimpy canopies only block the sun if it is directly overhead—great if you live at the equator. For everyone else, an extended canopy (also called an extended sunshade) are better at blocking all sun angles. Baby Jogger's canopies are a good example of extended canopies (pictured). The best canopies have multiple positions for flexibility. Fully enclosing canopies go a step further— they completely block out the sun from a stroller. These are great, but somewhat rare on the market.

FYI: If you live in an area with lots of mosquitos (we're looking at you, Florida), a bug net accessory is highly recommended.

◆ *All wheel suspension.* Stroller wheel suspension works like your car's shock absorbers, smoothing out life's little (and big) bumps.

7 WHAT STROLLER FEATURES REALLY MATTER . . . FOR PARENTS.

◆ *It's all about the storage.* Like napkins and toddlers, you can never have enough. We're not just talking about the size of the storage basket (but that helps). It's HOW you access the basket, especially if the seat is reclined. The best strollers add storage in areas you wouldn't think—on the hood, the back of the seat, a storage compartment with lid in a parent console for your phone and so on.

◆ *The right wheels.* Going for a nature walk on a dirt trail? Air-filled 12" rear tires are best. Navigating tight spaces at the Pikes Place Market in Seattle? Small 6" wheels enable tight turns.

◆ *Removable seat pad for washing.* Crushed-in cookies, spilt juice and the usual grime can make a stroller a mobile dirt-fest. Some models have removable seat cushions that are machine washable—other models let you remove all the fabric for washing.

◆ *Reversible seat.* When baby is young, you can have your child face you. Then when your toddler wants to see the world, the seat flips around.

◆ *The one-hand, flip flop friendly, standing fold.* The fewer the steps and hands you need to fold a stroller, the better. The best strollers have one-hand folds that stand when collapsed. If your stroller has a foot brake or release, make sure it is "flip flop friendly." Basically that means you can set and release a brake or folding mechanism *without* putting your toes underneath the lever and pushing up. Instead, you push *down* with your shoe/flip flop's sole. Voila! No messed up pedicure.

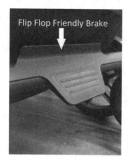
Flip Flop Friendly Brake

◆ *Height adjustable handle.* If you and your partner are two different statures, an adjustable handle is a must have.

Eco-friendly stroller certifications

There are three international organizations that test and certify textiles to meet environmental standards: OEKO-TEX, Global Organic Textile Standard (GOTS) and IVN Naturextil. All three of these certifications are optional—there is no legal standard for organic, non-allergenic, chemical free textiles in the US. Many of the stroller brands that are certified are European, with only a few US brands certified.

As of this writing, there is one eco-friendly certification on strollers sold in North America: OEKO-TEX. Here's some background:

OEKO-TEX is a German organization that offers "Standard 100 certification program for textiles at all steps in the manufacturing process. "Products marked with the label 'Confidence in textiles (Standard 100)' provide effective protection against allergenic substances, formaldehyde, heavy metals such as nickel or for example forbidden plasticizers (phthalates) in baby textiles," according to OEKO-TEX's web site. OEKO-TEX offers a second certification called Green by OEKO-TEX, which means the "materials (were) tested for harmful substances," the product was "made in environmentally friendly facilities" and it was "made in safe and socially responsible workplaces."

CONFIDENCE IN TEXTILES
Tested for harmful substances
according to Oeko-Tex® Standard 100
Institute

We found only two stroller makes who are OEKO-TEX certified: BumbleRide and Nuna. At the time of this writing, all of BumbleRide and Nuna's stroller fabrics were OEKO-TEX certified—however, check their web sites for specific models' information.

Best Lightweight Strollers

Up next, we recommend lightweight strollers in several categories:

- ◆ Best Lightweight Stroller (Overall)
- ◆ Best Budget-Friendly Lightweight Stroller
- ◆ Best Lightweight Stroller For Urban Parents (Winter/Summer)
- ◆ Best High-Style Lightweight Stroller

Best Lightweight Stroller (Overall)

We waded through 74 lightweight strollers—folding, unfolding, buckling, un-buckling—until we found the very best lightweight stroller: the ***Baby Jogger City Mini*** ($250).

Lightweight strollers are the holy grail of the stroller market—enough convenience features (easy fold, cup holder) for parents and comfort (canopy, seat pad) for baby, but not too much to add unnecessary weight. We generally define "lightweight" as strollers under 20 lbs. empty (not including baby!).

Our pick in this category is the Baby Jogger City Mini, an excellent 17.1 lb. tri-wheel stroller with oversized canopy and fully reclining seat.

Baby Jogger's quick fold technology is amazing—you lift a strap in the middle of the stroller and zip! It's folded. An optional car seat adapter can turn a City Mini into a travel system if you wish.

As a brand, Baby Jogger has a good reputation for quality. Now owned by Graco, Baby Jogger got its start by making (you guessed it) jogging strollers in the 80's. After going through a bankruptcy and ownership change in the early 2000's, the company pivoted to making easy-to-fold strollers in both the lightweight and multi-function markets.

The tri-wheel City Mini (single $250, 17.1 lbs.; double $450, 26.6 lbs.) is Baby Jogger's best-selling stroller, featuring a full recline and large canopy. In a recent refresh, the City Mini got a few tweaks: a slightly larger seat, an easier to access storage basket and an auto lock feature when the stroller is folded.

The secret sauce to the City Mini Series is the company's Quick-Fold technology: no complicated buttons or latches. No multi-step process. The Quick-Fold has super-sized Baby Jogger's sales in recent years and other stroller makers have rushed to copy it. Here's what City Mini looks like folded:

No, that isn't the most compact fold on the market, but the City Mini will fit into most trunks without a problem.

Parent feedback on the City Mini has been quite positive. They praise the overall ease of use and features like the large canopy, which puts the canopies on other lightweight strollers to shame. Look at the canopy (with the seat fully reclined) pictured on the previous page.

Finally, we should note that Baby Jogger sells a car seat adapter accessory ($25-35) for the City Mini that fits most major brands of car seats. This is one advantage the City Mini has over our other umbrella (lightweight) stroller picks—it can accommodate an infant car seat. You can buy the car seat adapter direct from Baby Jogger or from Amazon.

Baby Jogger also makes a raft of accessories for the City Mini: everything from weather shields to glider boards (for older toddlers to stand on), as well as a foot muff, cup holders and parent consoles. That's the advantage of going with a brand like Baby Jogger. Less expensive lightweight stroller brands typically have few (or no) accessories.

FYI: We should mention that Baby Jogger also has various spin-offs of the City Mini, including the newer **City Tour** ($200, a four-wheeled version with more compact fold) and **City Mini GT** ($360, with all terrain wheels).

If you live in a city with rough or broken sidewalks, the City Mini GT might be a worth the $90 upgrade.

Best Budget-Friendly Lightweight Stroller

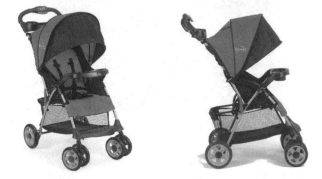

Kolcraft's entry-level strollers are winners. Dollar for dollar, these are the best affordable strollers on the market. Compared to other low-end brands (Graco, Cosco), Kolcraft shines.

The entry-level offering is the ***Kolcraft Cloud***, which comes in two versions. The basic Cloud umbrella stroller sold at Walmart for $29 is a simple umbrella stroller with cup holder, storage basket and extended canopy—a great deal for $29. The ***Cloud Plus*** (pictured above) adds a one-hand fold, multi-position seat recline and child snack tray for $66 (11.8 lbs.). There's even a ***Cloud Double*** side-by-side stroller for $83.

We like the affordable Cloud strollers—readers tell us they are a good value for the dollar, praising the simple fold and extended canopy (something often missing in the under $100 stroller market).

Best Lightweight Stroller for Urban Parents (Winter)

If you live in the city, you need a stroller that can navigate winter slush, ice and other non-weather city hazards (rough sidewalks). Our pick for these folks, the **Baby Jogger City Mini GT** ($360, 21.5 lbs.), is similar to the base City Mini but adds bigger, no-flat tires, as well as an adjustable handle bar with brake, a redesigned seat/canopy that provides more headroom, and an easier to access storage basket.

At 21.5 lbs., the City Mini GT pushes the outer limits of what we consider lightweight. But that's the trade-off for the bigger wheels, which add about four pounds over the basic City Mini.

Also: Baby Jogger has a raft of winter fighting accessories, like a $74 foot muff (for baby) and $40 hand muff (for parents). Add in the $40 weather shield and this stroller can battle whatever Mother Nature throws at you.

One caveat: the rear axle of the City Mini GT is about three inches off the ground. That means this stroller would struggle with deeper snow. If you regularly face deep snow, an all terrain stroller with higher ground clearance like the **BOB Revolution** would be a better bet.

Best Lightweight Stroller for Urban Parents (Summer)

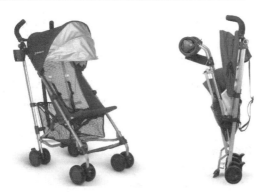

The **UPPAbaby G-Lite** ($180, 8.3 lbs.) is a super lightweight umbrella stroller with a standing fold and mesh seat with fabric padding. The G-lite doesn't recline, so it is best for babies six months and up. The G-Lite is your step-up in umbrella light weight strollers. Here's what we like:

◆ **Decent canopy with extendable sun shade.** Most umbrella strollers have very basic canopies. That's ok if you are in the mall—but once you are outside, there isn't much protection from the weather. The G-Lite's canopy has an extension that pops out to provide more coverage . . . and 50+ SPF protection.

◆ *Mesh seat.* Air flow is important to keep a baby/toddler cool in sweltering urban summers. The mesh seat on the G-Lite fits the bill.

◆ *Standing fold.* Once you fold an umbrella stroller, you'll notice a dilemma—unless the stroller has a "standing fold," you can't just lean it up against a wall in a restaurant because it will fall over. The G-Lite's standing fold is great for storage or use on the go.

◆ *Light weight.* We spec'd the G-Lite at 8.3 lbs, but that is without the canopy. With all the accessories (canopy, basket, etc), the G-Lite comes in at 10.7 lbs. Compare that to other "light-weight" strollers that are often in the 15 lb. range. Trust us, you'll notice that extra five pounds when you carry it around.

◆ *Flip flop friendly fold.* Some umbrella strollers require you to hit a foot lever to close the stroller—that can be difficult if you are in flip flops. The G-Lite has folding triggers that don't require any foot action. The G-Lite includes a cup holder, but a rain shield ($20) and travel bag ($50) are extras.

Flaws but not deal breakers. The G-Lite has a seat that doesn't recline—that means this stroller is best used for babies over six months of age. If your baby likes to nap in their stroller, the **G-Luxe** ($280, similar to the G-Lite but upgraded) with its reclining seat may be a better bet.

Overall, a few folks knocked the G-Lite for its value, or lack thereof. Yep, $180 is a chunk of change for an umbrella stroller—especially when compared with some of our recommended models for under $100. But the difference between a $30 stroller at Walmart and an UPPABaby is quality and durability. Cities tend to dish out more punishment to strollers, making the extra investment here worth it in the long run.

And UPPAbaby strollers have resale value—those $30 Walmart specials are worth $5 at a garage sale.

Best High-Style Lightweight Stroller

France may be famous for its wine and cheese . . . but strollers? Not so much. BabyZen's designer, Jean-Michel Chaudeurge, hopes to change that with stylish strollers that aim to complete with that other European designer stroller megabrand, Bugaboo.

Chaudeurge worked at Fiat before joining his son Julien and launching various baby gear ventures (Chaudeurge's design credits also include the Beaba Babycook food processor). BabyZen has basically one model in the US: the YOYO+ ($500).

The YOYO+ claim to fame is its one-hand unfold and super compact folded form that will fit in an airline overhead bin.

When the YOYO first came out, it didn't make much of a splash. But BabyZen refreshed the stroller (hence the "+") with a bigger basket, higher weight capacity, and padded carry strap. Yes, it is very pricey, but they do throw in rain protector and now the YOYO+ works with infant car seats (via car seat adapters sold separately). Too bad the cup holder is an extra $30.

Yes, if you tried to justify this stroller for overall value, it would be a tough sell. But the design is the star here: white wheels complete with suspension and the ability to morph from infant stroller (with lay flat seat—part of a newborn bundle that is an extra $250) to toddler stroller with a cushy padded seat.

Up next, let's talk multi-function strollers, the Swiss Army Knifes of baby buggies.

Best Multi-Function Stroller (Overall)

After researching and reviewing over 15 different multi-function strollers, we pick the **UPPAbaby Vista** ($840) as best multi-function stroller.

UPPAbaby hits all the right notes with their flagship model, the multi-function Vista (26.3 lbs.). Made with an aircraft alloy frame, the Vista stroller system includes a bassinet and toddler seat, telescoping handle and easy fold.

We liked all the included extras, such as a rain shield, mesh sunshade and bug cover. Plus the Vista uses rubber-like foam wheels that give a smooth ride, but don't go flat. Unlike the Bugaboo, you can fold the Vista with the seat attached.

Key features: a simple one-step fold (similar to their Cruz stroller), zip off washable bassinet fabric, removable wheels, a light-weight frame and the ability to hold two seats.

That's right, you can configure the stroller eight ways including with two UPPAbaby Mesa infant seats, two bassinets (an extra bassinet runs $200), or two toddler seats (second toddler seat called the RumbleSeat is priced separately at $180). Add a PiggyBack Ride Along Board and you can carry three kids of varying ages!

New in 2017, UPPAbaby took an inch off the width of the Vista and changed out the wheels. They've also added Vista models with leather accents for $880 to $900. If you get a non-leather version as a gift, UPPAbaby sells a leather covered bumper bar or a leather handlebar cover for $30 each. Other accessories abound including footmuffs, rain shields, stroller blankets, snack trays, seat liners and bassinet stands to name a few.

Parents love the Vista for its versatility and smooth ride. The only complaints: the price (yes, my first car was less expensive) and it's heavy! But if you want the best of the best in multi-function strollers, this is it.

Also Great: Britax B-READY

A close runner-up in the multi-function stroller race is the ***Britax B-Ready*** ($450-$500, 28.1 lbs.). It also has the second seat option, but lacks the cool quick-fold of the Baby Jogger. The B-Ready works out of the box with the Britax infant car seat, which is a nice plus.

We liked the B-Ready's ability to morph into different configurations—many more than the comparable UPPABaby Vista (which notably, runs $180 more than the B-Ready). Here's a visual overview:

And you can fold the B-Ready with the second (toddler) seat attached—that's something the competition can't do. But you won't get as many included accessories compared to the Vista like the bassinet and rain cover. A second toddler seat runs $180 while a bassinet is $180 and a car seat adapter (for the second position) is an extra $80.

Critics, however, knock the B-Ready's overall bulk and weight (about two pounds heavier than the comparable Vista). To Britax's credit, however, they have made small tweaks to improve the B-Ready (example: new rubber wheels replaced the previous foam versions).

So we have the function and value, but what about style? That's probably Britax's weakness . . . and we aren't just talking about the B-Ready's paint-by-number fabric color choices. Britax strollers lack a certain *je ne sais quoi* when compared with UPPAbaby's Vista.

Best Multi-Function Stroller for Kids Close in Age

If you plan to have two kids close in age, we'd suggest the **Baby Jogger City Select** ($500, 28.1 lbs.). It can be configured 16 ways with an optional second seat ($150), bassinet ($82) or car seat adapter (for Chicco, Peg Perego, Cybex, Maxi Cosi, Graco and Britax; $26 to $50). It's an excellent stroller with a quick fold.

New for 2017, Baby Jogger plans to release a "lux" version of this stroller, cleverly named the Baby Jogger City Select LUX. The LUX adds five more configurations, including a jump seat that can be used up to 45 lbs. The seat on the LUX version folds in a more compact manner—making the stroller 30% smaller when folded. At 28.4 lbs., the LUX is roughly the same weight as the original model. We like the new added rear wheel suspension. This stroller will sell for $629 (it should be on the market by the time you read this).

Overall, the Baby Jogger's City Select's quality is impressive— readers tell us they love it, especially when they have two babies close in age.

More stroller reviews on BabyBargains.com

We've got over 50—count 'em—50 stroller brands reviewed on our free web site at BabyBargains.com. So if you see a stroller online or in a store from a brand you've never heard of, odds are we got you covered.

Also: we have complete coverage of car seat adapters for strollers, with a chart that indicates which strollers works with which car seats (on the main page, click on Car Seat Adapters).

Best All-Terrain Stroller

The crown for best all-terrain stroller goes to the **BOB Revolution Flex** stroller ($384, 26.2 lbs.). It features a front swivel wheel, rear wheel suspension, multi-position canopy and seat recline plus padded handlebar. While not as easy to fold as a Baby Jogger, the Revolution's two-step fold is a close runner-up.

BOB has tweaked the Revolution over the years to improve its features. The latest models feature an adjustable crotch strap, new multi-position canopy and a storage basket with easier access. The version of the Revolution we like the best is the Flex, thanks to an adjustable handlebar.

FYI: There are four versions of the Revolution: Flex, SE, Pro and Stroller Strides. The SE (which stands for sport experience, $369) is a basic Revolution without the adjustable handle bar of the Flex. The Revolution Pro is the same as the Flex, but adds a hand brake: $432 single, $690 double.

The BOB Stroller Stride model ($385 single, $660 double) is basically a BOB Revolution Flex with an added handlebar console and tension tubing for resistance exercise.

If you live in a city with serious winter snows (Buffalo, NY, we're looking at you), this would be the best stroller, thanks to its higher ground clearance.

While the BOB Revolution is great for outdoor adventures, it isn't the best choice for running or jogging. Yes, the Revolution's front wheel does lock into a straight position—but we prefer strollers with fixed front wheels for running, based on numerous interviews with moms and dads who run with their strollers.

Good news—that's the topic up next!

strollers

Best Strollers for Running (and Power Walking)

Fixed-wheel jogging strollers with air-filled tires are best for folks who want to actually jog or run with a stroller—you can push them in a straight line. The disadvantage to these strollers: to turn them, you have to pick up the front wheel and move it. Hence, fixed wheel joggers aren't good for walking or shopping trips.

Another issue to consider: how young can your baby be and ride in a jogger? First, determine whether the seat reclines (not all models do). If it doesn't, wait until baby is at least six months old and can hold his or her head up. If you want to jog or run with the stroller, it might be best to wait until baby is at least a year old since all the jostling can be dangerous for a younger infant (their neck muscles can't handle the bumps). Ask your pediatrician for advice if you are unsure.

Another decision area: the frame. The cheapest strollers (under $200) have steel frames—they're strong but also heavy (and that could be a drawback for serious runners). The most expensive models ($300 to $400) have aluminum frames, which are the lightest in weight. Once again, if you plan casual walks, a steel frame is fine. Runners should go for aluminum.

Finally, remember the Trunk Rule. Any jogger is a lousy choice if you can't get it easily in your trunk. Check the DEPTH of the jogger when it is folded—compared this to your vehicle's trunk. Many joggers are rather bulky even when folded. One tip: quick release wheels help reduce the bulk, so check for that option.

So, which jogging stroller do we recommend? Let's break that down into two categories: power walking and serious runners.

Note that our pick for serious runners has a fixed front wheel; if you want a stroller with a turnable front wheel (more suited to the mall or light duty outdoor activities), go for the power walking pick or see the best all-terrain stroller on the previous page.

One final caveat: air-filled tires give the smoothest ride—but they require maintenance. Yes, they can go flat . . . and you have to remember to put air in them when not used for a while! A bicycle tire tump and patch kit would be wise investments.

If that sounds like too much hassle, consider a stroller with foam-filled rubber tires—no flats! These are more common an all-terrain or multi-function strollers. The trade-off is weight: foam filled tires are often heavier than air-filled ones.

Best Stroller for Power Walking

Our pick for the best stroller for power walking is the **Graco FastAction Fold Jogger Click Connect** ($170, 27 lbs.). It has a swivel front wheel that can be locked, plus a quick fold feature that earns kudos from readers. Add in a generous storage basket, parent console with cup holders plus an affordable price and you've got a great stroller for extended walking.

What's not to like? Well, this stroller is heavy—30% more than our pick for serious runners (below). And you can see from the picture above, when folded, the Graco FastAction Fold is quite large: 39"(!) in length, 23.6" in width and 15.3" in height. You might measure your vehicle's trunk before buying to make sure it will fit.

Best Stroller for Serious Runners

For serious runners and jogging, the best pick is the **BOB Ironman** ($420, 21 lbs.). It is a fixed wheel jogger with smooth 16" tires with steel wheel spokes and adjustable tracking. Thanks to an aluminum frame, this jogger weighs just 21 lbs. Cool feature: quick release wheels enable a more compact fold.

The Best Double Strollers

There are three types of double strollers that can transport two tikes: tandem models, side-by-side styles and sport strollers. Here's a quick 101 on double strollers.

A *tandem* stroller has a "front-back" configuration, where the younger child rides in back while the older child gets the view. These strollers are best for parents with a toddler and a new baby.

Side-by-side strollers, on the other hand, are best for parents of twins or babies close in age. In this case, there's never any competition for the front seat. The only downside: some of these strollers are so wide, they can't fit through narrow doorways or store aisles. (Hint: make sure the stroller is not wider than 30" to insure door compatibility). Another bummer: few side-by-side doubles have fully reclining seats, making them impractical for infants.

So, what to buy—a tandem or side by side? Our reader feedback shows parents are much happier with their side-by-side models than tandems. Why? The tandems can get darn near impossible to push when weighted down with two kids, due to their lengthwise design. Yes, side by sides may not be able to fit through some narrow shopping aisles, but they seem to work better overall.

Finally, if you want to exercise with your stroller, look to the *sport* stroller category for the best options. Most of the strollers in this category are commonly referred to as jogging or running strollers although most parents don't actually run with them. We prefer to use the terms "sport" or "all-terrain."

Best Double Stroller (Overall)

After researching and rating 19 double strollers, we picked the **Kolcraft Contours Options Tandem** as the best double stroller ($280 at Babies R Us).

The Kolcraft Contours Options Tandem is one of the best tandem stroller options on the market. It can take two infant seats (or one infant seat, one toddler seat), includes a universal car seat adapter and has a standing fold. At under $300, it also quite a bargain (other doubles are in the $400's and $500's).

The Options tandem stroller ($280, 32 lbs.) has seven different configurations with seats that can reverse or mix one (or two) infant car seats and a seat. We like the individual reclining seats, adjustable footrests and decent size canopies.

As a brand, Kolcraft is the exception to the rule that you need a successful infant car seat to succeed in the stroller market—despite the lack of any travel systems, Kolcraft has survived, thanks to an emphasis on under-served market segments (namely double strollers).

Kolcraft also has a couple different lines: the Kolcraft strollers are entry-level models, while their Contours brand strollers are a mid-price offering with upgraded features and fabrics.

FYI: Options is a Babies R Us exclusive.

There is also an upgraded version of the Options called the **Options Elite** ($300, 37.4 lbs; pictured on the previous page at right), which is a Buy Buy Baby exclusive. The Elite adds rubber coated rear wheels, side storage basket access and seat back storage. The Elite also has an extra, extendable canopy with mesh air vent as well as taller seats.

What do parents say about the Contours Options Tandem stroller? The comments are overwhelmingly positive. Parents especially like the versatility of the seat arrangements. Plus you can use almost any popular infant seat on the stroller. Others noted the stroller was easy to maneuver, often a problem with other cheaper tandem strollers.

Flaws but not deal breakers. The Contours Options tandem is an excellent double stroller with one big disadvantage: weight. At 30+ lbs, the Options is bulky when folded (it can easily eat up the entire trunk in a vehicle). While fans loved the multiple configurations and overall ease of use, the lack of a parent console (save one skimpy cup holder) is a bummer.

To remedy this, we'd suggest a universal parent console like this one pictured at right from Baby Jogger for $26.

Best Budget-Friendly Double Stroller

Our pick for best budget-friendly double stroller is the **Joovy Caboose Stand-on Tandem** ($100-$110, 26 lbs.).

This stroller really isn't a double stroller with two seats, but a "stand-on tandem"—the younger child sits in front while the older child stands in back (there is also a jump seat for the older child to sit on). This is a better solution when you have an older toddler who doesn't want to ride all the time in a stroller . . . but still gets tired and needs a place to sit on long outings.

Bonus: this stroller also includes a universal infant car seat adapter. At $100-$110, this stroller is a very good value—since most doubles are $200+.

Readers generally love this stroller, but a few critics note the wheels are designed for smooth surfaces, not rough or broken sidewalks. We'd agree—this isn't an all-terrain stroller.

Best Side-by-Side Double Stroller

Our top choice for best side-by-side stroller is the **Chicco**

Echo Twin ($190). Based on the popular Liteway stroller, the Echo Twin is a two-handled umbrella style stroller with rear wheel suspension, padded five-point harness and cup holder. Other features include independent four position recline on both seats, adjustable leg rest and compact fold.

A nice feature for parents of twins (or two kids close together in age): the compact fold and carry handle.

The Echo Twin has individually adjustable canopies that have zip-off rear flaps, which allow for additional airflow. The seats have a one-hand recline and they can be adjusted individually. Another plus: the recline here is a full recline, so babies as young as six months will be comfortable napping in this stroller.

The double wheels have both suspension (for a smoother ride) and swivel locks in front as well as a rear wheel brake.

Overall, readers tell us they love this stroller, especially for its compact size when folded. Amazon reviewers give this stroller a 91% positive rating (meaning four and five star reviews).

Flaws but not deal breakers. While the Chicco Echo Twin has mostly positive reviews, some parents (even those who love it) complain that the stroller is heavy. At 30 lbs., it's not a piece of cake to lift into your trunk, but that's true of almost every double stroller on the market today.

Others note it can be too wide (33.5″) to fit through doors and the canopies are rather small. Another disadvantage: there is no parent console, only a parent cup holder. And there isn't even a cup holder for the kids!

Also Great: Joovy Scooter X2 Double Stroller

The **Joovy ScooterX2** ($167) is a lightweight side-by-side twin stroller with an elliptical frame. It also features a deep (but not full) seat recline. Like all Joovy strollers, the Scooter X2 features an oversized canopy and large storage basket.

There are even two cup holders/storage pockets on the back of each seat. In a recent

refresh, the ScooterX2 gained larger wheels (7″ front, 9″ rear), new graphite frame and improved fold.

Best Sport Double Stroller

Our pick for best sport double stroller, the **BOB Revolution Flex Duallie** ($533) is an offshoot of the hugely popular Revolution single stroller. It has the same front swivel wheel, rear wheel suspension and individual multi-position canopies of the original Revolution plus a new adjustable handle and polymer wheels. These features make for a comfortable ride for both parents and kids.

Quality and durability are the hallmarks of BOB strollers. Yes, they are expensive (especially the Duallie versions), but they can take a beating and keep on rolling. Readers tell us they love their BOB's. On Amazon, four- and five-star reviews combine for an astonishing 94% approval rating for this stroller. Folks love the suspension and air tires, making it a breeze to push.

FYI: BOB is owned by Britax, so the BOB infant car seat adapter holds Britax seats. There are even special BOB versions of the Britax B-SAFE infant car seat; same seat, just matching colors.

Flaws but not deal breakers. BOB stands for Beast of Burden—and that accurately describes the weight of the Revolution Flex Duallie. At 34 lbs. this stroller is a *beast*. Yes, all that ruggedness has its price.

And as we mentioned earlier in this chapter, air-filled tires require maintenance . . . and can go flat at the most inconvenient times. A bicycle pump and patch kit should probably find a home in your BOB's storage basket.

Finally, the Revolution Flex Duallie does not include a parent console or kids snack tray. But . . . conveniently the company sells these as accessories. The console (specifically for twin strollers) is $23 while the snack tray is $40. It would be nice, since this stroller retails for $500+, if BOB could at least include a parent cup holder in the box.

The Best Diaper Bags

We consider ourselves experts at diaper bags—we got five of them as gifts. While you don't need five, this important piece of luggage may feel like an extra appendage after your baby's first year. And diaper bags are for more than just holding diapers—many include compartments for baby bottles, clothes, and changing pads. With that in mind, let's take a look at what separates great diaper bags from the rest of the pack. In addition, we'll give you our list of eight items for a well-stocked diaper bag.

7 Things No One Tells You About Buying A Diaper Bag

1 **THE SHEAR NUMBERS OF DIAPER BAGS CAN SEEM OVERWHELMING.** Yes, it seems like there is a separate diaper bag available for each of the four million moms that will give birth this year. So how do you know which one is best?

Here's our checklist: the best diaper bags are made of tear-resistant fabric and loaded with all sorts of useful pockets. Contrast that with low quality brands that lack many pockets and are made of cheap, thin vinyl—after a couple of uses, they start to split and crack. Yes, high quality diaper bags will cost more ($50 to $150 versus $30 to $45), but you'll be much happier in the long run.

Another item on our checklist: diapers bags that don't look like diaper bags. A well-made diaper bag that doesn't look like a diaper bag will make a great piece of carry-on luggage later in life.

2 **YOU MAY NOT NEED TO BUY A DIAPER BAG AFTER ALL.** Many folks have a favorite bag or backpack that can double as a diaper bag. Besides the obvious (wipes and diapers), put in a large zip-lock bag as a holder for dirty/wet items. Add a couple of receiving blankets (as changing pads) plus the key items listed in tip #3, and you have a complete diaper bag. You can buy many items found in a diaper bag (such as a changing pad) a la carte at most baby stores.

3 **DRUM ROLL! HERE ARE OUR EIGHT ESSENTIAL ITEMS FOR YOUR DIAPER BAG.**

◆ *Extra diapers*. Put a dozen in the big bag, two or three in the small one. Why so many? Babies can go through quite a few in a very short time. Of course, when baby gets older (say over a year), you can cut back on the number of diapers you need for a trip. Another wise tip: put whole packages of diapers and wipes in your car(s). We did this after we forgot our diaper bag one too many times and needed an emergency diaper. (The only bummer: here in Colorado, the wipes we keep in the car sometimes freeze in the winter!

◆ *Travel-size wipes package.* A good idea: a plastic Tupperware container that holds a small stack of wipes. Some wipe makers sell travel packs that are allegedly "re-sealable" to retain moisture; we found that they aren't. And they are expensive. For example, a Huggies travel pack of 16 wipes is $2. That works out to 12¢ per wipe compared to 2¢ per wipe if you buy a Huggies refill box of 624 wipes.

◆ *Blanket and change of clothes.* Despite the reams of scientists who work on diapers, they still aren't leak- proof—plan for it. A change of clothes is most useful for babies under six months of age, when leaks are more common. After that point, this becomes less necessary

◆ *Hat or cap.* We like the foreign legion-type hats that have flaps to cover your baby's neck and ears (about $10 to $20). Warmer caps are helpful to chase away a chill, since the head is where babies lose the most heat.

◆ *Baby toiletries.* Babies can't take much direct exposure to sunlight—sunscreen (30 SPF or higher) is a good bet for all infants. Besides sunscreen, other optional accessories include bottles of lotion and diaper rash cream. The best bet: buy these in small travel or trial sizes. Don't forget insect repellent as well. This can be applied to infants two months of age and older

◆ *Don't forget some toys.* We like compact rattles, board books, teethers, etc.

◆ *Snacks.* When baby starts to eat solid foods, having a few snacks in the diaper bag (a bottle of water, crackers, a small box of cereal) is a smart move. But don't bring them in plastic bags. Instead bring reusable plastic containers. Plastic bags are a suffocation hazard and should be kept far away from babies and toddlers.

◆ **Your stuff.** Be careful putting your wallet into the diaper bag—we advise against it. We left our diaper bag behind one too many times before we learned this lesson. Put your name and phone number in the bag in case it is lost.

4 **IF THE BUDGET ALLOWS, GET TWO DIAPER BAGS.** Buy one that is a full-size, all-option big hummer for longer trips (or overnight stays) and the other that is a mini-bag for a short hop to dinner or shopping. Here's what each should have:

◆ **The full-size bag:** This needs a waterproof changing pad that folds up, waterproof pouch or pocket for wet clothes, a couple compartments for diapers, blankets/clothes, etc. Super-deluxe brands have bottle compartments with Thinsulate to keep bottles warm or cold. Another plus: outside pockets for books and small toys. A zippered outside pocket is good for change or your wallet. A cell phone pocket is also a plus.

◆ **The small bag:** This has enough room for a couple diapers, travel wipe package, keys, wallet and cell phone. Some models have a bottle pocket and room for one change of clothes.

5 **IF MONEY IS TIGHT, JUST GO FOR THE SMALL BAG.** To be honest, the full-size bag is often just a security blanket for first-time parents—some think they need to lug around every possible item in case of a diaper catastrophe. But, in the real world, you'll quickly discover schlepping that big full-size bag everywhere isn't practical. While a big bag is nice for overnight or long trips, we'll bet you will be using the small bag much more often.

6 **FABRIC IS IMPORTANT.** Look for fabric that is easy to wipe clean or throw in the wash. (Sorry, stash away those expensive leather totes from your pre-baby years for some future day). Smooshed up crackers, wet clothes, and spit up are facts of life. So stick with easy clean fabric. And consider a diaper bag with a bright colored interior lining. Black linings make it hard to see items, but bright colors like red make it much easier.

7 **BE SAFE: DON'T HANG YOUR DIAPER BAG ON THE BACK OF YOUR STROLLER.** While you may see lots of parents hanging their diaper bags on the handles of their strollers, we generally don't recommend this. Kids can get injured when they are climbing out of the stroller and it flips up because the heavy diaper bag pulls down the back of the stroller.

Some diaper bags come with special stroller clips. If you're considering using those clips, try them without the baby in the stroller. Since every stroller is different, you'll want to confirm that the stroller won't tip with a bag handing on the handlebars. And some stroller makers also make a matching bag that will work with their stroller. If you're determined to hang your bag on the stroller, buying a bag from the stroller maker may be the safer way to go.

Our diaper bag picks are divided into the following categories:

◆ The Best Diaper Bag (Overall)
◆ The Best Budget-Friendly Diaper Bag
◆ The Best Designer Diaper Bag

The Best Diaper Bag (Overall)

After researching and reviewing hundreds of different diaper bag manufacturers and models, we pick the **Skip Hop Duo** ($48) as the best baby diaper bag.

Our readers love the Skip Hop line of bags (skiphop.com). Skip Hop offers nine different designs, but our favorite is the Skip Hop Duo ($40-$70).

Stylish, affordable and full of practical features, the Skip Hop Duo ($48) can handle just about anything for baby. With ten pockets (including two for baby bottles), contrasting liner, stroller straps, changing pad and more, the Duo is a winner.

The Duo is Skip Hop's largest bag with eleven pockets including a cell phone pocket, and magnetic closures instead of zipper. Yes, it has a shoulder strap too and changing pad, as you'd expect plus it comes in eleven colors and patterns:

Some parents say the bag holds less than they expected and the magnetic closures don't work as well if you stuff the bag really full. Those complaints aside, Skip Hop is a great option if you are looking for a full-size diaper bag with a bit more style. The Duo also comes in "Special Edition" versions with fancier fabrics (and only nine pockets).

Also Great: Ju-Ju-Be Hobo Be

The **Ju-Ju-Be** line of diaper bags gets raves from readers. Most of their designs are in the $150-$200, but the **Hobo Be** is a great option at only $78. This messenger style bag comes with five zippered pock-
ets, three main pockets, anti-microbial treated inner fabric, Teflon-treated outer fabric, a changing pad, and memory foam padded strap. A wide variety of colors and styles are available.

Best Budget-Friendly Diaper Bag

At first, you might think a diaper bag that costs under $50 isn't really that cheap. After all, you can find plenty of options in that price range. But those cheaper options usually only include a diaper changing pad. The **SoHo diaper bag** ($30) has seven pieces: the large main bag, zippered mini purse, insulated bottle bag, Grips stroller attachments, two accessory cases and changing pad. The diaper bag itself has a several outside pockets and zip closure on top. Score!

Best Designer Diaper Bag

The ***Kate Space Taden*** diaper bag is our pick for best designer diaper bag. Yes, Kate Spade is well known for a clean, simple design aesthetic and the company's diaper bags are no exception.

Our fave is the Taden, a nylon bag with a zippered pocket, two outside pockets (for bottles or sippy cups) and a removable changing pad. We found the Taden on Amazon for $152.

Other current Kate Space bag styles include the Stevie, Harmony, Brynne, Pauline, Hildy, and a backpack option. The designs you'll find on Amazon are mostly older models, ranging in price from $150 to $400.

Reader feedback on the Taden has been quite positive.

Up next, let's talk baby carriers—the other way (besides a stroller) to transport baby from here to there!

CHAPTER 9

Baby Carriers

Inside this chapter

Sure, baby wearing has been around for centuries, but a recent renaissance has sent the sales of baby carriers soaring. We've been fans of baby wearing since the 90's (before it was cool). So take a tour with us of the different types of carriers—we've got tips, advice and recommendations.

Baby wearing fans seem to divide into two camps: those that want to wear their babies for their first year. And those who are fans of extended baby wearing into toddlerhood.

As a result, we have basic carriers that work up to 25 lbs that are designed for babies up to 18 months. And newer carriers that now work up to 45 lbs. (for the curious, that is the weight of an average five-year old).

Just to make it more confusing, it seems like there are 437 different carrier makes and models on the market, from simple slings to fancy backpacks. And we've noticed over the years that every single one of those models has a parent who's a big fan.

How to find the right carrier for you? That advice is up next.

7 Things No One Tells You About Buying A Baby Carrier

1 WAIT! THERE ARE **THAT** MANY DIFFERENT TYPES OF CARRIERS?

Do you want a soft structured carrier? For infants or extended use? What about slings? What the heck is a Mei Tai? A rum-based drink from Hawaii?

Ok, let's take a deep breath. Carriers come in a variety of types. Let's review:

◆ **Front carriers** (aka Soft Structured Carriers) are the most well-known and popular of all the carrier types. The 800-pound gorilla in this category is the Baby Bjorn, which is Sweden's most successful export since ABBA.

Front carriers basically are designed like a fabric pouch worn on your chest with straps connecting at the shoulders and waist with buckles or snaps. These type of carriers are made for infants up to around 30 pounds although some hybrids like the Boba 4G can carry older kids up to 45 lbs. Nowadays, soft structured carriers are more flexible, allowing baby to be carried on your back and hip as well as in front.

◆ A sub category of front carriers is the *mei ta (also referred to as meh dai),* or *Asian carrier.* Inspired by carriers used in Asia (particularly China), mei tais have an unstructured body and are tied on rather than buckled. This allows for infinite adjustment.

◆ *Slings* and *pouches* (which are unstructured carriers) have been around forever. These carriers are basically pockets of fabric that can be adjusted with a ring or velcro. Babies can recline in slings or sit upright once they're old enough. Most slings and pouches are only rated up to 35 lbs., so they are more appropriate for infants.

◆ *Wrap around carriers* are one long piece of cloth that is twisted and folded to create a pouch for baby. Typically the fabric has some stretch to it. This type of carrier has the steepest learning curve for parents. Most designs are intended for smaller, younger babies up to 35 lbs.

◆ *Backpack or frame carriers* are designed for hiking with lightweight aluminum frames, high quality waterproof fabrics and ergonomically designed straps. Many include sunshades, lots of storage and adjustable seating as baby grows.

2 **THINK ABOUT HOW LONG YOU ENVISION USING A CARRIER.** The most common baby carriers (Baby Bjorn Original, for example) are designed for use up 25 lbs. The average boy would reach this weight around 18 months (girls a few months after that). Other carriers aim for extended use, up to 30 or even 45 pounds (that's a three, four or even five year old!).

Of course there is no right or wrong answer—it's your call.

If you only envision using a carrier in baby's first year—then focus on carriers that have the 25 lb. limits. If extended baby wearing is something you'd like to try, look at brands with higher weight limits, like ERGObaby, Boba, Beco and so on.

3 **JUST BECAUSE YOU LOVE A CARRIER DOESN'T MEAN YOU BABY WILL.** That's right—some babies can be darn right fussy about carriers. Your baby may love carrier A but hate style B, so hang on to your receipt (or buy from a source with a good return policy). Every baby is different, so a carrier that works for your sister-in-law may induce screaming fits from your baby. Some moms actually buy a couple types of carriers to see what works, then return the ones that don't.

4 **BABY WEARING LOOKS SIMPLE, BUT BE AWARE OF THESE KEY SAFETY PRECAUTIONS.** Back in 2010, the Consumer Product Safety Commission issued these baby wearing tips:

◆ Premature infants and those with low birth weight (under 7 lbs., including twins or infants with breathing issues such as a cold) should not be placed in a sling.

◆ Make sure the infant's face is not covered and can be seat at all times regardless of the type of carrier you're using.

◆ Frequently check on your baby to make sure he is breathing.

Check the graphic to see how to correctly and incorrectly wear your baby:

| **Right** Chin up; Face visible; Nose and mouth free | **Wrong** Baby's face is covered | **Wrong** Baby is too low | **Wrong** Baby is hunched with chin touching chest | **Wrong** Baby's face is pressed tight against wearer |

5 **SOME CARRIERS HAVE A STEEP LEARNING CURVE.** An example: wrap around carriers. These long pieces of fabric need to be wrapped surprisingly tight to keep baby in the proper position and support a parent's back. This can take some practice.

Even some soft structured carriers have lots of buckles, Velcro and adjustments that can get complicated.

Yes, slings are the easiest carrier to use, but still may require a little practice. Make sure you read the directions, watch instructional videos online and practice before you try your carrier with an actual baby. The first few times, you may want to have a second person handy to help you get all the adjustments correct.

6 **CHEAP CARRIERS COME WITH A HIDDEN COST.** Yes, there are $15 baby carriers at discount stores. What's the difference between this and our recommended carriers, which run about $150-$200?

A truth about carriers: a cheap carrier is no bargain if it hurts your back or is uncomfortably hot. And sadly, those $15 carriers score low on parent happiness, according to the many interviews we've done over the years with parents.

When purchasing a carrier, investing more money buys comfort and ease of use. For example, the fabric is softer when you spend more and the padding is thicker. Often hook and loop closures are industrial strength (Velcro vs. Aplix, for example) with more pricey carriers.

Deluxe slings may come with padded side rails and more expensive back pack carriers may have toddler stirrups to help older kids sit up comfortably.

7 **OPTIONAL ACCESSORIES ARE OFTEN WORTH THE PRICE.** Drool bibs that attach to carrier, sunshades for backpack carriers, extra long straps to fit a spouse—all worthy extras! One of our faves: teething pads for the ERGObaby carriers. Love 'em.

Organic fabric certifications

Several eco-friendly baby carriers tout various organic fabric certifications. Here's a quick 101 on what these mean.

There are three international organizations that test and certify textiles. These are OEKO-TEX, Global Organic Textile Standard (GOTS) and Textile Exchange (OCS). All three of these certifications are optional—there is no legal standard for organic, non-allergenic, chemical free textiles in the US. Many of the companies that are certified are European, with only a few US brands certified. Here's a bit about each of the three organizations.

◆ **OEKO-TEX** is a German organization that offers a Standard 100 certification program for textiles at all steps in the manufacturing process. Here's what the label means:

"Products marked with the label 'Confidence in textiles (Standard 100)' provide effective protection against allergenic substances, formaldehyde, heavy metals such as nickel or, for example, forbidden plasticizers (phthalates) in baby textiles."

OEKO-TEX offers a second certification called Green by OEKO-TEX, which means the "materials (were) tested for harmful substances," the product was "made in environmentally friendly facilities" and it was "made in safe and socially responsible workplaces."

◆ **GOTS (Global Organic Textile Standard)** certifies textiles as organic. To meet their qualifications, "only textile products that contain a minimum of 70% organic fibers can become GOTS certified. All chemical inputs such as dyestuffs and auxiliaries used must meet certain environmental and toxicological criteria. The choice of accessories is limited in accordance with ecological aspects as well. A functional waste water treatment plant is mandatory for any wet-processing unit involved and all processors must comply with minimum social criteria." Basically, beyond using organic materials, companies must also be socially responsible to their workers and the community.

carriers

◆ **Textile Exchange (OCS).** Previously referred to as the Organic Exchange (OE) Standard, the international Textile Exchange certifies textiles according to their Organic Content Standard (OCS). They verify the steps in the supply chain to make

certain the materials used in end products like diapers are sustainably sourced/grown, processed and manufactured.

There are only a few carrier manufacturers we can find with one of these international certifications. These companies typically sell both conventionally grown textiles as well as organic, so you'll need to refer to specific organic styles to get certified textiles:

Baby K'Tan (GOTS)
Beco (GOTS)
Boba (OEKO-TEX and GOTS)
Ergobaby (OEKO-TEX)
Mammas Milk (GOTS)
Moby (OCS)
Mountain Buggy (OEKO-TEX)
Tula (OEKO-TEX)

Carrier brands that claim to use organic textiles (for at least some styes) but do not have any info on certifications posted online: Peanutshell, ZoloWear, Lillebaby, and Stokke.

How We Picked A Winner

We evaluate carriers with in-depth inspections, checking models for overall quality and ease of use—for example, checking the ease of adjustment between smaller moms and taller dads, as well as detailed analysis fabric, fasteners and construction.

We also gather significant reader feedback (this book has over 1 million copies in print), tracking carriers on quality and durability. Besides interviewing parents, we also regularly talk with retailers of retailers to see which brands are most trustworthy and other key quality metrics.

The reliability of carrier manufacturers is another key factor—we meet with key company executives at least once a year. Since we've been doing this since 1994, we have developed detailed profiles of major carrier brands that help guide our recommendations. See our web site (BabyBargains.com) for links to individual carrier brand reviews.

The Best Baby Carrier (Overall)

ERGObaby's Ergo 360° ($160) is our top pick for best front carrier. Compared to its many rivals, the Ergo 360° has best-in-class quality, construction and safety. As the name implies, the 360° is a front carrier that allows you to face baby out as well as in, plus piggy back or on the hip.

ERGObaby debuted their first front carrier in 2002. Designer Karin Frost wasn't satisfied with carrier options when she had her first child, so she created a soft-structured carrier with multiple positions. First sewn in Hawaii, the original ERGO design worked in three positions: front carry facing inward, back carry and hip carry. ERGO refined the concept over the years, culminating with the 360°, which adds that fourth position of forward facing out.

The 360° is made with a structured bucket seat that keeps babies legs and hips in a correct position (no dangling legs). It comes with a wide waist belt, which can be worn high when baby is little and adjusted down to carry the weight of older babies and toddlers. The forward facing carry is recommended for babies six months old and older. An infant insert ($25) is required for newborns (and they have to face inward when small). Or you can buy a bundle of the carrier plus insert for $170.

The ERGObaby 360°'s weight range is 12 to 33 lbs. for the carrier only (with the infant insert, you can use it from 7 to 33 lbs.).

ERGObaby has expanded the 360° line by adding a Cool Air Mesh option, with "3D Air Mesh fabric" inserts to keep baby cool and is a bit lighter on moms and dads as well. At $180, it's more expensive than the regular 360°, but if you live in a hot climate or will only use it in the summer months, this may be the version for you.

Feedback on both versions of the 360° from parents has been

mostly positive. Ease of use is excellent, say readers.

Critics of this carrier say the hood is too small and doesn't store away. A few complain that the back latch is uncomfortable and hard to buckle. We also wish the infant insert was included and not a separate purchase. Despite these minor concerns, the ERGObaby 360° is an excellent carrier that wins our overall pick for Best Carrier.

Also Great: Cat Bird Baby Pikkolo

Runner up for the best carrier is the **Pikkolo** ($130) from Cat Bird Baby. This carrier is a mash-up of a front carrier and a mei tai with buckles instead of long ties. It's also more flexible than most other front carriers—it can be used in front facing both in and out, on the back and as a hip carrier.

Also Great: Boba 4G Carrier

The recently revised **Boba 4G Carrier** ($125) now includes an infant insert so it can be used with babies as little as seven pounds.

Other features we love include a removable sleeping hood included with a pocket. Removable foot rests for toddlers, a purse holder strap, smartphone pocket and a sliding chest strap round out the features.

Readers love this carrier—it is a worthy a look if you want a soft-structured front carrier.

The Best Sling Carrier

After comparing and testing more than ten different types of baby slings, we choose the **Maya Wrap** as the best sling carrier.

Maya Wrap has consistently been a favorite of our readers, who love its flexibility and comfort. Helpful instructional videos are available on their web site and a DVD is included with your purchase. The rings are made of ¼″ anodized aluminum, the fabrics are 100% cotton hand-loomed and are only made of one layer of fabric. As a result, the Maya Wrap sling carrier is quite lightweight and breathable. It comes in four sizes with nearly 20 fabric options.

Two versions are offered: the Lightly Padded sling ($80) and the ComfortFit sling ($95). The difference? The padded version has padding on the shoulder while the ComfortFit has no padding. One advantage to the ComfortFit—the shoulder fabric can be adjusted while the padded shoulder cannot. Parents seem to prefer the padded shoulder, however, and the ComfortFit is actually a bit more expensive.

Reader feedback on the Maya Wrap sling carrier is positive, although some parents complain about the long piece of fabric that hangs from the rings when the sling is being used. If you want to avoid a lot of extra fabric, you can size down your wrap so the hanging fabric is shorter. Another complaint: it can be painful to use with older babies or for long periods of time. We judged these issues to be minor and recommend the Maya Wrap as our top pick for sling carriers.

carriers

Also Great: Mamma's Milk Sling

Made of stretch cotton, **Mamma's Milk** sling carriers are probably the easiest to use of all sling carriers available, in our opinion. They are infinitely adjustable and use Aplix (a stronger version of Velcro) to keep the sling in the correct position for the parent. Comfortable foam padding is included in the area where toddlers' legs rest. Most of Mamma's Milk slings are made of cotton stretch fabric, although they also offer an one Solarveil (an open wave mesh fabric designed for hot climates) option and three organic fabrics. Bonus: detailed videos on Mamma's Milk's web site show how to adjust the sling.

Best Wrap Carrier

The **Wrapsody Breeze** gauze carrier ($83 to $92) by Gypsy Mama is our choice for best wrap carrier for it's front and back carrying flexibility and comfort.

Gypsy Mama makes the Wrapsody in three different fabrics: the **Wrap DuO** (can be used in water, $72), **Breeze** (cotton gauze,

$83 to $92), and **Hybrid** (t-shirt-like material, $98 to $120).

The Breeze wraps are the lightest weight, but not as stretchy. The Breeze fabric is hand dyed and batiked in Bali. Cool feature: it folds down into a built-in storage pocket, making it easy to toss in the diaper bag.

Gypsy Mama recommends the Hybrid wraps ($98 to $120) for beginners as they are "more forgiving of sloppy wrap jobs," says the company in a rather candid moment. The fabric is similar to a t-shirt and is very soft for both newborns and older kids.

The Wrap DuO is interesting: it's waterproof with two different weight limits: in the water, about 35 lbs.; 25 lbs. on land. Made of high tech sports knit, it's intended to keep mom and baby cool on those hot summer days.

We found the online instructions (both videos and printed) clear and easy to follow. Parents love the Breeze for warm climates/summer wearing.

The Best Meh Dai (Mei Tai) Carrier

After comparing and testing dozens of meh dai carriers, we have chosen the **BabyHawk by Moby** as the best meh dai carrier.

What makes BabyHawk different from other meh dai carriers? Flexibility. BabyHawk sells two types of carriers: a meh dai with traditional ties ($90 to $100), or a meh dai with buckles and ties ($130), cleverly called Buckle Tie carriers.

Want to custom design your own carrier? Yes, you can that here as well—select a strap color, regular or reversible pattern (from 50 options), strap length, accessories like a toy ring and so on. These run about $100. (The only bummer: you can't see what the final product will look on the screen).

The BabyHawk meh dai is a traditional Asian-style carrier with long straps at the shoulders and shorter straps at the waist that allow for infinite adjustment. These meh dais fit babies from 8 to 40 lbs. and allow parents to position baby at the front (facing in), back or on the hip. Made of 100% cotton, they come in over 25 pre-made designs.

The Buckle Tie baby carrier (formerly known as the Oh Snap!), has those long shoulder straps, but replaces the waist ties with buckles. These designs cost a bit more ($130 at retail, but often discounted online) than their traditional meh dais, but parents like the more supportive waist belt and buckle adjustment.

BabyHawk's secret sauce is the ability to custom design a carrier, as we briefly mentioned above. Start with a strap color (5 options) and main body color (over 35), and then decide whether you want extra long straps ($5), toy rings ($5 each), Oh Spit! strap protectors ($15) or reversible fabric ($20). Without all the extras, a basic BabyHawk is $100. If you just want to buy an in-stock meh dai, we saw over 30 options available when we last visited.

We like all the unique fabrics including nature scenes, Asian prints, and geometrics. Readers most like the customization options (but be forewarned: customized BabyHawks are non-returnable) and the comfortable fabrics. A few detractors complained that the straps were too long . . . and it takes a while to figure out how to use these carriers. If you're really petite, the buckle tie may not fit—go with the traditional meh dai instead.

Also Great: CatBird Baby Meh Dai (Mei Tai)

Catbird Baby manufactures one of our favorite front carriers, the Pikkolo, so we were excited to see they added a meh dai option a few years ago. Priced at $100 and available in 14 fabric options, this is a great choice for parents who want carrier flexibility. You can use the Catbird meh dais in four positions including front carry forward facing.

For parents with older, heavier babies, Catbird sells a support belt ($25) to make it more comfortable. In fact, this is our only complaint about the brand: it would be nice if the support belt came with the meh dai. Despite this minor quibble, readers give the Catbird Baby excellent reviews and the reasonable price leads us to rate them highly.

Yes, meh dai carriers do have a bit of a learning curve; fortunately Catbird Baby's web site has several instruction videos.

Best Backpack Carrier

After comparing and testing nearly a dozen backpack carriers, we picked the **Kelty Transit 3.0** as our choice for best backpack carrier.

Love to hike? A frame carrier is the best option for hikers—these carriers have more support for parents and comfort features for babies than typical baby carriers.

The Kelty Transit 3.0 ($195) is our favorite for its comfort and ease of use. Yes, $195 is a chunk of change for a carrier—but how much did your hiking boots cost? Sure, you can hike in tennis shoes for less, but specialized gear makes hiking more comfortable for everyone.

The Kelty Transit's adjustable lumbar support wins kudos and parents find it easy to get on and off. Most importantly, the Transit is very comfortable to wear on long hikes.

We liked the little extras such as the sun hood, changing pad, toy loops, organizer pocket, and hip belt water bottle pocket.

What's not to like? Readers say it can be hard to get a good fit for petite parents. And the initial adjustments when you first put it on require a bit of patience.

Also Great: Deuter Kid Comfort II

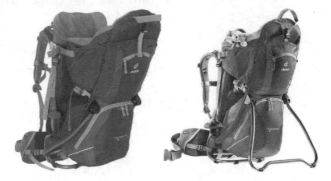

If your best friend offered to buy a backpack carrier as a gift, the **Deuter Kid Comfort II** ($250) would also be an excellent choice. Features include a contoured hip belt, zipped compartment under the seat, 35-point harness, side entry, large mesh storage pockets, and breathable seat cushions. A sun roof and rain cover are sold separately. It's got everything you could ever need: adjustability, storage and great safety features.

Reader feedback on this carrier is excellent—it only missed being our top pick because the similar Kelty carrier mentioned on the previous page is $50 less.

CHAPTER 10

CONCLUSION

What Does it All Mean?

How much money can you save if you follow all the tips and suggestions in this book? Let's take a look at the average cost of having a baby from the introduction and compare it with our Baby Bargains budget.

Your Baby's First Year

ITEM	AVERAGE	BABY BARGAINS BUDGET
Crib, mattress, dresser, rocker	$1570	$1433
Bedding / Decor	$350	$222
Baby Clothes	$615	$301
Disposable Diapers	$865	$400
Maternity/Nursing Clothes	$1300	$550
Nursery items, high chair, toys	$515	$225
Baby Food/Formula	$1015	$350
Stroller, Car Seats, Carrier	$730	$490
Miscellaneous	$490	$500
TOTAL	$7450	$4323
TOTAL SAVINGS:		***$3127***

WOW! You just saved over $3100! We hope the savings makes it worth the price of this book. We'd love to hear from you on how much you saved with our book—feel free to email, write or call us. See the "How to Reach Us" page at the back of this book.

What does it all mean?

At this point, we usually have something pithy to say as we end the book. But, as parents of two boys, we're just too tired. We're going to bed, so feel free to make up your own ending.

And thanks for reading *Baby Bargains*.

conclusion

APPENDIX A

Registry Cheat Sheets

SAMPLE
REGISTRY

Time is tight—we know. So to help juice your baby registry, here are the Baby Bargains Registry Cheat Sheets.

These sample registries follow our recommendations for each chapter of this book. Enjoy!

Good

Item	Baby Bargains recommends	Price
Crib	IKEA Sniglar	$70
Mattress	Safety 1st Heavenly Dreams	$52
Dresser	Ikea Hemnes Double Dresser	$250
Changing pad	Summer Infant Contoured Changing Pad	$20
Glider Rocker	Ikea POÄNG rocking chair	$129
Bedding	American Baby Co. sheets (4)	$43
Wearable blanket	Halo SleepSack	$17
Breast pump	Medela Swing mini-electric	$112
Bottles	Dr. Brown's Original Bottle Starter Kit	$16
High Chair	Fisher-Price Space Saver	$42
Bathtub	First Years Sure Comfort Deluxe Tub	$16
Potty seat	Fisher Price Froggy Potty	$13
Audio monitor*	VTech Safe & Sound Digital Audio Monitor	$50
Video Monitor	Infant Optics DXR-5	$99
Play Yard/Bassinet	Graco Pack N Play On the Go	$53
Bouncer	Fisher-Price Infant to Toddler Rocker	$25
Humidifier	Crane Adorable Ultrasonic Cool Mist	$30
Swing	Fisher Price Snugabunny Cradle 'n Swing	$105
Safety gate	KidCo Safeway Gates (2)	$86
Thermometer	Vicks Baby Rectal Thermometer	$11
Infant Car Seat	Graco SnugRide Click Connect 35LX	$160
Convertible Seat	Cosco Scenera Next	$47
Stroller	Kolcraft Cloud Plus	$66
Diaper Bag	SoHo diaper bag	$30
Carrier	Maya Wrap Lightly Padded Ring Sling	$80
Clothing	Wait until after showers; see Chapter 4	
TOTAL		**$1622**

Better

Item	*Baby Bargains recommends*	Price
Crib	DaVinci Kalani	$220
Mattress	Moonlight Slumber Little Dreamer	$197
Dresser	Eco-Chic Baby Clover Five-Drawer Chest	$550
Changing pad	Summer Infant Contoured Changing Pad	$18
Glider Rocker	Best Chair Jacob upholstered glider	$450
Bedding	Aiden + Anais sheets (4)	$116
Wearable blanket	Halo SleepSack	$17
Breast pump	Philips Avent Double Electric Comfort	$200
Bottles	Dr. Brown's Original Bottle Starter Kit	$16
High Chair	Jovvy New Nook	$120
Bathtub	First Years Sure Comfort Deluxe Tub	$16
Potty seat	Fisher Price Froggy Potty	$13
Audio monitor*	VTech Safe & Sound Digital Audio Monitor	$50
Video Monitor	Infant Optics DXR-8	$165
Play Yard/Bassinet	Graco Pack N Play On the Go	$25
Bouncer	Fisher Price Infant to Toddler Rocker	$40
Humidifier	Honeywell HCM-350	$63
Swing	Fisher Price Snugabunny Cradle 'n Swing	$105
Safety gate	KidCo Safeway Gates (2)	$86
Thermometer	Vicks Baby Rectal Thermometer	$11
Infant Car Seat	Britax B-Safe 35 Elite	$200
Convertible Seat	Chicco NextFit	$280
Stroller	UPPAbaby G-Lite	$160
Diaper Bag	Ju-Ju-Be Hobo Be	$78
Carrier	Boba 4G Carrier	$125
Clothing	Wait until after showers; Chapter 4	
TOTAL		**$3321**

*Audio monitor is optional—you can get either audio or video. You most likely will NOT need both!

See the next page for the best picks.

registry cheat sheets

Best

Item	Baby Bargains recommends	Price
Crib	Pali Imperia	$400
Mattress	Naturepedic Organic Cotton Lightweight	$260
Dresser	Eco-Chic Baby Clover Five-Drawer Chest	$550
Changing pad	Summer Infant Contoured Changing Pad	$18
Glider Rocker	Dutailier Glider Recline + Ottoman	$442
Bedding	Carousel crib sheets (4)	$120
Wearable blanket	Halo SleepSack	$17
Breast pump	Medela Pump In Style Advanced	$180
Bottles	Avent Classic Infant Starter Set	$33
High Chair	Graco Blossom	$143
Bathtub	Primo EuroBath	$21
Potty seat	Baby Bjorn Toilet Trainer	$24
Audio monitor*	VTech Safe & Sound Digital Audio Monitor	$50
Video Monitor	Infant Optics DXR-8	$165
Play Yard/Bassinet	Graco Pack N Play On the Go	$53
Bouncer	4Moms MamaRoo	$160
Humidifier	Honeywell HCM-350	$58
Swing	Fisher Price Snugabunny Cradle 'n Swing	$105
Safety gate	KidCo Safeway Gates (2)	$86
Thermometer	Vicks Baby Rectal Thermometer	$11
Infant Car Seat	Chicco KeyFit 30	$200
Convertible Seat	Britax Boulevard ClickTight	$304
Stroller	Baby Jogger City Mini	$250
Diaper Bag	Skip Hop Duo	$48
Carrier	ERGObaby 360° baby carrier	$160
Clothing	Wait until after showers; see Chapter 4	
	TOTAL	**$3858**

Grandparents

Item	Baby Bargains recommends	Price
Crib	Dream on Me portable crib	$110
Mattress	Safety 1st Heavenly Dreams	$52
Bedding	American Baby Co. sheets (4)	$43
High Chair	Fisher-Price Space Saver	$42
Thermometer	Vicks Baby Rectal Thermometer	$11
Safety gate	KidCo's Safeway Gates (2)	$86
Convertible Seat	Cosco Scenera Next	$47
	TOTAL	**$391**

Audio monitor is optional—you can get either audio or video.

APPENDIX B
Advice for multiples

TWINS

Yes, this year, one in 32 births in the US will be twins. Here's our round-up of our picks for the best gear for parents of multiples.

◆ **Cribs.** Since twins tend to be smaller than most infants at birth, parents of multiples can use bassinets or cradles for an extended period of time. For those on a tight budget, we like a portable playpen with a bassinet feature as an alternative (**Graco Pack N Play** is one popular choice for under $100). We also like the **Halo Bassinest Swivel Premiere Sleeper** ($250).

Here's a neat idea for parents of multiples—how about a crib that converts to two twin beds? HGTV Home Baby (made by Bassett and sold at Buy Buy Baby) makes the Hayden collection, a crib that converts to two twin beds. Yes, most twins sleep in separate cribs; so one could sleep in the Hayden and the other in a simpler IKEA model.

◆ **Nursing help.** Yes, nursing one baby can be a challenge, but two? You might need some help. To the rescue comes **Mothering Multiples: Breastfeeding & Caring for Twins and More** by Karen Kerkoff Gromada ($18.95). This book was recommend to us by more than one mother of twins for its clear and concise advice.

Looking for a nursing pillow for twins? Check out **My Brest Friend's Twins Plus Deluxe** pillow for $55 to $80. Moms note this pillow helps keep their babies in the correct position so they can nurse in tandem.

FYI: Skip buying a glider-rocker if you plan to nurse your twins. The large nursing pillows won't fit! Instead, go for a loveseat.

◆ **Car seats.** Most multiples are born before their due date. The smallest infants may have to ride in special "car beds" that enable them to lie flat (instead of car seats that require an infant to be at least five or six pounds and ride in a sitting position). The car beds then rotate to become regular infant car seats so older infants can ride in a sitting position.

Some hospitals sell infant car beds—they can be used for premature infants up to nine pounds. The key feature: a wrap-around harness to protect a preemie in an accident. FYI: ALL premature infants should be given a car seat test at the hospital to check for breathing problems—ask your pediatrician for details.

As you might guess, some car seats fit smaller babies than others. We like the **Maxi Cosi Pria 70 with TinyFit** ($232), which starts at just 4 lbs. This version of the Pria has an insert specifically designed for pre-emies; it is an excellent car seat.

multiples

Another idea: check with your hospital to see if you can RENT a car bed until your baby is large enough to fit in a regular infant car seat.

◆ **Strollers.** Our complete wrap-up of recommendations for double strollers is in Chapter 8 (see Double the Fun in the lifestyle recommendations).

Our top pick for tandem strollers: the **Kolcraft Contours Options Tandem** ($280, 32 lbs.). Cool feature: the seats reverse to face the parents or each other. The runner up: the **Chicco Cortina Together,** which accepts two infant seats ($300).

For side-by-side strollers, we suggest the **Chicco Echo Twin** ($190, 30.5 lbs.; Target exclusive). It comes with a one-hand recline and sip off rear canopy. We also liked the **Graco Fast Action fold Duo** ($280, 33 lbs.) with big storage basket and canopies with sun visors. Finally, if grandma is buying, we like the **Baby Jogger City Mini Double** ($450, 26.6 lbs.), with its excellent extended canopies and quick fold.

◆ **Deals/Freebies.** Chain stores like Babies R Us and Baby Depot offer a 10% discount if you buy multiples of identical items like cribs. Buy Buy Baby has a similar program—and they even allow you to use one of their 20% coupons in addition to a 10% twin discount (for the second item only).

The National Mothers of Twins Clubs (nomotc.org) has fantastic yard/garage sales. Check their web page for a club near you.

Another good source: *Twins Magazine* is a bi-monthly, full-color magazine published by The Business Word (twinsmagazine.com).

◆ **Clothes and Diaper Bags.** For clothes, make sure you get "preemie" sizes instead of the suggestions in our layette chapter—twins are smaller at birth than singleton babies.

One of our readers with multiples sent us an extensive list of tips from her experience with twins. Go to BabyBargains.com/twins to download this free PDF.

With twins, you'll need a bigger diaper bag. We recommend **Skip Hop's Forma Pack and Go Diaper Tote Bag** for $40. It comes with two smaller zippered backs, a changing pad, exterior zippered compartments, one mesh packing cube, one insulated packing cube, changing pad and more. It's also water resistant. A good value at $60!

◆ **Our message boards.** On our message boards, you'll find all sorts of help as a parent of multiples. Our Bargain Alert forum features discount codes and other sales info for baby-related sites. There is a freebie list that is updated frequently: babybargains.com/freebies. And if you just need another mom or dad to chat with, go to the Baby Bargains Lounge.

INDEX

index

index

NOTES

index

BabyBargains.com

What's on our web page?

◆ *Detailed product and brand reviews.*

◆ *Message boards with in-depth reader feedback.*

◆ *The latest coupon codes and freebies!*

◆ *Social media feeds with safety recalls & breaking news!*

◆ *Updates and changes since this book went to print.*

BabyBargains.com
Email: authors@babybargains.com
Facebook: facebook.com/babybargains

More great books!